Full
Circle

T0383696

Edith Kurzweil

Full Circle

A Memoir

With an introduction by
Walter Laqueur

Routledge
Taylor & Francis Group

LONDON AND NEW YORK

First published 2007 by Transaction Publishers

2 Park Square, Milton Park, Abingdon, Oxfordshire OX14 4RN
711 Third Avenue, New York, NY 10017

Routledge is an imprint of the Taylor & Francis Group, an informa business

First issued in paperback 2017

Library of Congress Catalog Number: 2007021241

Library of Congress Cataloging-in-Publication Data

Kurzweil, Edith.
    Full circle : a memoir / Edith Kurzweil ; with an introduction by Walter
    Laqueur.
        p. cm.
    ISBN 978-1-4128-0662-6
        1. Kurzweil, Edith. 2. Women sociologists--United States--Biography.
    3. Jewish sociologists--United States--Biography. 4. Holocaust survivors-
    United States--Biography. 5. Women periodical editors--United States--
    Biography. 6. Partisan review (New York, N.Y. : 1936) I. Title.

HM479.K87A3 2007
301.092--dc22
[B]

                                                                    2007021241

ISBN 13: 978-1-4128-0662-6 (hbk)
ISBN 13: 978-1-138-51027-2 (pbk)

Contents

Illustrations follow page 184

Introduction

Walter Laqueur

This is the story of one of eighty thousand—the approximate number of the young Jews in their teens who lived in Grossdeutschland when the Nazis came to power in Germany and Austria. Of these boys and girls about two-thirds escaped in time. These were the lucky ones. Emigration for the older generation was much more difficult and escape from Eastern Europe, the big concentrations of European Jewry, was virtually impossible once war had broken out. Of these lucky ones several thousand have written their stories in later years—most not for publication but for a small circle of friends and family. As a historian of this generation I have probably read more of these accounts than anyone else. Despite this massive exposure to the fate of this generation to which I also belong I still find these memoirs of absorbing interest, intellectual and emotional. So, I am certain, will others, even though the events described in these memoirs must seem light years away to those born in the postwar world. A major effort of imagination is needed even to begin to understand what it was like to be fifteen or eighteen years of age when World War II broke out.

But is it not the same story all over again? It is the same—always very different, except that some lived and others died young. Some left their countries of origin together with their families, or, as in the case of Palestine, as members of a group; there was safety and reassurance in belonging to a group when facing adversity and danger. Others had to make their way alone through the minefields of the late 1930s and early 1940s and this at an age when normally boys and girls of similar background were preoccupied with sports, dancing lessons and, if they were of an adventurous bent, rowing on the rivers and camping in the forests of Europe.

All these young wanderers were wholly unprepared for the tribulations facing them; they were the last of Stefan Zweig's "World of Yesterday."

They came from families in which the offspring, if no longer well guarded, certainly had not yet to fend for itself. They had no money nor useful contacts in foreign lands; they did not master the languages that could be of vital help; they were not familiar with alien customs and ways of life; they did not know whom to trust and how to evade danger. There was no safety net for them; it was a question of swimming (which no one had taught them) or drowning. Some were lucky and made it to the very few countries in which eventually possibilities and careers opened to them about which they could have only dreamt in the dark years. Many were less fortunate, ending up in places such as Shanghai that could at best offer only temporary shelter. The history of the emigration of this generation is very often one of moving from place to place and from country to country.

Some of this generation had spectacular careers in later life—in the academic world, business, and even politics, and there is the temptation at the distance of sixty or seventy years to focus our attention on those outstanding ones. But we should never forget that accident often played a decisive role in the lives of members of this generation. All of us remember the many relations and friends who failed to escape and who ended up in the extermination camps of Eastern Europe. Others did manage to flee but were caught by the advancing German armies in 1940-41. Yet others were killed while fighting Nazi Germany. There are endless bad luck stories of those who never made it in their new homes—which never became home. New immigrants were seldom welcomed with open arms in any place.

How to explain with all this the large number of success stories among this group of people? I don't think they were more gifted than those who came before or after, and there were no more saints and geniuses among them. It was simply that they faced much greater challenges—first to survive, and later to make their way in a wholly unfamiliar world. And the price of failure was infinitely higher than before or after, very often there was no second chance. Again, the role of accident was often crucial. I have been told by those who survived the "selection" to the gas chambers of Auschwitz that they were usually saved owing to mere accident—being smaller of stature than others or somehow less conspicuous in other respects. The same seems to have been true with regard to success or failure in more auspicious circumstances—it was simply a question of being in the right place at the right time.

The first part of the story of Edith Kurzweil, up to her arrival in New York, borders on the miraculous. Born into a well-to-do Viennese Jewish family, aged thirteen, she found herself at the outbreak of the war in a children's home in Brussels. Her parents had made their way to the United States, but owing to the many bureaucratic complications so frequent and typical at this time the children, Edith and her younger brother, were still stranded in Europe. In April 1940, the Germans occupied Holland and Belgium and amid the great escape southwards of hundreds of thousands there were these two children, entirely on their own. Helped occasionally by the goodness or the pity of strangers (and no doubt a powerful guardian angel) they made their way in this utter chaos first to Toulouse, later to Barcelona, Madrid, and Lisbon where tickets on a New York-bound ship were waiting for them. Thus bypassing the Slough of Despond and the Hill of Difficulty they finally reached the House Beautiful, the city of New York, where apfelstrudel and Wiener schnitzel were waiting for them in the parental home.

At a very early age the writer of this memoir had experienced more uncertainties, adventures, and dangers than do most people who live to a ripe old age. A case could therefore have been made to end at this point (or soon after) the story of a near-miraculous escape, of two children lost in war-torn Europe. But readers quite naturally would like to know more about the subsequent fate of the author, not only her first steps in America. Edith Kurzweil has provided this in a very honest account, which at times must have been painful to write. She had not expected to have to spend her days sewing hatbands into hats or to cut diamonds rather than enter college life—to help support her family. Far from self-satisfaction despite all her achievements she focuses to a considerable extent on personal difficulties in the acculturation of a young European adult in war time America: the failure of a first marriage, the early death of her second husband with whom she lived in Milan.

Edith Kurzweil returned to New York after eight years in postwar Italy and resumed her studies while bringing up her three children. She became a distinguished scholar with a special interest in European intellectual history of the twentieth century and the history of psychoanalysis. Her early publications prompted William Phillips, the co-founder and editor of Partisan Review, to invite her into the elite circle of New York intellectuals. She ended up as the magazine's editor, close to the center of New York and Boston (and Wellfleet) intellectual life. But this is another story, not coming "full circle," but the narrative of another existence.

Preface

When I was about to turn seventy, I contemplated writing a memoir, because, like everyone else, I then had more to look back on than to look forward to; because I was (and am) convinced that forgetting one's past empties one's present; and that reflecting upon one's long ago deeds and behavior may lead to larger insights, and to a better understanding of the world we inhabit.

But which one of my worlds ought I to start with, given my peripatetic life? And how could I get across that after having given the slip to the Nazis, I refused to count myself among their victims?

"You were one of their victims," said my husband, William Phillips, "so explain why you dislike being called a survivor."

"You must write about your early childhood and your courage as a fugitive," said old-timers from Europe.

"What about your impressions of New York as a teenager, when you worked in sweatshops?" a few others wanted to know.

"What a ball you must have had while living in Italy during its 'economic miracle,' remarked a number of envious ones. Some sociologists were surprised that I had not pursued one or two areas of research; why I had jumped from participant observation of Italian entrepreneurs to French intellectual thought, and then from comparative psychoanalysis to Holocaust literature and European politics.

"You must write about all the interesting people you've met as editor of *Partisan Review*," and about your exciting life with William Phillips," said a few socialites. How can I do all that in 300 pages, I asked my publisher. (Fortunately, not many persons have been indiscreet enough to want me to give them the low-down about my marriages.)

All of these questions are valid, insofar as my existence has been, not only a reflection of turbulent times, but a manifestation of some of what my generation of immigrant girls from Europe (and other macho societies) experienced while getting to and into America, not just physically but emotionally and professionally. And of the countless twists and turns that tend to depend on luck, and yet more luck. Of course, I have kept asking myself whether or not I would still be so anxious about missing trains, or would still feel that I had to know "everything," if I had had the luxury of an uninterrupted life. And if, instead of writing a memoir I had followed in the footsteps of Johann Strauss's Rosalinde, in *Fledermaus*—dancing while singing *Glücklich ist wer vergisst was nicht mehr zu ändern ist* (happy is she who forgets what no longer can be changed.)

When, in the 1960s, I finally entered graduate school, and came upon Georg Simmel's essay, "The Stranger," I recognized myself. By then, I had acquired good friends in all social classes, and in various countries, and could well be perceived by some as being here today and gone tomorrow. Was that why a few women from Milan and Manhattan, from Paris and London, and from some hinterlands, told me secrets they kept from those near and dear to them? Or did they take me into their confidence because I know how to listen in a number of languages?

Wherever I happened to reside, I assumed I would remain for the rest of my life. As a child in Vienna, I was certain that my future would be played out in a whirl of waltzes; and that I would drink *Kaffee mit Schlagobers*, and consume gooey pastries in open-air coffee houses on lazy afternoons. Then, my father's America had been depicted in the imposing, silver-covered tome, *How They Got Rich and Famous*, mine in Karl May's *Winnetou* and in Margaret Mitchell's *Gone With the Wind*. His heroes had been John D. Rockefeller and J. P. Morgan, mine had been Old Shatterhand, Winnetou, and Scarlett O'Hara. After fleeing to Brussels, I put my energy and anxiety into speaking French—in the proper regional accent—as I got ready for family life in Paris. Now, my heroes were Clark Gable, Joseph Cotten, and John Wayne. And since I wasn't as cute as Deanna Durbin or Shirley Temple, I planned to turn myself into a famous author, another Pearl Buck. While snatching myself and my younger brother from the Nazis' *razzias*, I consoled myself that I would write about those frantic times—unaware that this would take me over sixty years. Of course, my memory is as flawed as everyone else's, and is partial as well as more extensive than I could possibly put into a short book.

* * *

Now that we pride ourselves on living in a multicultural society, and no longer even expect immigrants to speak English, or to "melt into the pot," foreign accents have stopped being a handicap. But when I arrived in America, unaccented English was required for professional employment, and for all "desk jobs." Many occupations were closed to Jews. I almost automatically have come to judge what I observe, whether trends or events, by comparing them to these days, or to other countries and milieus. Some of my off-hand comments and clever conclusions have earned me praise, others have gotten me into trouble. But I relish feeling at home while abroad, while being both insider and outsider.

I should add that I have extraordinary visual recall of some traumatic incidents, and have totally wiped out others. Many idioms and cultural customs inevitably are lost in translation, even while recalling people's gestures and facial expressions that convey specific contexts and ironies. For the sake of brevity I have skipped frolicking interludes, such as dances, cruises, travels, and worries about, and most events with, my children. But I have sketched some of the history against which my life was played out, because during thirty years of teaching in universities, I found that most members of our younger generations do not know much about the past. How else, for instance, could I get across that my upper-middle-class father sent me to work in dingy and totally unsuitable surroundings, not because he was a monster, or because he was a macho, tyrannical white male, which he was, but because he had become a frightened foreigner and a *schnorrer*—who could not bear losing control over his life, and over his daughter? Or explain why I went into an unsuitable marriage by the time I was twenty years old? True, I did it to get out from under, but how and why was I able to hide that from myself for over ten years?

In the 1940s, the plight of refugees like myself—a category that referred to European Jews who had escaped from Hitler—had no government agencies to turn to for financial help. We were of little interest to fellow workers, fellow students, or social scientists. Nor did most of us want to call attention to ourselves. The women's movement was not yet on the horizon when I was divorced in 1958—five years before Betty Friedan published her bestselling *Feminine Mystique*.[1] This liberation from my failed marriage was lonely and difficult, against parental advice. I could not have done it without therapy. That was when I began to catch up with some of my hidden self. I soon met my second husband, and, with my two children, went on to lead a joyful expatriate's life in Italy. At Milan's British-American club, I got to know more about my fellow Americans, and their true diversity than I had at my jobs or in the suburbs of New York. When eight years later, Robert Kurzweil died, after a short and terribly painful bout with cancer, we had returned to New York, and I went back to college. By 1973, I had earned my Ph. D., and began teaching.

On the way, I brought up my children, had many joys and many setbacks. While growing up, I had caught and soon overcome every imaginable childhood disease, which made my mother call me her Jack-in-the-box: she couldn't foresee the numerous tragedies that would hit me, or that I would end up dealing with them nearly as expeditiously as I had with scarlet fever, measles, mumps, chicken pox, and diphtheria.

This memoir of my life in the thick of the twentieth century interweaves political events and my take on them during the worst of times as well as during the best of times. Did the Viennese saying was *e net weiss macht me net heiss* (what I don't know doesn't bother me) make for my eternal optimism, or was it due to denial?

In 1957, I described myself as a chameleon, the animal that adapts to its surroundings by changing the color of its skin. After a few years with Robert, that portrayal no longer was accurate. Maybe, as Edmund Burke might have put it, wrestling with my father strengthened my nerves and sharpened my wit, so that his imperious demands and sarcastic asides spurred me on. More likely, the successive waves of my chopped-up life, like the waves that follow a hurricane, carried me forward on their cusps to increasingly attune myself to others as well as to my inner self— which led me to oppose the father, whom I could not help but adore and respect until his death. But he never forgave me for not falling into line—which was the only way I could survive.

Anyway, that is what I think today, on April 15, 2007.

*   *   *

I owe thanks to all those friends on both sides of the Atlantic who kept asking me to write about my topsy-turvy life, and to those who read and commented on earlier accounts about my flight from war-torn Europe. Some of them also wanted to know how I fared later on. Others were curious about my ex-patriot years in Italy and my return to New York. Still others were interested in my take on New York intellectuals and in gossip about the writers around *Partisan Review*.

In particular I am lucky enough to have had the ongoing guidance and encouragement of Doris Lessing, Walter Laqueur, Robert Miller, Rachel Rosenblum, Daniel Dayan, and, earlier on, Diana Trilling. Moreover, my publisher's, Irving Louis Horowitz, and my editor's, Laurence Mintz, guidance helped me shorten and improve the manuscript. Lately, I have had the good fortune to reconnect with Ilse Garfunkel and Walter Reed—

cohorts during my wartime flight from Brussels to southern France. Both were generous in sharing their memories of these dangerous times.

Last but not least, I am grateful to my children, Allen Kurzweil, Ronald Schmidt, and Vivien Schmidt, who helped refresh some details of more recent events. And to my late husband, William Phillips, whose love and sharp questions kept me on target.

Part I

1

The *Anschluss*

In March 1938, when Hitler marched into Vienna, I was a skinny girl of thirteen, a stellar student at the Wiener Frauenerwerbverein, and an aspiring swimming champion. Like many daughters of upwardly mobile and assimilated Jewish families, I was slated to acquire a profession in the arts, some sort of off-shoot of the Wiener Werkstätte, "because one never knows what might happen." But no one in my family seriously believed that I would ever really need to work, that I would not be happily married by the age of twenty-one, like my mother. Or that Austria, however anti-Semitic some of its citizens might be, would willingly welcome any *Anschluss* to Germany. Even after Sigmund Freud's books were burnt there in 1933, he too was certain that his Austrians never would follow suit. Along with Karl Kraus, the editor of *Die Fackel* (The Torch), my parents believed that psychoanalysis was the sickness it set out to cure. However, they all were at one in their ambivalence about being Jewish. Neither dreaming of converting nor of practicing their religion, most of Viennese godless Jews made fun of their parents' conventional views, and of conventions. Like my parents, they kept their children in the dark about politics and other serious matters. "*Was e net weiss macht me net heiss*" (what I don't know doesn't bother me) was one of the countless proverbs most Viennese parents lived by.

So when late on that fateful Friday afternoon my mother and I were done with shopping for material for the following fall's clothing, and my father was skiing in Switzerland, I was stunned to hear on the radio that Austria's chancellor, Kurt von Schuschnigg, was resigning—"in order to avoid bloodshed." On the following morning, my mother was informed that our brand-new American Ford had been requisitioned to welcome Hitler.

"What will Papa say when he gets back and his car isn't in its proper spot," was all she could say.

Starting at dawn on that morning, miles and miles of the German Wehrmacht, of black-clad SS (Schutzstaffel) and brown-shirted SA (stormtroopers) were passing below our windows. They filed by in tight formation, or stood upright in open trucks, belting out their seductive marching tunes and giving the Hitler salute. How I wished to be one of the children hopping and singing alongside. My friend, the superintendent's daughter, Lori, was among them. Airplanes were circling overhead, blackening the sky with their flyleaves, asking every Austrian to personally welcome Hitler.

"Die Fahne hoch, die Reihen dicht geschlossen" and *"Heil unserm Führer"* were the catchiest tunes I had ever heard. Now, my mother no longer worried that I might turn into a spoiled brat, but expected me to grow up overnight.

"We are in for rough times," she said, as I accompanied her to visit our friend and lawyer, Karl Ettinger. On our way, I noted passers-by who greeted each other by shooting up their right arms; others who sported the wide red armbands with their round white circle and black swastikas everyone has come to know from the movies; and yet others who wore swastika pins in their lapels. In the distance, we heard the rhythmic shouts of *"Deutschland erwache! Juda verrecke!"* (Germany awake. Jews perish). My mother's grip on my arm tightened as we hastened ahead. Fearful that our phone was tapped, she had to talk to Karl Ettinger in person: a greedy competitor had gotten a warrant for my father's arrest —for allegedly practicing unfair competition. They were phoning him, debating whether or not he ought to return. (From a letter I found after my mother's death, my father seems to have regretted his obstinate decision to come back to Vienna.)

On that Sunday morning, my mother dispatched me to consult with yet another friend, the director of the Hotel Bristol, across the street from the Vienna Opera.

"He will know how to manage getting our car back before Papa's return. Fortunately you don't look Jewish," she said, "so they won't stop you. Make sure to pay attention to what he tells you, and be careful."

By then Jews were prohibited in that area, which was close to the Hotel Imperial, where Hitler was to stay, and to the Heldenplatz, where he was to give his now famous speech sealing this annexation. While making my way through the frenzied crowd, and panicked by the Jew-hating and Jew-baiting slogans that came at me from every side, I tried to get away quickly but had trouble fighting my way against the advancing throng—like swimming upstream under water without coming up for air.

The newsreels of that triumphant takeover, which are routinely replayed on television, cannot convey the frenzy and excitement of the onrushing crowd. I do not recall whether I was more afraid of being crushed or of being recognized by someone who knew I was Jewish.

Soon, bad news piled up—about a relative's or acquaintance's mishap or arrest, or someone's suicide. Were my own free-floating fears justified, or just products of my imagination? Whenever the doorbell rang we shuddered: unannounced house searches were becoming more and more frequent. Oppositionists, that is, communists and socialists who had not been imprisoned or left the country after Chancellor Dollfuss's murder in 1934, laid low or were arrested. So was my father on Wednesday, March 15, the day after he returned from Switzerland.

Now, my mother stood on endless lines in front of the *Landesgericht* to bring her husband food and clean laundry, and to get five minutes worth of advice. By the middle of June, my father was summoned from his cell and given a choice: to sell the business for a small fraction of its value and leave Austria, or be deported to Dachau. He signed and—after many mishaps—left for Paris.

Before the Anschluss my fairly fickle mother had been in charge of *Kinder, Küche*, and frivolities, but now took over the family's reins. Suddenly, this allegedly brainless, irrational, and witless housewife was catapulted into a much more dangerous situation than her husband had ever encountered. She took over instinctively, as if she had been waiting in the wings. She wheedled her way into offices of obnoxious Nazis, decided to register us for visas at the American consulate because "*Doppelt hält besser*" (make doubly sure); dispensed advice; and accompanied my grandparents to whatever doctors they were in need of.

Just then, I was becoming aware of my body and of boys. But since I no longer had school friends with whom to discuss intimate matters, I blushingly turned to our housekeeper, Anni, for my sex education. She told me more than I needed to know. While taking my brother and me to the Waldmüllerpark, she made eyes at every German soldier we passed. I don't know whether I was embarrassed because she picked them up and allowed them to steer her onto the grass behind the bushes, or was eager to spy on what went on. Mostly, I was worried that they might ask about my religion. To ward off all potential danger, I told myself that if, for instance, I could jump rope one hundred times without tripping, or count to fifty without breathing, we would get home safely. She also filled my head with blow-by-blow descriptions of how she had seduced the cute Frantz from Munich and the feisty Fritzl from Freiburg. In my head, magical thinking, free-floating fears, and romantic dreams became inextricably entangled.

When I ran into the stub-nosed, freckle-faced Lucy Pressburg, she invited me to join some of the Hakoah swimmers who were meeting under the auspices of the Maccabi Hazair, along with a bunch of sixteen-year-old boys from the Sperl Gymnasium and a troupe of boy scouts. As the youngest, I was tongue-tied, kept smiling, and learned what Zionism was about. I didn't really want to end up in Palestine, but was afraid to say so. Neither did the scouts. But as our desire to escape the Nazis escalated, our enthusiasm for Zionism grew exponentially. By Rosh Hashanah, in late September, I had convinced myself that I wanted to make aliyah: one evening, after dancing a lively hora, and singing the Hatikva, we embraced and solemnly pledged to meet at the Wailing Wall in Jerusalem, if not sooner then at noon, on Rosh Hashanah in 1943.

After the club quarters in the inner city had been closed down, Mausi, the scouts' leader offered his apartment in the heart of the Jewish District as the weekly meeting place. I had a crush on the round-faced Mausi: he made up for his short stature by clever and playful situational jokes. According to Lucy, he was in love with her. (She confided that Rappan, the best looking of the bunch, already had kissed her, and that she didn't know whom she favored.) Still, I was overjoyed when Mausi, shortly before *Kristallnacht*, picked <u>me</u> to provide the cake for the following meeting. Maybe he wasn't in love with Lucy after all? I never questioned the depth of her devotion to either of these boys.

By then, *Umschulungskurse*—fly-by-night instruction in private apartments—had sprung up around town, for spoiled Jewish matrons who were readying themselves to earn their keep. The wives of lawyers, businessmen, and bankers knew that their husbands' skills would be obsolete in a foreign country, and were "equipping" themselves as milliners, dressmakers, and so on. My mother learned how to bake for large groups and to make hand-stitched gloves. So did her sister, Ilka. My clumsy cousin, Blanka, was briefly working at a hairdresser's shop, and joined her mother when she was volunteering at the nearby soup kitchen. And I became a (paying) apprentice to a dressmaker, Frau Silbermann.

"What you know they can't take away from you," had become my mother's motto.

"You start by basting hems and finishing seams, and after a while you'll be allowed to hem and embroider the dresses my customers order for their emigration," said my new boss.

I disliked Frau Silbermann, a bustling, heavy-set gossip who I believed was holding me back from turning into a future Coco Chanel. She did not assign me challenging tasks, was afraid I would ruin a raglan sleeve, or a silk blouse. At this pace, I was sure that I never would become an accomplished *couturière*. In my fantasies, I expected to help support the family on the sale of the stunning, glamorous clothes I was projecting in my mind, and to become rich and celebrated.

Frau Silberman lived in the Tempelgasse, across the street from Vienna's largest, orthodox synagogue. On November 9, 1938—a gray afternoon—we heard banging and drunken yelling below her apartment. It was the start of what has become known as *Kristallnacht*. I had a first row seat to the event: hordes of stomping, pink-cheeked, storm troopers in brown, and black-clad SS men—along with ordinary Viennese—were throwing Torah scrolls, bibles, and other holy articles into the street. Parts of wooden pews followed, accompanied by whistling, and by yelled obscenities about *Saujuden* (Jewish pigs). Two local *strietzies* (street bums) stood by smiling, idly smoking their cigarettes; a few others set fire to the holy articles that now littered the gutters, before hurling blazing torches into the temple itself. No fire engines arrived. While the synagogue burned to the ground, I was afraid that the flames might send sparks through the smoke and break one of our front windows, and that we might hear insistent knocks by uniformed Nazis at the rear door. The (Aryan) dressmakers in the shop were aghast at this dreadful spectacle. One of them exclaimed, while clearing her throat:

"How can we trust these Nazi hoodlums when you see what they're up to? They'd better not come here, or we'll show them. Frau Silbermann, you just leave them to us." These simple gentile women, who did not have to fear for themselves, were horrified at the violence below, especially at the desecration of bibles cast into the raging fire. Seeing me shake with fear, Gertie, a stocky, blond and plain-looking fourteen-year-old apprentice, who by landing this job had been able to escape from her drunken father, slovenly mother and ten brothers and sisters, offered to walk me home. She was fond of me, not only because I was below her in the hierarchy and thus relieved her of some onerous chores, but because I paid attention to her endless babble.

"I'll protect you," she volunteered, "so stop shivering."

Like Lori and Anni, Gertie was streetwise. They all had a way of swinging their ample rear ends to attract male attention. Gertie's savvy stood me in good stead: she escorted me to my grandparents' apartment because it was so much closer than my own. We sneaked through the by then ghoulishly quiet streets. Nearly paralyzed by the lurking danger and petrified of moving in the dark, I kept clinging to Gertie's arm. Each time we passed someone, or saw a shadow round a corner, my heart beat faster. At one point, Gertie declared while pointing at a huge poster: "If they stop us, I'll tell them you're my cousin Herta from Neusiedl. You know, she has a much bigger nose than you, and her skin is much darker. She looks almost like the picture of the ugly Jew on this wall."

After that night, my mother strove to get us out—with or without her. She was worried not only that my uninhibited, willful brother might get into a fight with a street urchin, but that I too no longer was safe. She had heard about children's transports to England, and decided to inquire about them. "The sooner the better," had become her credo, along with "act now think later." Moreover, she had been given notice that by December 31 we had to vacate our apartment. In desperation, we planned to move into the extra bedroom of my uncle Poldi's and his wife Lia's flat in my grandfather's apartment house on the Gaudenzdorfergürtel, and to pack and store the furniture and belongings we expected to take with us to our as yet unknown destination.

The statuesque, slovenly Lia lorded her Aryan blood over us. We rarely saw Poldi who silently walked in and out. I felt sorry for him and was repulsed by Lia's noisy ways. She wore thick mascara, and did not seem to take off her Chanel suit, maroon with navy trimming, which was stained around the armpits from perspiration and torn on its left side.

"Don't you dare even stare at that hole, or she'll get your poor grandmother to buy her a new outfit," ordered my mother.

This oppressive and cramped atmosphere certainly added to my mother's determination to send us abroad. On a dismal January afternoon she arrived home, laughing hysterically and sniffling compulsively while patting her dripping eyes and nose with a white handkerchief, embroidered with butterflies and violets.

"What has happened this time," I wondered while she slipped off her coat. She plopped on Lia's couch in the vestibule, patting it on both sides of her and motioning my brother and me to sit down. While putting her arms around us, she cleared her throat, and with a quivering mouth, declared: "I have arranged for you to leave this hellhole, you're going away to where you'll be safe. I have registered you to get on a children's transport to Brussels, where Weinwurm, you remember your father's friend, don't you, will greet you. You are joining a bunch of kids in Cologne, on February 10th."

While an embroidered butterfly seemed to be fluttering on the swollen eyelids she kept dabbing, she turned more and more solemn: "From now on, Ditterl, you will have to take care of yourself and of your brother. You have to promise to take my place. As for you, Hanserl," she continued while turning to my uncharacteristically subdued brother who seemed to be shrinking into the pillows, "you will have to listen to your sister. Until we meet up with Papa in Paris, you will have nobody else to rely on, only each other. You have to do what Ditta says even if you think she's wrong."

Soon, my mother sobbed uncontrollably, while we both embraced her—Hansl whimpering silently, and I biting back my tears. We vowed never to quarrel again. But we immediately started to argue whether or not we could play monopoly on the train as we had done on our way to Italy the previous summer, or would be limited to playing cards.

The next three weeks flew by. Whereas before my mother's motto had been that "children should not get everything they want," we now splurged on elegant clothes and pricey accessories. My mother bought me whatever I desired—shoes and dresses on the Kärntnerstrasse and the Graben, even the latest style in pocketbooks, a burgundy one with a zipper and a navy blue one with a shoulder-strap at Lederer's, and a beige camel hair coat as well as a blue pin-striped one for spring, at Leschka's. These items were to last forever, through a lifetime in poverty. And we visited my mother's countless relatives to say our last good-byes. There were so many of them, all of whom I had met at one time or another at my grandparents' Sunday gatherings: they were full of advice I didn't think I needed, and which they dispensed with damp eyes and sad, earnest nods. My brother and I accepted their laments as graciously as the chocolates and sweets they lavished on us. But my thoughts were already in Paris. I couldn't even figure out whether my mother was more upset at our imminent departure, content that we were about to be "safe," or primarily preoccupied by all the details she had to be on top of.

I pictured this trip as an adventure and allowed my fears to surface only in my dreams, mostly about getting lost in spooky woods or being abducted by slave traders. But as I saw more and more Stürmer-type posters going up that depicted Jews as *Untermenschen*—less than human—and heard about more and more roundups, I was convinced my mother had made the right decision. I envisioned my departure as a dangerous but enlightening voyage that would allow me to taste life in a boarding school, and to conquer the wide world.

On the way to the fourth floor, to sleep one last time under Lia's roof, we visited my paternal grandparents. While ringing their bell, I was overcome by dizziness and nausea. We had done the last of our shopping. While my beloved Marie prepared a festive dinner, both my mother and my grandmother were hovering over me, certain that I was too young to be suffering from "nerves." Instead, after I surreptitiously and proudly showed my first brassiere to Omama Weisz, they agreed that my dizziness was due to its tightness around the chest. (I still was flat and unlike some of my friends had not yet gotten my period.)

Now, my grandparents kept repeating that they might never see us again, and I kept remonstrating that they were being silly, while not persuaded that they were wrong. Not that anyone as yet had any inkling of what came to be called the final solution. I knew only that they were old, were fearful of travel, and that we might not have the money to return to Vienna even if, as my grandfather still said, "This situation can't last, Austrians cannot tolerate a maniac like Hitler for long."

Altogether, I refused to think that I might encounter any perils. Beyond the German frontier, all would be fine and dandy, at worst a challenge I would meet head on. One last time, my Omama was rummaging in her *Wäschekiste* (laundry bin) for chocolates, while unable to control her tears and voicing dire forebodings. While hemming and hawing, she noted that I was already as tall as she: "You are growing into a beautiful girl, Ditterl, and you have to start protecting yourself against men. Don't ever trust them, Ditterl," she went on, "you are attractive and intelligent and will go far. But getting involved with the wrong one could be your downfall."

I was flustered. My grandfather was as taciturn as ever. I had known him as a forbidding presence in his office—handing out stamps and petty cash to employees, and a shilling as well as colorful stamps to me whenever I popped in. Now, he cleared his throat and gave each of us ten shillings—ten times what we had received on our customary Sunday visits—which was all we were allowed to take across the German frontier. As was his habit, he was warming his back against the tall chimney in their living room, with his left thumb under his suspenders and puffing at the cigar he held in his right hand. While he patted me on the head, I acted the perfect Pollyanna. But he addressed Hansl: "We're at the end of the line my boy, you're the third generation. The first one starts the family enterprise, the next one builds it up and expands it, and the third one squanders the fortune his grandfather and father have slaved for. What will happen to you, I don't know, but I'm sorry to deprive you of your opportunity."

Shades of *Buddenbrooks*, but the stereotypical prediction of all successful Viennese entrepreneurs, of Jews and Gentiles alike.

2

Exodus

At dawn on February 9, 1939, my mother, my brother, and I arrived at Vienna's *Westbahnhof*, nearly two hours ahead of time. The platform was empty, except for railroad workers checking parked trains, a few policemen in blue, and clusters of Wehrmacht in grey and green, trim SS personnel in black and SA in brown. I put on my most grown-up face and made believe I didn't notice them—intent on hiding my fear.

"Thank God you two are getting away from all that," my mother whispered under her breath, "but when will I see you again? Who can understand what Hitler has done to us? What have we come to?" Again, she begged me to make sure to take care of the eleven-year-old Hansl now that I was fourteen years old. "You know that our Hanserl so easily gets himself into trouble," she went on, "and only you can keep him out of it, now that you are a big girl." Once more her eyes filled with tears. My own thoughts, though totally unfocused, were on the future. As had become my habit, I reacted with a determined show of calm while suppressing my all-encompassing worries. Soon, I saw my maternal grandmother approach in the distance, almost hidden by the huge food basket she carried. We were not going to starve on our overnight trip to Cologne. With a sob, she embraced me, unclasped her thick golden link bracelet, and handed it to me, saying, "wear this, to remember me by." As we mounted our train, I unexpectedly and silently began to invoke a string of disasters that might befall us. And I didn't understand why I suddenly was choking on my tears and breaking out in a sweat. Strangled by anxiety and nausea, I told myself that I would have no trouble escaping would-be abductors and white slave traders—who I gathered sold girls to men in some wild, uncivilized country, and where they might be tortured. For the moment, however, the black-booted SS men around us were the true menace. As the station platform was teeming with more and more of them, and they were getting onto trains, I worried whether they were there in order to watch us. But I kept smiling vacuously and tried not to let on to my sudden and inexplicable dread, and my nausea. I touched the heavy golden chain on my wrist, checked its safety chain, thrilled at its glistening smoothness, and was gratified that my grandmother had given it to me rather than to one of her other granddaughters. But I also recalled with foreboding that we were forbidden to take any valuables out of Germany—by now called the *Altreich*.

In the end I panicked. As the dispatchers began to bang shut the heavy doors, and the train was about to move, I reached out of the window to return the coveted jewel to my grandmother. What if one of the border guards would grab me off the train and punish me for smuggling? (It was what I had been afraid of when hiding a bottle of wine after a summer in Italy.) He might imprison me, beat me up, and turn me into a galley slave. That was why just as the locomotive's whistle blew, the railway men gave the wheels their last bangs, and our train began to chug slowly out of the station, and already before my grandmother started to sob loudly and insisted on touching our hands just once more, "for the last time in her life," I could barely control my agitation.

As the train's wheels rolled faster and faster, my rounded mother and my even more rounded grandmother appeared to get smaller and smaller. With dripping eyes and noses, their feet seemed to be running in place as the train was gaining speed. I kept hearing their admonitions and advice over its noise, over the whistle's piercing shrieks: stick together, write every other day, be careful and brave. And I vowed again, over the din of the accelerating train that I would take good care of Hansl, no matter how much he might irritate me; that I would record "everything" in my spanking new beige, leather-bound diary with its golden key; and, most of all, that I would write at least twice a week. The grownups, of course, were aware how difficult it would be for an unworldly, sheltered kid like me to be on her own, particularly in such ominous circumstances. They knew I would be homesick, lonesome, and insecure. As for me, I knew only that I had to be competent, to rise to all emergencies in the way I thought grownups always do. That was how I managed to bury my fears, hiding from myself that I was consumed by terror.

Were the Nazis getting away with murder because Jews did not accept the Christian God? I had not believed what I had been told about God in religious classes. But if my cousin Blanka was correct and God could see whatever I did, I had better be careful. Still, she had been good all along, and God had treated me better: I was on my way to Brussels, and she wasn't even sure she could get to Palestine—even though she was knocking on countless doors to collect money for WIZO (Women's International Zionist Organization).

I had stopped being a child. But instead of turning into the adult I imagined I had become, I metamorphosed into a vigilant fugitive. In the process, I transformed the chameleon-like characteristics of the fearful and goody-good Viennese schoolgirl into what I might call its bona fide refugee equivalent. I knew that I had best not stick out, not make waves, and keep my clever rejoinders to myself. By focusing on that rather than on the shock of being responsible for myself and my brother, I presented an ever stronger façade while blinding myself to my feelings of insecurity.

In the end, our exit from Austria turned out to be uneventful. Still, in my frame of mind I was sure the Nazis had come for us when, soon after we passed Linz, three jowly men with beer-barrel stomachs and tell-tale swastika armbands made themselves at home in our compartment. They were being friendly, even expansive, and asked us why we were traveling alone. Since I would not have trusted them even without their swastikas, I instinctively recalled what the brazen, self-assured Lori had told me about her trips to Melk where she used to visit her aunt: I invented an aunt in Cologne and had her married to a German shopkeeper. They seemed to believe my improvisation, and Hansl inadvertently (?) helped out by interrupting me, saying that he was starving and had to eat "right away." I don't know whether these men suspected that we were Jewish, or cared, but it didn't hurt that I offered them some of my grandmother's delicacies. They couldn't stop salivating over the strudel. Would they think it was poisoned if they knew that a Jewish woman had baked it?

I kept reassuring myself that our tickets and money were still in my pocketbook at least every half hour, while agonizing about our arrival in Cologne. What if our compartment were to be uncoupled by mistake? What would happen if our train would get there too late to meet up with the others? Would they wait? Would the guards at the Belgian frontier let us cross? What embarrassing questions might any of the conductors who kept coming to check our tickets ask me before punching them? Would they kick us off the train if they found out that we were Jewish? My brother was uncharacteristically silent. We watched the countryside slide past us as we had done on our summer vacations in Austria, Italy, Hungary, and Yugoslavia. We passed the time by competing about counting more cars, or cows, or telephone poles. I vaguely thought of my cousins, Eva and Marianne, who already were in Shanghai, and of my best friend, Lotte, who was about to leave with a *Kindertransport* for

England. But mostly, we kept stuffing ourselves. After it turned dark, and throughout the night, I alternately dozed off to the steady drone of the train's wheels, relived the turbulent recent past, especially *Kristallnacht*, that finally had caused my mother to send us on this lonesome, frightening journey. I now recalled how Omama Fischer had saved me from humiliation by furnishing the *Oblattentorte* for the meeting at Mausi's house—after my mother had refused to supply it. ("Stop being so hard on her," I had, with satisfaction, overheard my grandmother chide my mother, by saying "she is beginning to grow into a teenager.") Now, romantic dreams and nightmares intermingled. I allowed Mausi to kiss me, but the billowing, smoky clouds of *Kristallnacht* made me push him away; Frau Silbermann was chewing me out for improperly sewing a buttonhole, and giant rowdies ran after me; they caught and almost killed me, but I escaped by jumping into the flames, was suffocated by them and then woke up happily. At that point, I consoled myself by thinking of the reunion with my father in Paris, and of strutting up and down the Champs Élysées.

Neither Hansl nor I noticed just when we crossed into German territory: there no longer was a frontier, and we were napping. But I observed that the passengers getting on spoke in increasingly unfamiliar and to our ears unpleasant German accents. I missed the softer, more familiar Austrian ones. I was Austrian enough (and would be for years to come) to be suspicious of these *"Piffkes"*—a derogatory term all my countrymen kept using even after they had welcomed the Nazis and appeared to have turned into the happy citizens of the *Ostmark*.

Our train rolled into Cologne's terminal nearly two hours late. I had kept checking my watch, the map on the wall of the compartment, and the stations we passed, and was ever more upset at the growing delay. We didn't even have enough money to return to Vienna. What would I do? But the moment we stepped off that train, a tall, blond man in a loose-fitting raincoat spotted us and said that he had been on the lookout for us. He deftly grabbed our suitcases while telling us to hurry. The other children already were assembled nearby on the large square, in front of the famous Cologne cathedral. The man was annoyed when I asked whether I'd have a minute to look at the inside of the cathedral.

"This is no time for tourism," he informed me superciliously as he herded everyone back to the station and onto the train that would take us to freedom.

*   *   *

I had never gone to a summer camp where, my overly protective mother was sure, I'd acquire bad habits. Thus I never had become aware of the loud and exhibitionist behavior children assume when among themselves. After we settled into our seats, I was appalled at these kids' manners, but soon assumed that they simply were being German: noisy showoffs and busybodies (*Geschaftlhubers*). I never expected that my fellow travelers might be looking down their noses at our Viennese ways, or make fun of our accent. Their ages ranged from four to fifteen. But not all of them were raucous and boastful: two of the older boys were motioning to their ill-behaved younger pals to pipe down, by shushing them and putting their forefingers to their lips. We seemed to have the entire passenger car to ourselves. Any outside observer could have taken us for a group of children on a typical excursion organized by the Nazis' popular vacation program for children, *Kraft durch Freude*.

When reviewing Bernt Engelmann's book, *In Hitler's Germany* [2] (1986), I realized that we probably were among the children saved by the members of "Herr Desch's" courageous, underground network: a small contingent of ordinary Germans, defying the new racial laws, managed to smuggle out politically endangered persons, mostly Jews, and hundreds of their children. These youngsters, Engelmann states, would "meet at the Central Station in Cologne," some destined for England, others for France and yet a few others for America. They would travel on "a single group ticket as far as Liège . . . which the chaperon would show to the conductor once in Germany and once in Belgium . . . and the conductor count[ed] to make sure the number on the ticket [was] right—that's all. . . . They care[d] that the numbers [were] accurate." According to Engelmann, "Herr Desch" could freely travel to London, to buy fabrics for his tailoring business, which specialized in Nazi dress uniforms. He was a "supporting member of the SS," and thus was "supervising" his transports—protected by the SS insignia on his lapel. Was I one of the children he scared while saving them? (He had to make sure that the German kids who were slated for vacations alone would be kept in ignorance and that the Jewish ones would get out.)

When I asked my mother many years later under what auspices our escape had been arranged, she did not remember. And she did not seem to wonder then or later how it had been possible for us to leave Vienna without passports. She assumed that the money provided by the Belgian branch of the family business was all it had taken to get us to safety.

As it turned out, my bottomless repertoire of forebodings had been unwarranted. Ultimately, the border control in Aachen was pro forma. We got through without a hitch: no one wanted to confiscate either of the thin golden rings my grandmothers had pressed upon me, nor my watch or golden necklace. Nor were we detained. The strutting customs inspectors in grey uniforms with dark green trimming officiously mounted the train, caused a lot of confusion and commotion, and made a few spot checks. After I had spent fifteen minutes in intense dread they waved us on our way.

As soon as we had safely crossed the Belgian border, one of the oldest and most pretentious boys clapped his hands and called everyone's attention to himself by loudly proclaiming to his eleven-year-old sister that their parents had hidden the family jewels in one of her bags, and that he had to take charge of them. Now, he swaggered over, and with a flourish lifted her suitcases from their overhead perch and took his time rummaging inside. After locating two diamond brooches, a string of pearls, a few gold bracelets and rings among her underwear, he held them up high and dangled them for us all to see. I was infuriated at the nerve of this show-off. I wondered what would have happened to us if this loot had been detected. How could his parents have been so irresponsible and have endangered us all? But mostly, I was angry with myself for having been too scared, or too stupid, not to hold on to my grandmother's bracelet.

*   *   *

Karl Weinwurm, a former hockey player for Hakoah, and who still worked for what remained of the family enterprise, waited for us in the bowels of the immense central station in downtown Brussels. His physique, and especially his potbelly, belied the fact that he had ever done any sport. Still, he had convinced the Belgian rescue committee to include us among the few hundred German refugee children the authorities eventually would allow into the country. I did not yet grasp how ludicrous it was for this portly, awkward bachelor to act as our surrogate father. Before then, I had met him only during the occasional midday meals he had shared with us in Vienna. There, I had had trouble taking my eyes off his hulking body and the neat round hole in his left temple: he had been hit by a bullet during World War I, my mother had said, which made me assume that he had been a hero. How come, I had kept wondering, he seemed so boring, and could talk only about moving marble slabs from one location to another, or debate whether or not to help himself to yet another piece of meat. And why did he always walk around with his lips squeezed tight and drop the corners of his mouth? Did he really sneer at everything and everyone?

Despite all of that, I was delighted to hear Weinwurm's booming voice in that imposing dome covered railroad terminal. After he barreled through, he just about succeeded in pressing fifty francs into my hand: "Use it for whatever you may need," he whispered to me, aware that we were being summoned. A slight, pasty-faced man with a Piffke accent and red-rimmed eyes behind thick spectacles was speaking through a megaphone: "Hurry up, hurry up. Boys line up on the right and girls on the left, and don't forget your luggage." It was only then that we found out that boys and girls would be separated, that my brother would be living in Anderlecht and I in Zuen. A number of the younger children started to whimper, and to clutch the hands of their older siblings. Now, Hansl clung to me, tightly gripped my arm, and insisted he wouldn't leave me. I was just as upset. But I urged him to obey and promised to telephone early the next day. We parted reluctantly. Exhausted and full of apprehension, we mounted the grey school busses that would transport us to our Belgian "homes."

Unlike all of our new buddies we felt privileged: our father was in Paris and we expected to join him soon. I already sensed that the *home d'enfants* we were heading for would be more of a Dickensian orphanage or prison than a Trotzkopf-type adventure. However, I consoled myself by considering Brussels as no more than a stopover on the road to "gay Paree." I certainly did not envisage that for sixteen months the lackadaisical Weinwurm would rule over me and my leisure time.

3

Brussels

The Jews who escaped from the Nazis had to live in countries whose languages they didn't understand, and had to adapt to local customs that made no sense to them. In order to properly navigate, while trying to pretend they knew what they were doing, they had to reinvent themselves, and to create personal myths that would allow them to hold on to their convictions in a way that also would accord with their new lives. How else could they explain—to themselves and others—what previously had been normal and now seemed bizarre? This was difficult enough for families that were immigrating together. But those whose members left separately, and who had different experiences, needed to create their own survival myths. For instance, my mother was bound to resent remaining in Vienna while assuming that her husband was having a good time in Paris, and that her children not only were safe in Belgium but happy. My father, whose charmed life had been based on his entrepreneurial skills, had to reestablish his business, in order to overcome his depression and to reunite us and reestablish our former way of life. My brother was young and fortunate enough to continue putting his energies into playing soccer, thereby hiding his longing for his mother. I escaped into glorious fantasies of an as yet vague intellectual and glamorous future. But could such divergent myths portend well for a harmonious family life?

Actually, loneliness swallowed me the moment I got onto our bus to Zuen, and heard the director of the *home d'enfants* shout through his megaphone, "Welcome girls, I'm Monsieur Alex Frank. I now will distribute your nametags. My wife will assign you to your rooms as soon as we arrive at your new home, Général Bernheim, in Zuen." I dozed off and awakened only when the silence in this gloomy, rumbling vehicle was broken by the occasional sob of a little girl. After the bus's lights went on, we met Madame Frank, a mouse of a woman, who was planted at the entrance to our new home. In the semi-darkness, she had no shape or face, as she was bent over her large list. After hearing my name, I too was directed up the central staircase, "to the corner room on the far right, on the first floor. Yours is the bed in the right hand corner, under the window. You are sharing a sunny room with three other girls."

My fantasies of boarding school camaraderie, intimacy, and exhilarating adventure went up in smoke. I longed for my mother. Still, Little Dorrit and David Copperfield had been younger than I when they had had to look out for themselves and to outsmart the adults around them. So had Trotzkopf, the heroine of my favorite girls' books. I put on a good front, purposefully ignored the seediness of my bare quarters—and was relieved when the clanging of the cook's cowbell summoned us to supper.

Back on the ground floor, Madame Frank shooed us down a narrow, spiral staircase to the spooky basement. She compensated for the unease she felt at her newly acquired authority over so many kids, by ordering: "*macht schnell*" and "*dépèchez-vous*," as we ducked under the single, loose light bulb that dangled by a long cable from the ceiling at the top of these steep, creaky steps. The illumination cast eerie, dancing shadows, suggesting that what we would come to refer to as our "castle" was inhabited by ghosts. These underground dining facilities adjoined the kitchen, and were lit by more floating light bulbs: they reminded me of Vienna's Kapuzinergruft—the catacombs that housed the tombs of the succession of Austrian Kaisers. Our dark, wood-paneled rectangular space, with its musty smells, used to be the staff's living quarters in this formerly elegant mansion, much as in Upstairs-Downstairs. Now, an odd assortment of rickety chairs scraped unpleasantly against the wooden floor and produced jarring noises as we sat down around the huge u-shaped makeshift table.

We perked up when large baskets of bread were being passed around, and deep bowls of farina were slammed in front of us. The little ones now interrupted their whining, but resumed it when they found the bread too dry and the farina lumpy and cold. The cocoa with skin of boiled milk floating on its top was unappetizing. Julie, our nanny, and Annie, our cook, used to melt a bar of Bensdorp chocolate into our farina, which came with pictures of movie stars: they were the rage among my classmates. We collected and exchanged them—just like American kids trade baseball cards, or more recently Pokemon cards.

No one ate much that night. I already had overheard the fat, uncouth cook snarl at a sniveling youngster: "*Tais-toi, tu as de la chance d'être ici*" (just be quiet, you're lucky to be here). The harshness of her *tais-tois*—among the words my French mademoiselle had taught me years ago—was reminiscent of the Nazis.

This was only the first time I resented relying on the charity of strangers. When I called my brother the following morning he immediately griped about his inedible farina and disgusting cocoa. But whereas I felt humiliated, he became defiant: "I'm just not going to eat anything," he vehemently declared. I lapsed into my older sister role, telling him that the food wasn't all that bad, and to give it another try.

Monsieur Frank, a Jewish high school teacher from southern Germany, was as stiff as the rod he was alleged to have threatened to apply to some of his charges' backsides. His nose and forehead beneath his receding hairline seemed forever pulled up into a sneer. He wasn't around most of the time. His wife, the designated charwoman, had a scowling face and couldn't quite manage to smile. This pale dumpling of a woman was in perpetual motion—fixing the bobby-pins in her light-brown hair, tucking straggles into the topknot under her head scarf, while wringing out mops and rags into her bucket of water. Cleaning up children's messes, alternately wiping runny noses, dusty windows, and creaky floors, were her life. She had distributed the assorted cots and beds—most of them topped by lumpy mattresses—to rooms ranging from sizable living spaces to tiny servants' quarters; had sewn gauze curtains for countless, odd-shaped windows. No one appreciated her labors. And we unfairly blamed her for our woes.

After our ramshackle château had been abandoned by its wealthy owners, the surrounding fields gradually were being crisscrossed by roads and sold off as commercial property. Clinging vines covered its ornate turrets, which to me seemed appropriate for Rapunzel or Sleeping Beauty. Brambles and weeds had replaced formal gardens. No one even attempted to tend to this wild growth. The working-class families who had settled nearby could not afford to heat and inhabit this white elephant. Tall iron fences kept out stray dogs, trespassers, and squatters. Clearly, our residence had come down in the world almost as much as we had. Indoors, the walls were badly cracked and bare of pictures, although tell-tale signs of where works of art had hung remained; the imperial staircases needed painting; the creaky parquet floors lacked carpets but disclosed where these previously had been; the few pieces of furniture needed repair; the doors squeaked; the drip-drip of the plumbing rarely stopped; and a number of floorboards were loose enough to conjure up spooks. Were my nightmares caused by my circumstances or by this tawdry habitat?

I met my roommates after that first supper. Bouncy, stocky, literal-minded Ilse Steinhardt was the oldest. She asserted her superiority at once by bragging about the boyfriend she had left behind in Nuremberg. Erika, whom I judged to be a crybaby, was skinny and short, with a washed-out face that receded behind enormous, black-rimmed spectacles. I took a dislike to Marianne Scheuer, a scrawny, thirteen-year old loud-mouth with flaming red hair, watery blue eyes and dark freckles, who excelled at stirring up trouble. Our routine of lounging, eating, and changing our clothes was conducive to trouble-making and brooding. The older girls lorded it over the younger ones, the Berliners over the Frankfurters, the ones from Munich deemed themselves better than their neighbors from Nuremberg, and so on. Small-town girls disdained country yokels.

The only thing that united us was being Jewish. I was the most as-similated, the least savvy about religion. Marianne came from Hannover, from a close-knit and observant Jewish community. Ilse's boyfriend was half-Jewish, which she skirted; and I don't recall anything about Erika. Before long, each one of us was arguing for the superiority of her own family's beliefs. Trying to score points, and competing, helped distract us from the homesickness we couldn't face. Not only the little ones wet their beds; we all whined, became aggressive, cruel, obsequious, and hostile. We suspected we would never again return to our homes, and were waiting for American visas.

We lived from mail to mail. I corresponded with my mother, my grand-mothers and my father. We read and reread the letters we received, and agonized over answering them. I poured my anguish into my (locked) diary. And we babbled endlessly, without ever trusting one another. We argued about tidbits of news, wondered about when Hitler would die, and what we would be eating for lunch or supper. We kept accusing one another of taking up more than our allotted space, the way Hansl and I had done over the exact amount of elbowroom in the back of our father's car.

Since we had no closets, we kept our belongings in the suitcases under our cots. Our clothes were always wrinkled, and we procrastinated in ironing them. We cleaned up our domain only when we no longer could get out of it. With much ado, we would go through the motions of the household tasks that previously had been taken care of for us. I didn't like helping wriggly little kids slip into their shoes, which I considered "maid's work"; or to bicker and take care of myself in hochdeutsch (high German); and to try unlearning the Viennese colloquialisms I grew up with. Whenever I fell into them, I became the object of derision. To soothe myself, I would hurry across the road whenever the coast was clear, to buy crunchy cookies and cheap chocolate. Eating temporarily seemed to quell my anxiety.

When taking the bus to visit Hansl, the driver didn't understand my school French. I had to learn the Belgian pronunciation in order to get around. There was vague talk of enrolling us in the local school, but nothing ever came of it. Yet I desperately wanted to master the French language.

Madame Goldschmidt and Madame de Becker, of the committee that had organized and enabled our escape, seemed the only ladies I then met who resembled my mother. But during their visits, they rarely spoke to their little refugees. Before their arrival, the Franks checked that our beds were made properly, that we cleaned up our rooms and ourselves. They made their rounds with the littlest ones at their side, encouraging them to "tell the nice ladies" how much they liked their food, and the Franks. The latter probably did take the place of their parents. But I could not admit to needing anyone. However, Madame Frank called the doctor when we were ill, and in this limbo, where the past and the future seemed more tangible than the present, being sick was time out from chores.

Thus I welcomed my sore throat and aching wrists, which the doctor diagnosed as rheumatic fever. He ordered bed rest. Neither he nor the Franks connected my illness to my inadequate diet. I took the fact that Madame Frank spotted a louse in my by then carefully kempt pompadour hairdo much more seriously. One morning, after noticing that the five-year-old Rosa kept scratching her blond, curly head, she found out that it was teeming with lice. So were her roommates' heads. To stop the epidemic, Madame Frank enlisted the older girls, including myself, in a crusade against lice. She shaved the heads of children under seven, and gave short, ungainly crew cuts to the others. And she doused all their heads with petroleum jelly. Every evening, she checked her assistant checkers heads.

One night, after Madame Frank had discovered a louse in my long, wavy mop, she readied her shears, eager to pounce. But as she came at me, I said, "don't get near me, please," while backing up onto the left side of the divided, regal staircase. When she refused to listen and kept coming closer, I turned and ran up two steps at a time, and down on the right side. She was close behind me, and every time she lost ground, she would stop, turn around, and try to catch me in her outstretched arms. But I anticipated her every move and would spin around once again. By then she was yelling angrily and the girls were clapping and cheering me on. I won.

I don't know whether Madame Frank was more upset because I might be spreading the epidemic, or because I had undermined her already questionable authority. Of course, my louse was nauseating to me. I spent the following week getting rid of its potential offspring by saturating my hair again and again with the sticky, smelly petroleum paste, and by washing it every few hours. In the process, I managed to have straight, sleeked-down hair, and imagined myself as Theda Bara whom I knew from her "Bensdorp" picture, or as Madame Butterfly— although I didn't recall her bitter death, only her romance-driven life.

* * *

Ever since we had gotten to Belgium, my father had been planning to visit us. Finally, he had the necessary travel permits. Already before calling me downstairs after he had rung the bell, Madame Frank had complained to him about my wild, bushy—and unsanitary—hair. He later recalled, "While Madame Frank was talking at me, I saw a small ape-like creature at her side. She told me that you were unmanageable, uncooperative, and headstrong. That much I could believe, but I knew she was on a tear when she said that you set a bad example to the others." My father actually was proud that I had defied Madame Frank, especially after I explained to him what accounted for little Rosa's grotesque appearance.

My father was as ignorant of his children's psychic life as the rest of debonair Viennese men who strongly resisted knowing what Freud, in essence, had learned from their behavior. And more than most of them, he gladly had relegated "the children's upbringing" to his wife. Had he not been confronted with the prospect of having to explain upon our "imminent" arrival in Paris why his daughter was masquerading as a son, he might well have closed his eyes to my misery. But he was appalled by the fact that I was wasting my time, which was an unpardonable sin in my family's book of ethics. And he had disliked Madame Frank at first sight. He found her unattractive and righteous, both characteristics he condemned in women. So he complimented me on having had the guts to confront her, and on my shoulder-length hair. And he decided that I needed to get away from there.

Objectively, my brother was not much better off. But since the boys' mansion had much outdoor space, the director, Monsieur Gaspar De Waay, had organized his charges into teams. Increasingly, Hansl was embroiled in ferocious fights over soccer scores; and in frays over the size of desserts. Moreover, the boys were given an hour or two per day of some sort of haphazard in-house schooling. Hansl was glad to get out of regular schoolwork and, instead, to improve his athletic skills. Also, he never had been prone to moping and fretting as I was. He tended to settle his scores physically and instantly. So it seemed as unnecessary to move him as it was imperative to get me into a place where I would do more than lie around and brood.

My father could not tarry in Brussels without risking the loss of his temporary, and precarious, residency in Paris, so Weinwurm came to the rescue. He had located a *pensionnat de jeunes filles*, whose board of directors had decided to accept a few refugees at half the usual cost, and who would attend public schools. That was how I came to be a resident at the Maison Yvonne Vieslet, which was named after the heroic girl who had informed on the Germans during World War I, and whom they subsequently had executed. When I moved in at the beginning of April, I did not yet know that I was jumping from the frying pan into the fire.

* * *

The Chaussée de Vleurgat is a steep, cobble-stoned street that descends from the then posh Avenue Louise to the Place St. François, which still distinguishes itself by its landmark church and the tall antenna of the Belgian radio. Adjoining number 51, a nondescript Belgian version of a five-story brownstone, stood a walled-in convent school of gray cement to the north, and a narrow five-story blackened brick building with a slanting slate roof, and with rectangular window boxes burgeoning with red and white geraniums, to the south.

Upon our arrival, an obsequious black-clad maid showed Weinwurm and me into the director's, Madame Despois, overstuffed parlor. With a magisterial gesture, she pointed us to our chairs and immediately informed us, pompously, about financial obligations and the ground rules *pour toutes les filles*. I found her intimidating, especially when she lifted her lorgnette to peer at me, and her eyes looked like a pair of large, blue marbles. I almost sensed already then, that her oppressive order would be as upsetting as the Franks' helter-skelter; and that she might be as self-satisfied by her Christian charity as Madame Frank was by her devotion to cleanliness. In any event, my free-floating unease found its target.

Whereas in Zuen I had been among the oldest children and the *lingua franca* was German, I now was the youngest and had to live and breathe in French. Mademoiselle, Madame's daughter, who soon was summoned to show me around the premises, sensed my discomfort. The flowery brown wallpaper spread gloom, and so did the narrow room with its seemingly worm-eaten furniture I was to inhabit. It held two creaky armoires, two narrow cots, two caned chairs and two marble-topped commodes—each equipped with a chipped washbowl of thick, ecru porcelain and a pitcher.

As the graceful Mademoiselle left, my roommate Emma—the daughter of an American doctor who years ago had divorced her mother, a heavy-set, Belgian nurse—returned from school. Long, sleek, black hair surrounded her chalk-white, even featured face. She wore a dress that nearly replicated the stiff uniforms her pontificating mother never seemed to take off; and she was a goody-good who was too scared of Madame to bad-mouth her even when she was out of earshot. (I think the uncontrollable anxiety that still hits me when afraid of being late is connected not only to my mothers' anger when kept waiting, but also to my fear of Madame.)

My Belgian life was full of chatter, but I have forgotten what animated it. I probably used *formidable* and *oo-la-la* more frequently than any other words. I was frustrated by many a French phraseology, by trying to translate German sayings, and by assuming that my life depended on being perceived as native. While immersing myself in my dictionary, in Alexandre Dumas's tales, in Balzac's, and in whatever reading was at hand, I imagined I was maintaining a confident façade while feeling totally at sea. I often didn't know how to pronounce the words I read, and whether or not they were still being used.

The girls around me spoke with a variety of pronunciations. It took me some time to learn that most of Madame's *filles* came from Flemish speaking parts of the country and expected to perfect their own French, and to obtain proper manners. Among them were the beautiful sisters, Marlène and Jeanne, whose parents worked in the Belgian Congo. All of the girls referred jokingly to their differences, to their Flemish or Walloon origin. I envied them all for being Belgian.

No army was as regimented, or lived by the clock more than we did. Madame's chimes woke us at 6:45 A.M. and summoned us to breakfast at 7:15 A.M. During that half hour we had to run with our water pitchers to the bathroom at the landing below, fill them with icy water, and carry them back for our ablutions, throw on our clothes, and make our beds. Madame would be positioned at the entrance to the pine-paneled, ill-lit dining room, with her lorgnette dangling to her navel—the only ornament on whatever baggy dress she happened to be wearing, except for the embroidered or pearl-studded choker that held up her turkey neck. Like a pint-sized general, she stood there to inspect her twenty-five charges. Her supercilious stares and rigid posture invariably reasserted to me that I was there on her sufferance—a refugee kid on a scholarship, a temporary and expendable lodger whom she could kick out for the least of infractions.

At 7:35 A.M. we were to have wolfed down our *tartines* (bread with butter and jam) and coffee with milk—in a ladylike manner. That bell would remind us to scuttle upstairs for our schoolbags and coats before dashing off to school—which started at 8:00 A.M. Thus we were constantly skipping down or climbing up the narrow staircase, and bumping into each other while struggling to appear the "graceful, young ladies" we were being groomed for. We had no time to ourselves—except on the walk back from school. I basked in this half hour respite from supervision. At 3:45 we were summoned to tea with more *tartines*, and between 4:00 and 6:00 o'clock we were silently hunched over our homework, in the dining room. Between 6:00 and 7:00 we were "free"—to wash and mend our clothes, to finish whatever homework was left undone, to take care of our correspondence.

Upon entering the dining room at 7:00 P.M., Madame would inspect us, calling attention to a run in a stocking, poorly kempt hair, excessive make-up, a wrinkled blouse; and our "bonsoir Madame" was to be as respectful as the mornings' "bonjour Madame." In the process, my false smile became permanent. (Years later, when reading the *Madeleine* books to my children, I knew I had been Ludwig Bemelmans's daughter.) I poured my gripes into my letters. Because mail from Vienna was being censored, my mother and grandmothers refrained from writing about their ever more restricted lives. In my golden cage, I kept myself nearly oblivious to their increasingly endangered circumstances.

In later years, when I recalled life at the *pensionnat*, my mother kept recounting some of her ordeals under the Nazis: having to walk across Vienna in fear of being picked up by police; dealing with tax collectors and commissars; taking grandparents to unfriendly doctors. Thus she was unable to be sympathetic: in her mind, I was living in the lap of luxury, as was her husband in Paris—who complained of his shabby room in a pension off the Champs Elysées. His letters to me, however, seemed to grasp my distress. For instance, when I mentioned that I was putting on weight, he responded that "some people eat to live, and others live to eat." He increasingly appreciated my caustic and often scathing observations, and praised my growing proficiency in French. I never felt nearer to him than on my birthday, on June 3—when he sent me a dozen red roses. Until that day, Madame had dismissed him casually as yet another one of those "refugees who are malingering in Paris." He wrote, "You will receive lots of flowers in your life, because you are growing into a beautiful young lady." And he went on to say that he wanted to send me my first bouquet, since every girl always remembers this occasion as her initiation into womanhood. Madame lent me a pink vase, and I joyfully skipped up the stairs because she had promised me a birthday cake to be shared among *toutes les filles*. I had been worried that if my father were to overlook this to me most important day, I soon would die. The flowers had removed the impending disaster.

*   *   *

Emma was polite and *comme il faut*, but her closemouthed manner irritated me. Instead of the *confidante* I had hoped for, I found her snobbish even when she quietly and considerately tip-toed through my half of the area to hers. An open archway connected us to the adjoining room, which Ilse and Marianne soon came to occupy. By then, I looked forward to their arrival, if only to take time out from speaking French. But Madame informed me that it was up to me not to lapse into German.

"It would be rude, *ça ne se fait pas*," she stated emphatically. In some weird way, she connected the *sales boches*, as the Germans were called during the First World War, who she said had chopped off Belgian children's hands, with anyone who spoke German. (This is not to say that I wasn't still being jarred by Ilse's and Marianne's Pieffke accent.)

After a few months, the laughing, spunky, red-haired Janine Dupont, the daughter of a Flemish post office official in Ninove, befriended me. She seemed to clue in to my discomfort by nodding sympathetically when we bumped into each other on the stairs, and soon explained some words I didn't understand. She advised me on how to avoid getting into trouble, and let me in on local customs. But contrary to my mother's unshakable conviction, I never had "learned without studying," although I often had pretended to do so. Challenging thoughts alone could take my mind off worrying about every conceivable bit of nonsense.

I was rudderless, and grasping for some unavailable anchor. I envied the other girls because they went home on weekends, to parents, boyfriends, movies, siblings, and dogs. When I felt too sorry for myself I retired to the toilet to cry "for no reason." (Now, I occasionally wet my bed, and fear of discovery added yet another load to my ever darkening moods.) My own (better) weekends were crowned by Sunday lunch with Weinwurm and my brother. During our first two outings, we were shown the main sights of Brussels; on subsequent ones we went to the movies. I must have bored this forty-five year old bachelor as I went on talking about Madame's injustices. Neither could Hansl's aimless jabber about bunkmates who cheated at soccer have absorbed him. He must have looked forward to the movies as much as I did.

* * *

Basically, after leaving the *home d'enfants* I lived entirely among Christians. I tried to hide that I was Jewish, or to pretend to myself that it didn't matter. For instance, on Sunday mornings, Madame, Mademoiselle, her prosperous daughter, Madame Stark, and her two blonde tots, came over for breakfast before going to church. When Marlène and Jeanne were around, they went along, since they too were Walloon, and Catholic. They never said out loud that I was a sinner, but I remembered from my friendships with Catholics, and from my many visits to afternoon mass with our nanny, Julie, that people who don't go to confession, who don't cross themselves when passing a shrine, and who do not take holy communion, are doomed. So, their sanctimonious smiles upon their return from church set me on edge. I also recalled the life-size crucifixes on Austrian country roads, from which Jesus kept on bleeding, and the tales about saints who had protected Julie, and the pictures of haloed Madonnas our succession of cooks had hung over their bed. Now, a crucifix hung over the door in my room. Every morning, Emma, with drooping shoulders and hunched back, would kneel by the side of her cot, and while fingering her rosary say a rushed Hail Mary. In her most mincing manner, Madame thanked God for our daily bread and crossed herself before every meal. I wished I could pray to Jesus, or to someone who would protect me.

Of course, I was perpetuating my family's ambiguity about religion. When Mademoiselle asked me the following December, whether I wanted to help her decorate our Christmas tree, I was flattered, but immediately wondered whether she included me in the preparations and the celebrations for the holiday festivities because she took pity on me or because I had nowhere else to go. Christmas in Brussels was lonely, and without presents. I was upset when Madame told her grandchildren the story of Christmas, emphasizing that Jews had refused to give lodgings to Mary, the mother of God. For a moment, I again felt I was held responsible for Jesus's crucifixion. I wished my best friend Lotte were here.

Since my religion was the reason for my presence in Brussels, I often blamed it for my to me inexplicable moods. Instead I kept fastening on tangibles: having to be signed in and out, and having to sneak across the street to buy sweets, because Madame watched our entrances and exits from her parlor by peering at the outside mirror whenever the opening of the front door activated the chimes.

As everywhere when discipline is too strict, the girls had devised ways of circumventing it. I felt flattered when the buxom, saucy seventeen-year-old Georgette invited me to join her and Madeleine's slumber parties. These ritual events took place after Mademoiselle's final inspection and lights out, at 8:45 P.M. After having synchronized our watches and hung a bedspread across the window to hide the light, at exactly nine o'clock, we pressed down the heavy, bronze door handles, making believe that only one door was being opened. To fool Madame, the girl elected to go to the bathroom again would match the opening of that door with the closing of all the others. The fun was in outsmarting Madame. Actually, these escapades were totally tame: all we did was to stuff ourselves with the pretzels and cookies we had bought on our way home from school, and to gripe about Madame.

School was the only "normal" activity approximating my former life. At the bottom of our street we would turn left and saunter up the steep, cobble-stoned Chaussée d'Yxelles and near its top would enter the wide archway that led into the Lycée's courtyard—hoping to arrive before the bell rang. While my classmates recited their *notre père* (Vienna's *Vater Unser*) I would think of the mannequins I had seen in the shop windows and the lives I imagined for the bustling housewives we had passed.

I relished window shopping. By admiring the latest fashions, handsome stationery, outlandish hats, and shiny, modern furniture, I imagined belonging. Ever more voraciously, I lived the adventures of Alexandre Dumas' heroes and Dickens's waifs, pondered the fates and moral choices by the *Comte de Rassignac* and *Père Goriot*, and the tell-tale life of *Eugenie Grandet*, and alternately identified with Albertine or one or another of Proust's characters. And I increasingly blamed my inexplicable wretchedness on Madame. At the Lycée, I befriended a few of my classmates, lapping up what they said about boys.

When we were taken to hear Beethoven's Fidelio at the opera, *La Monnaie*, the hazards posed by males reached their climax. We had primped and dressed up before getting onto a tram. Suddenly Madame ordered us to get off and jump into several taxis: Madeleine and Georgette had "made eyes at boys." "What one of you does reflects on all of you," she declared furiously with her customary *pudeur* (modesty mixed with shame, or prissiness). I didn't really grasp what had gone on, but was stung by having to stay in our box during intermission. Yet, I was grateful to Madame for this outing.

* * *

I had assumed that by the end of June, we would be united with my father. But the international situation worsened. Czechoslovakia had been overrun by the Nazis, and my father's cousin, Uncle Fritz (Uncle Sammy's son and my father's minor partner in Prague), had fled to Canada—thereby forfeiting another chunk of the family's assets. In addition, the French, who were being flooded with refugees, were shutting their borders ever more tightly against immigrants. My father asked me to be patient and remain in Belgium a bit longer.

Because Madame now got ready to spend the summer in her hometown in the Ardennes, and Mademoiselle planned her yearly travel abroad, we needed to find another haven. That is why Madame, Weinwurm, and Ilse's and Marianne's guardians, decided to ship us off to the sister home for the aged, the Foyer de la Femme kept in Lombartsyde—a tiny village on the Belgian coast, not far from Westende. I looked forward to another junket: it would be a fitting diversion while waiting to saunter from the Eiffel tower to the Concorde, and from Montparnasse to Place Pigalle.

4

War and Flight:
From Lombartsyde to Toulouse

When my girlhood model, Trotzkopf—the German-speaking heroine of teenagers, somewhat akin to our Bobbsy Twins—entered her teens, she alternately was "shouting to the skies and distressed to death." I had identified with her enthusiasms and was certain that I never would be prone to irrational ups and downs. Because I was a refugee, I assumed that my thoughts were driven by these circumstances alone, and never attributed my moods to my overly sensitive psyche, or to teenage insecurities.

My ups were rare, but the spring air, and our occasional visits to the nearby bois (Brussels's Central Park) perked me up. And the upcoming beach vacation promised to liberate me from the tedium of Madame's routines. Ilse, Marianne, and I imagined Lombartsyde as yet another resplendent seaside resort, another Cesenatico or Viareggio, peopled by elegant vacationers, and by gallant young men playing soulful tunes on guitars and harmonicas. In anticipation, we acquired cheap bathing suits, shorts, and halter-tops. And we debated what summer clothes to pack. Once again, my travel bug infected me.

A week or two later we set off for the railroad station. There, we were joined by the laid-back mademoiselle who was to guard us in Lombartsyde. We were full of expectations. But upon the train's arrival our spirits took a precipitous dive. As is typical of the northern Atlantic coast, we were greeted by dense fog, and were informed by the taxi driver that our beach was two kilometers down the road rather than near the village, on the other side of the towering dunes we could make out in the distance. Our new home, which was inhabited by seven or eight old ladies, faced the village plaza. They greeted us suspiciously, while inspecting us over the rims of their thick spectacles, and informing us, firmly, that we were not to disturb their calm—as we noisily bounded up the stairs to inspect our two connecting rooms.

We routinely walked to the beach mornings and afternoons, and complained that the hangout atop the dunes—the only place of interest—was forbidden territory. Still, while sitting on beach towels in the sand, we kept our eyes on the passing truck drivers and the few fishermen who took turns dancing with the sexy woman bartender. And we listened to the haunting tunes from the jukebox—such as Edith Piaf's "*J'attendrai le jour et la nuit, j'attendrai toujours*," and Charles Trenet's "*Je chante*." Since occasionally the to us attractive teenage brothers from Antwerp, Raymond and Robert, also hung out there, these evocative tunes transported me to the romantic future which, until then, had been encompassed by waltzes in three-quarter time. Would I ever be able to glide across a dance floor in the arms of an attractive man? The ocean was icy cold, and we did not even try to swim. So, I daydreamed about some of the could-have-beens. I had been expected to follow in my mother's footsteps, who had won the *Quer durch Wien* (straight through Vienna) swimming championship before I was born. Thus, I had been in the running as one of the girl swimmers for Hakoah. Just as my brother had been destined to go into the marble business and to play soccer. And where would I be now, if my mother had allowed me to go skiing with my father in Davos, just before the *Anschluss*? Might I have escaped the Nazis? What were my friends and cousins up to? And where were they? Daydreaming had taken the place of most of reality.

*   *   *

My father had expected my brother and me to leave for Paris before the end of August, but at the last moment called up to say that we ought to wait another week. By then, the Germans had invaded Poland; my father left Paris, hoping to sit out the war on the French coast. But he soon was interned, first in Lisieux and then in Deauville—as an enemy alien. Our guardian precipitously left for her hometown, and so did the few vacationers who had stayed at the village's only hotel. The Maison Vieslet was not to open before September 18, so we had nowhere to go. Until then, I had not seriously followed political events, although I was vaguely aware of the war in Spain and that the good guys were not doing well. Now, we listened to the news on the radio, but nevertheless were determined to make the most of our unexpected "freedom." We refused to come face to face with our panic, and I forgot my nightmares by the break of dawn. Every morning, we resolutely headed for the forebidden hangout, alternately spent our scarce francs by feeding ourselves and the jukebox. But we behaved *comme il faut*. We spoke only French and added

"The White Cliffs of Dover," "The Siegfried Line," the *Marseillaise*, and catchy French marching songs to our repertoire.

Sitting atop the dunes, we observed the Belgian army go off to war. My heart sank, when watching these sloppily attired men saunter south. I didn't think that they could defend themselves against the Germans' Wehrmacht. Some were clad in ill-fitting army uniforms—with or without voluptuous girls hanging on their arms—others wore civilian clothes. The anxiety in the pit of my stomach mounted when seeing yet others carry backpacks, while dragging their feet and putting uncorked wine bottles, flasks, or decanters to their lips. Their slapdash ways and lackluster eyes spoke of their distaste for war. I recalled the Germans' entrance into Vienna, who so ardently sang their upbeat Nazi tunes while raising their arms in the Hitler salute. I was full of forebodings for the patriotic delusions of this motley bunch. But not for my own.

The parental letters that waited for me in Brussels made clear that I had to become their go-between: no mail could cross the Maginot line. I took my responsibility seriously, passing my father's messages on to my mother, and vice versa. As her letters became shorter and shorter, and their tone more and more plaintive, I put on increasingly solicitous airs, reassuring her (and myself) that all would be well after we were reunited. Yet, I was convinced that the Nazis soon would descend upon us, although I also assumed that by adjusting ever more thoroughly to Madame's routines, and by perfecting my French, I was keeping them at bay. I accelerated my consumption of whatever chocolates and cookies I could lay my hands on, and, like Madame de la Marquise, told myself that all was well—while my world was collapsing around me.

I was jolted when my father wrote that we no longer could afford for me to pursue my studies at the Lycée, and that I had better learn a trade. For the first time, he informed me that my grandfather, Opapa Weisz, "was sent away from home on his fourteenth birthday, carrying two pairs of socks, a shirt and some food in his backpack, and was told to find a master who would take him on as apprentice." Since we had become impoverished, the letter went on, I would have to be prepared to support myself—and that we would have to replicate my grandfather's road to success.

"*Der Mensch denkt, Gott lenkt*" (man proposes, God disposes) was yet another proverb embraced by the Viennese. Not until decades later did I realize that my mother had substituted her husband for God, and that for many years her children did not question their father's authority. I followed his advice as if it were the gospel. I venerated him. Actually, he himself was deeply identified with his father, as he so frequently would articulate. Like Madame, he was perpetuating, and proving, the ancestral belief that ambition and hard work lead to wellbeing and happiness. That I might be able to support myself by following an intellectual endeavor had occurred to neither of them. On that ominous fall morning, Madame sweetened my sacrifice by telling me that in trade school I would have to sew pretty clothes for myself, and could acquire hats if I were to take up millinery as well. I no longer hesitated and registered at the École professionelle pour jeunes filles on Avenue Louise.

Now, Weinwurm supplied me with money for dress materials, felt forms and trimmings, and I immersed myself in shopping for cheap fabrics which, once again, I manipulated between forefinger and thumb, the way I had seen my mother do when she had let me accompany her. I persuaded myself that I was leading a normal life by trying not to make waves and swallowing whatever (real and fictitious) indignities came my way. Indeed, like a typical teenager I took myself extremely seriously, whether practicing the rolling French "r's" in front of my mirror, choosing a felt form, evaluating the weave of a fabric, brooding over petty slights by Madame, or by anyone else. I was extremely touchy, but didn't know it. I substituted my diary for a best friend. What positive energy I had went into planning for my weekends.

*   *   *

In the course of the summer, Ilse and I had grown closer. Now, we thought that it would be fun to go out on the town together. To that end, we inveigled our guardians, who were bachelors, to invite both of us for lunches. For as long as we were together, they wouldn't have to bother picking us up, because Madame would be willing to have them sign our *billets de sortie* in town. They eagerly agreed. After a few such outings, Ilse whispered that she had a secret:

"Cross your heart and hope to die," she said with much agitation on a Monday morning, while we were walking to school. I did.

"I don't know what to do," she went on, "Weinwurm is in love with me." "When did he tell you that," I wanted to know, "after all, you have never seen him without me." With a disdainful glance, she went on to call me an innocent child, saying that he didn't have to speak, because "he made it crystal-clear by moving his hand up and down my leg while you were watching Jean Gabin walking around the dangerous Casbah." We whispered about this crisis during every free moment. Again and again, I wanted to know whether she loved him. Most of the time, she thought he was too old and fat for her. But she didn't want to give up our delicious meals and our good times on the town. A few months later, her guardian seemed to admire me as much as Weinwurm admired her. However, I was spared a decision after receiving a scathing letter from my father, informing me that Weinwurm had charged him for all sorts of expenses that were cutting into our "dwindling family resources." He went on in this vein, asking about specific expenditures, from restaurant bills and carfares to postage stamps, from entrances to movies to my spending money. I felt shamed and upset that Weinwurm's generosity was not based on sympathy for me, but on greed. (Until the end of their lives, my parents would trot out this episode to prove that I "always was extravagant and demanding.")

From then on, Ilse and I arranged to meet our guardians for their signatures alone. We went to the movies—some of them forbidden to minors—by ourselves. We were turned off by the display of female flesh, but excited by the fact that we were outsmarting Madame. We disgustedly moved from seat to seat in these half-empty, cavernous theaters whenever a man sidled up to us. On Sundays, I picked up Hansl in Anderlecht. With or without Ilse, we took in a double feature, and ended up at our favorite restaurant, the automat on rue Neuve. There, we got more for less money, could pick from the juicy delicacies in their glass-enclosed cubicles, and felt at ease talking to the people around us. In a letter to my mother, I wrote that Hansl and I never fought, and bought birthday presents for one another. I felt overly protective of him.

At school, over half my time was spent on learning my new trades, and the rest on academic subjects, such as history and French. I don't recall much of any subject matter, except the outing to celebrate our benign king, Leopold III, and the young crown prince, Baudouin. When on that bright sunny day they had stepped onto the flower-filled balcony of their palace, I clapped enthusiastically. Was it because all my life I had heard praises of Kaiser Franz Josef, or because I thought that if all else failed, a prince might rescue me?

Only sixty years later, when reading some of the letters I then wrote to my mother, did I realize that my ability to deal with increasingly difficult circumstances had not matured me. It then didn't cross my mind that writing in French might have an estranging effect on my mother, or that what a kid wrote to a parent might not be important enough for the censors to bother with. Or that my pseudo-adult airs might not have gone over too well. That I rebuked my mother for her short communications must have upset her, not only because she always had felt handicapped by her inability to express herself as well as her husband, but because her letters would be censored. Throughout her entire life she would tell me: "Your father writes good letters," which meant that he managed to get her to accept his infidelities as a necessary component of an otherwise flawless character.

*   *   *

As my French was improving, I tried out new phrases and colloquialisms, concocted nostalgic poems for all occasions, and fantasized about our happy future in America. Not much later, I earned first place in my French class. Madame, who hadn't paid any attention to the grades of her refugees, now was proud of me. She offered me seconds at Friday lunch, the day we had my favorite food, *moules et pommes frites*. But I didn't give an inch. I wanted her to appreciate me rather than my grades. In fact, nothing she did could have pleased me.

Toward the end of September, Elzbieta, a quiet, black haired girl with transparent blue eyes joined us. Her father was a senior officer in the Polish army, and she hadn't heard from him since the German invasion. Over our midday meal, she recounted how, with her mother, she barely had eluded the Germans while fleeing from Warsaw. At her request, everyone now was invited to listen to the news bulletins in the dining room before dinner. We were informed that the Maginot line was impenetrable, that the Belgian army was on high alert, and that the Allies soon would win the war, even though the stalemate was lasting longer than foreseen. Apparently, I wasn't the only Pollyanna during what later on would be called the *drôle de guerre*. Still, the war cast a pall over everyone.

The day after Christmas, Janine's parents, warm as simple people often are, invited me for a few days to Ninove. They lived in a comfortable, modest house, behind a white picket fence. While rolling in the powdery snow with Janine, her dog and a few of her neighbors, in this clean-smelling country air under the sort of sunny sky Brussels never seemed to manage, I was transported back to Austria, mostly to the small family hotel in Küb am Semmering, where my mother, brother, and I had spent our winter holidays. There, we had shared a huge tree with the owners and other guests, who also kept returning year after year, and had walked through the crunchy, white snow to listen to the Christmas hymns at midnight mass. Now, I thought of the identical twins, Dorrit and Marlene, with whom we had gone skiing and sledding, and had gotten into serious snowball fights. I was almost certain that they had become ardent Nazis.

At school, I befriended the only other Jewish refugee from Vienna, Lisl Wertheimer. She lived with her mother. Lisl was lithe and slim, with a straight, thick brown mane of hair she wore over one eye, like Veronica Lake. She was mischievous. I admired her, if only because she was supporting herself and her mother by sketching gloves for a fashion magazine. She was nearly three years older than I, and had a slightly balding boy friend who, every afternoon, picked her up with his car. One day, she confided that she wore no underpants. "Georges prefers it that way," she added laughingly when she noticed that I was shocked. "You'll soon find out why." The more my ears were being filled with sexual innuendo, the more perplexed I became.

*   *   *

When, on an impulse, my mother had registered us at Vienna's American consulate, she didn't imagine that we really could end up in America. But by the time the war broke out, my father's brother, Felix, was in New York and had sent us affidavits. Finally, in March 1940, our number came up. This allowed my mother to escape from Vienna, for Genoa, on April 6, 1940. From there her ship would leave on the 15th, a day before Italy entered the war on Germany's side. It was touch and go, and our household goods never made it. My father was called a bit later and received permission to present himself in Paris for his visa. This allowed him to book passage on the *Champlain*—which was to depart on May 14 from Le Havre. Weinwurm was contacted as well, but took his time before escorting us to Antwerp to obtain our German passports (with the telltale "J" and compulsory middle names of Israel and Sarah), and to undergo the necessary physical exams for our visas. Finally, on May 6, Hansl and I were ready to leave. I was excited at the prospect and had corresponded with my mother about whether we should get a boat from Antwerp or Rotterdam.

On May 10, I woke up to the ominous drone of airplanes. The sky was black with what seemed like thousands of bombers and the countless leaflets they were dropping. The Belgians were asked to surrender. March 10, 1938 all over again. The Germans had outflanked the Maginot line, and were moving to France through neutral Holland and Belgium. Within a week, both countries would lay down their arms, aware that resistance would be suicidal. On that fateful morning, however, I was concerned only for myself and my brother. What will we do? I thought while jumping out of bed. How will we get to Paris? And where is Papa?

Since I was more certain than ever that the Germans could not lose, I alternately froze with helplessness and spun dreams of escape.

Now, the Belgian girls quickly packed their belongings and left for their homes. The Luftwaffe kept roaring and circling overhead. Emma's mother arrived. Taciturn and efficient as usual, she had Emma out in a flash, to send her off to New York—to the ex-husband she detested. Marianne and Ilse already had gotten to America. A day later, I was the only girl in the *pensionnat*. Madame and Mademoiselle were closing up, planning to leave for the family's ancestral village. Without telling me, Madame had been in touch with Weinwurm, and they had decided that I was to join Hansl and the other refugee children in Anderlecht. On May 14, she suddenly summoned me downstairs and said: "Pack your things at once. Take only as much as you can carry, and be ready to leave within fifteen minutes." I cannot recall anything happening between May 11 and 13. Now, I jammed what I could into my suitcases, grabbing clothes without the least reflection. And I forgot my (locked) diary. (Until I visited Brussels with my mother, in 1956, I cringed at the thought that Madame might have read my hateful thoughts about her. And, when in the early 1980s, I was invited to talk at a conference of psychoanalysts, and the organizers put me up at a nearby hotel, I could not help reflecting that in spite of the building boom and its international importance, Brussels still was the gray and damp city it had been upon my arrival from Vienna.)

*   *   *

As I was about to close my suitcases Madame yelled excitedly up the staircase, "*Dépêches-toi, Dépêches-toi*, I just spoke to Madame Frank. You must get to the Home Speyer, in Anderlecht, at once. A few buses will take all you little refugees to the train station, and from there, to France. They'll be leaving late this afternoon. *Dépèches-toi*, you can't afford to miss them."

Had the German invasion turned Madame, who never raised her voice, from a model of decorum into a fishwife? Or had common sense suddenly removed her petit bourgeois pretensions? After bumping my belongings down the staircase, Madame rushed me out the front door, wishing me luck and embracing me for the first and only time. Tears were welling up in her eyes as she looked around her deserted establishment, mumbled something about the *sales boches* who once again were threatening her life, her country, and "innocent children" like me. Although I still held her exaggerated and obsessive discipline against her, I suddenly felt inexplicably close to her, and remorseful. Had I misjudged her? Was she fond of me after all?

However, as I rushed out, I had no time for idle reflections. My mind was on saving myself. Would the ominous bombs drop nearby? Would I be hit? And how would I find my way to America?

The street was deserted. The owner of the candy store, a bumbling oldster who had been advising me on the tastes of Belgian chocolate bars, along with the other nearby shopkeepers, had shuttered their doors. Two families were busily stuffing their cars with as many of their belongings as they could. They were tying mattresses, and even a baby carriage, onto their roofs. The eerie silence was broken only by the steady knocks of my two suitcases bumping against the cobblestones. At the bottom of the Chaussée de Vleurgat, no tram was in sight. The first one slowly creeping around the bend turned out to be too crowded. What would happen to me if I couldn't get to Anderlecht, or if I arrived after the busses already had left? How would I ever find Hansl? Why hadn't Weinwurm given me my passport?

Brussels had taken on a tomb-like aura, the typical image of an abandoned town before a foreign invasion, the eye of the storm. People either already had departed or were staying indoors, behind closed shutters, resigned to their inevitable fate. A long line of cars was snaking around the gasoline pump on Place St. François. Belgians were getting ready for their country's funeral, like automatons programmed by the oft-told reminiscences of those who had lived through the First World War.

My immediate forebodings were unwarranted. I arrived in Anderlecht just as Monsieur DeWaay, was helping the last of his charges mount the busses, while checking off their names.

"We've been waiting for you," he said, as I was crossing the street. "But you can't possibly carry all that stuff," he continued while pointing to my bulging suitcases.

"Take out everything you won't need, you're running for your life, not going to a ball. The boys are carrying nothing except bread." I quickly unloaded shoes, a few books and my beige camelhair coat.

"Could I keep these things here," I implored, adding: "the coat will get too dirty anyway." I was immensely relieved upon hearing my brother yell out from the other bus:

"Why didn't you come sooner? You're slow as a snail. Did you have to get your beauty sleep?" By the time we arrived at the teeming train station, some boys were making fun of the "frivolous" girls who had brought "frilly" clothes. Jesting and good-natured teasing temporarily took our minds off the approaching Germans. Madame Frank was herding us together, repeatedly counting to make sure that none of her large flock was lost. In her broken French, she told us not to speak German. Her husband was in the army. Monsieur DeWaay was taking possession of "our" boxcars, and was making sure they would be attached to the very next train. (Over fifty years later, at a Heurigen in Vienna, I met a woman who had been in another such *home d'enfants*, and who had run into Alex Frank in 1945. She informed me that he had been a high functionary of the Communist Party; that he had had a large role in the resistance; and that he subsequently had settled in East Germany. How could you not have suspected it, she marveled.)

I watched the pandemonium around me as if in a dream, and put my trust in the adults, assuming they would get us through. By the time we finally clambered into our cattle cars, around 10:00 P.M., I was exhausted, weary and disgruntled. Madame Frank designated a few of the older girls, including myself, to calm the little ones. Although we were riddled by anxiety, we tried to be considerate, while intent on grabbing the most comfortable "seats" on the bumpy, smelly straw-covered floor. We were dead tired, when a few hours later the train began to move from one track to another, and we half-heartedly hummed the Marseillaise.

At the crack of dawn, we still were not far from Brussels. Our slow-moving snake of a train had lost its direction. As it lurched around countless curves, I embroidered once again on former summer vacations, and totally forgot that some of those days had been exceedingly boring. I dreamt of my mother's picturesque pamphlets and travel brochures, and considered myself lucky to get to see France.

Would there be inspectors at the French frontier? I suddenly thought, and then recalled that I had nothing to hide. When I realized that I had forgotten my address book at the *pensionnat*, I was upset that I no longer would be able to write to my pen pal in Australia, and to the Israeli boy who, in Igls, had frightened everyone with the horror stories of werewolves and savages he told after nightfall. (One evening our shins briefly had touched, and I had wondered whether one could get pregnant that way. My mother said not to worry when I finally found the courage to ask her after we were back in Vienna.)

Each time the train jerked to a halt, I would come to and stiffen up to avoid bumping into one of my neighbors. We were uncharacteristically polite to each other, painfully aware that we would have to get along. Gradually, I was conscious only of the stench, and of my cramped, aching limbs. Soon, most of us paired off with partners of our own size, propping ourselves against the back of the kid behind.

The train moved south and north and east and west, lurching uncertainly to its unknown destination. It stopped for hours in the midst of freshly sown cornfields and in dark tunnels.

"Are we there yet," the younger children would ask repeatedly, and no one could tell them. Some tracks had been bombed and others blocked. We had to trust the engineer to get us to safety, unaware that he too was in limbo. He was navigating on one of the two tracks that still led south, but could not know at what point it might stop. At each station yet more cars were added to the locomotives that were barely pulling us.

After two days (instead of the normal three hours) we reached the French frontier. We had heard wild rumors from railroad workers, and from refugees on neighboring trains, that it might be closed. No one, of course, could sort out facts from hearsay and speculation. Fortunately, the boys had brought bread. From time to time, just as I got lightheaded and thought I might faint, Monsieur DeWaay would produce a jug of water to pass around. We were relatively considerate, but whoever took more than a few gulps was rebuked by devastating stares and shrill, angry hoots.

While peeking through the oblong crevices or round holes in the wooden slats that enclosed our boxcars, we saw throngs of people on nearby roads: exhausted bicycle riders, pedestrians with bundles on their backs; farmers pushing carts and donkeys; small *Deux-Cheveaux* their owners kept propelling forward; families in carts drawn by horses that foamed at the mouth; abandoned automobiles that had run out of gas; and family groups that sat beneath shady trees, surrounded by their belongings. If I had known of Hemingway's moveable feast, I might have called this mass exodus a moveable famine. How could these poor souls have a chance against the advancing German army with its formidable tanks and planes, and against the sadistic SS and the Gestapo?

One morning, we stopped outside a major station. The sky was the deep blue I had imagined French skies to be, the sun was softly shining, and we were immersed in a deadly calm. The jarring clatter of the train switches and the puffing of locomotives had stopped altogether, and so had the roar of airplanes. A cheery Red Cross lady, whom as if by magic Monsieur DeWaay had conjured out of thin air, appeared with her mobile cart, offering hot chocolate and fresh doughnuts.

"You're lucky to be here," she said. "Didn't you hear the ghastly bombs that came down during the night? Do you mean to say that you slept through last night's attack?"

That was how I found out that a train at a siding about fifty yards from us had been hit. Too numb to feel anything, and overtaken by a sort of fatalism, I contentedly munched on my breakfast and did not even ask whether anyone had been hurt. Now, some of us kept bragging about how clever we had been at eluding the Germans, and were convincing ourselves that our luck would hold. As we were constructing myths of escape, we blithely denied to ourselves that German planes might return at any moment. Instead, I worried that Monsieur DeWaay, who like a jumping-jack kept moving on and off the train, might not get back on. What would happen to us without him?

My trip into the blue was far from what I had envisioned, and had absolutely nothing in common with the one Clark Gable and Claudette Colbert had embarked on. But because they had ended up in some previously undiscovered paradise, I again relied on being saved by counting to fifty without breathing, or by standing on my toes while getting up to one hundred even as the train was rounding a curve. As we began to move more rapidly, Monsieur DeWaay seemed to be a bit less agitated; and Madame Frank started us on singing peppy, French marching tunes and soft, German lullabies.

The younger children got sick first and some of them threw up; we had no toilet facilities and had to use the odd containers Monsieur DeWaay furtively appropriated from here and there. Since boxcars have no windows, and the narrow air slats let in the occasional rain as well as the humidity of the morning dew, the putrid smell of excrement mingled with that of perspiration and vomit. By the fifth day most of us felt nauseated. Our limbs were black and blue from the bumps we got when the train was careening and coming to abrupt stops; we were achy from the cramped positions we had been forced into; our clothes stuck to us; and we stank. Ever so often, someone needed iodine for a cut, aspirin for a headache, or ointment for a bruise. Madame Frank's medicine chest, which she carried in the deep pockets of her dress, seemed bottomless. And in her awkward fashion, she soothed those who couldn't stop sobbing or calling out for their parents. Only the steady sound of the moving train was comforting, insofar as with each rotation, it was taking us further away from danger.

I sighed with relief when we stopped in Lyon: finally a landmark I knew to be to the south. Where was my father? Had the *Champlain* taken off for America on May 14? If so, was he on it? I shuddered as much at the thought of having been left behind, as I feared that his ship might be sunk by German submarines. And I rehearsed just how I would tell him about our tumultuous trip. As he had advised me, I concentrated on every minutia of this exodus, on every sound and smell, spinning out how I would write about it when I grew up. Like Robinson Crusoe, I saw myself as living a perilous yet unforgettable adventure: as the hero of my own tale I would forever remain a step ahead of the Germans, and after my triumphant escape I would live out the rest of my miraculous life, full of adventures and brilliant admirers. Still, by peering through one of the "peepholes," I grasped that my journey was part of a human stampede.

On the eighth day or so, we reached Toulouse. The station was overflowing with humanity. All of France appeared to have gotten there ahead of us. People were sprawled across their motley, makeshift luggage, falling over each other, and trying to capture a bit of space on the few wooden benches every time an occupant arose to get on the snaking queue to the *toilette*. Babies were whimpering; gaggles of small children were hopping about, dozing off, sucking their thumbs and cradling their stuffed animals; exhausted parents kept shouting to their offspring to stay close by. Some were awaiting trains that never came. Optimists were on the lookout for relatives, peering into boxcars, calling out their names, or asking around whether any of the newcomers had run into them. Pessimists studied obsolete timetables, wondering whether to follow the Germans' propaganda and to return back north, and whether to believe that they would not retaliate. Yet, there also developed the sort of camaraderie only the most alarming situations can bring about: strangers asked each other for advice about lodgings, and exchanged confidences.

The natives, whose dialect alone would have set them apart, never had been aware that there were so many people in the world, much less that they all could fit in their backyard. They did not know what to do with them, where to put them up, or how to feed them. Inevitably, hustlers approached the seemingly affluent and offered them sleeping quarters they often did not dispose over.

Monsieur DeWaay played on the sympathy strangers tend to display toward children. And on his Communist Party credentials? Clever and insistent, he had us assigned to a bucolic village—the tiny hamlet of Seyre par Naillou, whose inhabitants we were about to double. Like so many other backwaters in that forlorn region, Seyre had been depopulated long ago, when its young people had started to leave the farms to make their mark, and to better themselves in the cities. The French army had drafted the remaining able-bodied men. In the 1920s, the elder of the de Capèle family, which since the twelfth or thirteenth century had owned the entire countryside—its hills, valleys, cattle and crops—had converted two granaries into an orphanage. At the onset of the war, the remaining orphans had joined the army or had otherwise dispersed. Now we were to fill their places.

5

From Seyre to the Melée of Toulouse

I don't recall sleeping during that night at the railroad station, but cannot forget awakening at dawn to glorious sunshine, and to more *dépêchez-vous*. Now, we were being herded onto yet another train for the rather short trek to Villefranche du Lauragais. Roofless cattle cars awaited us on a siding far outside the station. Reinvigorated by the pure country air, we perked up as our train ambled through the rolling countryside, and joked that we were like cows being transported to their slaughter. I idly marveled at the green hills and plowed fields in the radiant dawn, at their irregular yet harmonious patterns, and at the neatly kept farmhouses and green carpets of grass. Blue cornflowers and red poppies were swaying with the wind. On this leisurely ride, we stopped every few kilometers to let a farmer or two get on, and enthusiastically returned the greetings by bustling gardeners and yeomen. As they looked up from their chores they waved and shouted their welcomes. I let myself loll in the bucolic peace, and reveled in the let-up from our tumultuous trip, while taking deep breaths.

In Villefranche du Lauragais, we were met by Jacques, a cocky, barefoot fourteen-year-old local boy. He bragged that he knew every rut and furrow, every stone and brook in the region, and that he would get us to Seyre by the quickest route—across fields. "Just follow me," he kept repeating, while explaining his momentous mission to everyone we met. Speaking in his school French with a large sprinkling of the native patois, I had trouble following him. (The nearly toothless "oldster" who stopped me on a visit to Seyre, in 1988, introduced himself as that Jacques and instantly began to reminisce about that day.)

The village was nearly ten kilometers away, "up over that hill and on top of the one behind it," Jacques said while pointing southeast by thrusting out his chin. We trudged for the rest of the day, dragging our belongings across bumpy dirt roads and lush meadows, complaining periodically about sore feet, hunger, and thirst. When my feet hurt, I briefly flopped down under the nearest tree and waited for the younger ones to catch up. I took comfort in sniffing the cow dung and apple blossoms, in the plethora of lilacs, marigolds and blooms I could not identify, in watching exotic butterflies, and the abundance of lush goldenrod and buttercups, dandelions, and daisies bending in the breeze. As my fears were receding, I listened to the sounds of this rolling farmland, to the scraping crickets, the incessant chattering and trilling of songbirds, and the occasional screech of a raven.

Finally, Jacques pointed to trees surrounding a *château* atop a distant hill, informing us that that was where we were heading. Upon rounding the last curve of the faint footpath along the right side of a steep, grassy incline, we came upon Seyre. (When I tried to locate the village in the late 1960s, this path already had been paved.) The right hand side of its relatively broad (and only) street was flanked by about a dozen narrow one-story row houses, each of whose gray stone façades was broken up by a tiny window and a door. On our left stood the two empty, flat-roofed granaries-cum-orphanages of brick and cement, which would be our new home. At the end, on the right, was the tiny tavern that doubled as the post and telephone office. From there, a small footpath led downhill, bordered by a handful of detached houses and granaries. At the far end of that lane, surrounded by open fields, stood the water pump that served most of the village.

As we straggled into the main street, the wife of Monsieur le Maire, Madame de Capèle, came to greet us. She haltingly explained that her husband was in the army and that she and her new baby had had to move out of their *château* at a moment's notice—while pointing to it, among its tall trees. It had been requisitioned by the French army, which also had fled south. Madame Frank, who intuited the insecurity of this proud yet unworldly woman, offered to help with the baby.

The zealous inhabitants of Seyre were ready for our arrival. They had refurbished our cavernous kitchen; gotten the antiquated coal stove into shape; had found outsize buckets for cooking, a few crude restaurant utensils, odd plates and tin silverware, which were neatly stacked on makeshift tables—old doors placed on top of wooden saw horses. A few aged, wrinkled inhabitants milled about, along with the bumbling "village idiot," while feisty women kept running to their own homes to round up whatever necessities seemed to be missing. Monsieur DeWaay strutted about, taking his glasses on and off, cleaning them, inspecting and advising. Much as a commander would assess the territory he had just conquered, he decided where his troops would lodge: "Boys upstairs and girls downstairs," he ordered. I secured the southern right hand corner of my dorm by depositing my luggage on the straw covered floor. Some of the boys were mobilized to fetch more straw, which encouraged the staple wisecracks about spoiled females; others helped villagers carry additional boards and saw horses—to enlarge the dining facilities. We borrowed benches from the whitewashed church at the left end of the street—which was a few steps from the château.

I soon helped set the tables and cut bread. By the time we were done, the hearty peasant women, who until then had not had any direct contact with the ravages of war, brought in immense buckets of hot food. I no longer recall what we ate that night, but I was grateful for this first hot meal in over a week. We unwound. It didn't seem to matter to the villagers that German was the lingua franca amongst us, either because they still were so removed from the northern part of the country and had trouble with classical French, or assumed that that was the Belgians' language.

After that supper, we marched to our sleeping quarters to the tune of the Marseillaise. My corner space allowed me to extend my arms, but I hadn't expected straw to be so scratchy. Nor had I anticipated waking up with two sets of legs on my shins. Kicking off Ilse Schragenheim's and Inge Berlin's feet, I sensed that from now on we would arise at daybreak; that the itching straw and the biting bugs, along with the crowing cocks and clucking chickens, not to speak of the lack of electricity, would determine our schedules. Monsieur DeWaay had organized us into work-ing teams, and had made a chart assigning us to rotating weekly chores. Having drawn breakfast duty, I soon was in the kitchen, cutting up huge loaves of heavy farmers' bread. Others set out the assorted pitchers of fresh milk and placed plates on the tables before the younger children were allowed to enter. While kitchen duty fell on everyone over eleven or twelve, the oldest ones once more were to take care of the younger ones. I was assigned the nine to eleven year old boys.

Now, I envisioned myself as a model counselor. I invented tasks I assumed "my boys" would enjoy, and invented oral exercises to help them improve their French. We hiked to Naillou and other villages, and found shady spots for pastoral picnics. But my obstreperous charges had their own ideas. They didn't want "a girl" to tell them what to do. And they were my brother's pals, which they believed gave them the right to bedevil and tease me as he did. (Years later, my brother recalled Seyre as a three-year, happy sojourn.) But we all made believe we were safe, and concentrated on the pleasures and abandon life in the country could offer.

I was exasperated when "my boys" didn't listen to me, presented me with frogs and grasshoppers after they realized I loathed their touch; hid pretending they were lost; dared me to jump across the fast-moving, silvery brook I preferred to sit by and watch; and "accidentally" fell into it. Still, I ran after them with animal gusto, avoiding the occasional horse apples, enjoying the liberty to flit about, pointing out an orange and blue butterfly to one, searching for four-leaf clovers with another. In these slumbering, southern meadows and pastures I unwound. We were in limbo, and the Germans were far away. While marching across neatly staked out fields, we readily adapted to the slow, harmonious rhythm of country living.

Most evenings after supper, Monsieur DeWaay gathered his counselors around him to air our gripes and plan the next day's activities. To put down the "insubordination" of my sassy charges, he suggested that I join up with Werner Rindsberg (a.k.a. Walter Reed), the boy leading my brother's group. We organized them into soccer teams, which were a roaring success. But while Werner and I conferred about choosing the most suitable meadow to play on, my brother heckled: "Why don't you kiss?" That made me anxious and uncomfortable. Werner was athletic, a quick runner and about my height. If he heard this innuendo, it didn't seem to bother him. I soon palled around with Inge Berlin, the oldest of our bunch. She had a heavy walk to match her ample girth, wore a long, dark blue skirt and gold-rimmed spectacles. Straight, pale blond hair, which was tied in back by a spangle, framed her pale, even-featured face. Madame Frank had entrusted Inge with the key to the larder—the house next to Madame de Capèle's. We were assigned to supervise the girls' weekly (outdoor) bath. The boys had to carry countless pails of water from the pump, which we would heat on the stove and then pour into the huge beer barrel that served as our tub. One by one, by ascending ages, our giggly girls would mount the makeshift stepladder and self-consciously heave themselves over the barrel's rim. We scrubbed them. By the time we got to the eleven-year olds the water was gray, with soapy grime and hair swimming on its surface. The older girls refused to take their clothes off "in public." We never really bathed but instead waded in the brook and, however rarely, washed our hair in the icy water under the pump.

While Madame Frank and "Tante Lucienne," Monsieur DeWaay's wife, cooked, and we roamed the countryside—speaking to farmers and farmhands, kidding around with the soldiers who hung about the entrance to the château—Monsieur DeWaay procured groceries and ration cards, and complied with formalities in Villefranche and Toulouse. From one of his trips he brought back a handsome (unmarried) couple in their late twenties, comrades he had known in Brussels, and who were to help take care of us. They announced that they were Communists almost the moment they arrived. Bursting with energy and enthusiasm, Jean and Jeanne reorganized our groups and zeroed in on our scant knowledge of sex. And they decided that everyone over thirteen or so needed to be enlightened.

To that end, Monsieur Jean assembled the boys, and Mademoiselle Jeanne the girls. As we sat cross-legged on the earthen floor of Madame Frank's living room, and candlelight kept flickering across our confused and flustered faces, Jeanne did her best to ignore our scarcely concealed and bewildered snickers. So far as I recall, she did not suggest that we ask questions, but quickly launched into supplying us with biological facts. At least to me, she offered more information than I could absorb. Because she had no blackboard, she said, she was drawing pictures of the male and female sex organs on notebook paper. She passed these around while explaining the mechanics of sexual intercourse. After she said something about having left behind her collection of "dildos"—I never had heard of the word—and wondered aloud what the invading Germans would think upon finding it, I began to feel sick, thinking of what Madame's reaction would be when finding my diary. I don't recall any mention of love and romance—which was the only thing I ever connected to the deep and blushing glances some of our girls fleetingly, and ever more frequently, exchanged with our boys. When they came out of their classroom on sex instruction they seemed to snigger and titter even more than we did.

Jean's and Jeanne's arrival allowed me to save face, mostly for myself, about what a flop I was as a counselor. They taught us to build campfires, organized staggered singings, such as *Alouette, gentille alouette…*," folk and scout songs, stirring marching tunes, and the Internationale. They instituted scout-type activities, overnight excursions for select groups, treasure hunts for the little ones. We soon were engaged in team sports, in competitive ball games and other group endeavors, such as potato races, mushroom and strawberry picking. I was assigned more household chores, from sewing mattresses out of potato sacks to washing dishes and serving our hot mid-day meal.

Since Madame Frank had to stretch our rations, she threw whatever vegetables, meat and bones she could lay her hands on into the daily flour and potato soup, our lunch time fare. Heaps of bread were placed on the tables, to dunk in the soup. Because the kitchen was at the farthest end from the dining room, the designated waiters had to carry the buckets through a long corridor. This allowed ample time to reach elbow-deep into the pot, to fish out one of the rare pieces of meat, and gulp it down. (Breakfast consisted of bread with lard or jam, and dinner of bread with cheese.) I felt guilty for stealing, and sighed with relief every time I wasn't caught, petrified that someone might spot me with my hand in the soup, yet determined to stop being a goody-goody.

On June 3, my birthday, I reluctantly asked Monsieur DeWaay whether I could send a postcard to my mother. He not only granted my wish, but told me that Weinwurm had given him our passports, and that I ought to try getting to America. So I sent the following message to my uncle's business address:

Dear Mutti:

A few days ago we arrived in Seyre. We escaped from Brussels and are safe. Can you send us money and tickets to come to New York? Much love and kisses, Ditta and Hansl. This is the address: Seyre par Naillou, Villefranche du Lauragais, Toulouse, France.

For years, my parents would recount the excitement and relief they felt upon getting this message. About two weeks later I received a cable saying that arrangements had been made to send us twenty dollars, and that tickets to leave for America were in the works— signed "parents."

That was how I found out that my father was safe. Within a few days the woman in charge of the P.T.T (post, telegraph and telephone office) came running to tell me the money had arrived. Now, I threw myself headlong into preparing our departure: our visas were expiring on September 6.

In the letter I had sent to my mother to Genoa before she left for New York, dated March 31, 1940, my handwriting is clear, the content full of what a compliant, proper girl would write. I asked questions about relatives, and complained that she had not been writing freely. My long letter from Seyre, dated July 26, 1940, is that of a responsible, insecure but budding adult: This is what I related, again in French:

My very dear parents,

Finally I can write to you, knowing that this letter will arrive soon, given the current situation. You asked me to write via airmail but you did not realize that this is not always feasible. I hope that my telegram arrived. But its text no longer is correct. Yesterday I received $20. which are worth 870. frs. Today I received 1000. frs. from the firm in Dervillé [my father had contacted them]. I complained 7 days ago because I had not heard from you. But 6 days ago our director received confirmation that the money had arrived with much delay, asking whether we were still here. So all is in order, and I now have:

870. from the dollars

1000. Dervillé

83. Belgian francs minus the 33.90 for the telegram, because you did not send enough for return postage, minus money for stamps.—I have no idea what the trip from Toulouse to Lisbon may cost, but I hope that our money will suffice. We are missing only the two transit visas. —Two days ago Madame Braunstein [one of my father's business contacts] wrote a very friendly letter. Her husband is in the army, she is working in a military hospital. She will try to help us, and she has written to Madame Goldschmidt to whom our director wrote about our case (she is one of the ladies of the Committee in Brussels, maybe you know her). Our director takes good care of us, but everything is very difficult. You were in France during the war, we are here after it ended. Half of France is occupied, Belgium is occupied—and there are many refugees around here from these regions. People don't have rooms to sleep in. Many are content to find a small corner to put down their blankets. If you were to see all this you would write differently. You still had a chance to leave and I am pleased you did. You are advising me to go to Marseilles: but we would need extra money. I mean we would have to have money to buy food. One has to run around to get potatoes and when one does it's a holiday. And you cannot forget that we are 100 persons, persons who eat a lot. We're always outdoors and get hungry. When we are hungry we need about 16 large loaves of bread for supper. So far we have been all right, and we never have left the table hungry. And, after all, we still have beds of wood, even if ten are sleeping on six beds, and we're better off than other refugees.—We two are lucky because we will be leaving, but we're the only ones, the others don't know what they will do and no one knows. In any case, they have a life without the least hope that this life will change. This is still all right for the little ones, but it's different for the big ones. There is only one girl older than I, and a number of boys. Three have been sent to a camp and two have returned, and two girls are still there. One must also do something for them. But the screening commission [criblage] cannot save everyone, there are too many. I am writing you all that to give you some idea of what is going on here. Under normal circumstances, one receives a transit visa without any difficulty, but now every country is so full of refugees that they don't want more people than they already have. Under normal circumstances one sometimes finds pity. Now it is normal to be refused, and people are used to seeing misery, and you see more refugees than natives.—Compared to all the other refugees we're very well off, we are in a tiny village, and the group of orphans from Brussels are its only refugees. I don't know of any refugees better off here or in Villefranche, and I believe that after seeing others while coming from Brussels to Seyre in our boxcars. I don't agree with you that I will immediately forget all that has happened, because one doesn't easily forget such experiences.—Hansl is fine, he will write to you, if it isn't much don't be angry at him, he is, as you, Maman, know, "our Hanserl" who disappears when he has to write or do anything reminding him of school. —I have received a postcard from Charles [Weinwurm] and he still is in the camp and I wrote to him. —I have the impression that things will work out with our departure and that we will rejoin you soon if there are no more accidents, but one always has to count on more difficulties. I also have written to Mrs. Schwarz, American Joint Committee, without receiving an answer. I had no address in Lisbon but I hoped the letter would arrive anyhow.—I receive your mail within 7 to 8 days, the first letters took longer. You wrote that you are living with friends who are in the country. Will you move when they return or remain with them? Write also about private matters. You, Maman, you never write anything at all and I don't like it. —Also, there are few trains from here, for a while there were none. And I want to ask you something else: There is a girl here, Inge Helft. She has family in New York but can't write to

them because her mother is in England and she gets money for only one postcard per month. The address: Mr. Kurt Gans, 1710 Avenue H, Brooklyn. She would like you to let them know that she is fine, etc., and give them her address. You would do her a great favor and I'm sure you'll do it. I think I have written enough for today and that you will be content. Now Hansl will write a long letter. I embrace you, your daughter, Ditta

His letter:

Dear Parents,

Ditta already has told you everything. I am amusing myself. Now I am sitting at Ditta's dormitory window to write to you. She is a little sick but it is nothing. During the last days I had to spend all day carrying wood for the fire, and then I have to go to bed. So I have to write quickly. I sleep with 9 on a bed for 6. I hope to see you soon.

Many kisses, your son, Hans.

At that point, Monsieur DeWaay decided it was time for me to accompany him to Toulouse—to arrange for tickets, and for the permits and visas we would need before being allowed to leave. We walked the ten kilometers to Villefranche and got on the next train. Monsieur De Waay had more of an inkling than I of the endless formalities I would have to get embroiled in; and that it would be a while before Hansl and I were on our way. He advised me to get the ball rolling by starting to tackle the Spanish consulate. As he handed me a map of Toulouse, a thick cheese sandwich, and my ration card, he suggested, "Use this card in place of a *carte d'identité* and pass yourself off as Belgian if you're stopped. And whatever you do, don't let on that you understand German. Everyone in Toulouse hates the *boches*. Remember, people can't tell the difference between a Jewish girl from Austria and a bona fide Nazi."

After we agreed to meet for the return trip at 5 o'clock, I set off to conquer this teeming city by trying to melt into its bustling crowd. I did not yet know that this would be the first of many trips to Toulouse, the start of my voyage to America.

*   *   *

Nowadays, Toulouse is a well-kept, sedate town, with gardens surrounding many of the rose-toned, imposing and scrubbed buildings—the typical seat of a French *départment*. But in 1940, it was crawling with humanity. Then, foreign consulates were located in the center of town. I had to head into this maelstrom—my idea of Calcutta at its worst. I was paralyzed, gripped by anxiety and unsure about how to insert myself into the motley crowd. Women were pushing their belongings in baby carriages while carrying toddlers on their arms, corpulent and officious looking gentlemen lugged bulging briefcases, beggars in rags asked for handouts, and portly farmers led heaped carts pulled by tired horses—loaded with potatoes, kale, corn, and other vegetables, and with rosy peaches, red apples, and ripe cherries. These tillers of the soil were circumventing the rationing system that had just been put in place. I bumped into soldiers in wilted khaki uniforms, into white-clad sailors with their cocky red pompoms on their berets, and into the inevitable wheeler-dealers; and I tried not to notice, or stumble over, the sleeping bodies in doorways. The town was so overrun with humankind that one could barely make out the low-slung houses.

I had put on my most adult looking dress, the lightweight, navy print with huge white flowers I had made at the École. I had gotten used to running around barefoot or in tennis shoes, so that I was a bit unsteady in my sturdy pumps. Pretending self-assurance, I decided to head for the Spanish consulate. But I had no idea where it was or how far I would have to walk. And I couldn't rush for fear of tripping or jostling someone who might question my right to be where I was. Without a passport or the *laissez-passer* required of enemy aliens, I imagined I'd land in jail if apprehended. Monsieur DeWaay had intimated that my age was my protection, but I assumed that anyone doing grown-up things might be stopped and interrogated by the police. To keep my composure, I kept rehearsing the clever phrases I would recite to impress the Spanish consul by my maturity, picturing how I would pose in half-profile while address-ing him; and I was determined not to gesticulate, which the Nazis had said was a Jewish habit.

To begin with, I had to decide whom to ask for directions. The first two passers-by either didn't hear my whispered request or ignored it. But the third one I stopped said:

"Go straight ahead, Mademoiselle. You cannot possibly miss the Span-ish consulate, it is the most crowded place in town, looks like they're giving away money."

When I reached this magnificent, ornate structure, the mob trying to get inside by way of its wide steps, seemed to be breaking down the mas-sive portals. Whenever the door was opened from inside, at about twenty minute intervals, five to ten persons were let in, too few to make a dent in what should have been a line but was more of a milling mass. Around twelve-thirty, a pretentious, swarthy clerk in a blue serge uniform, and with slicked-down, pomaded hair, opened the door a crack to announce that the consular staff was going to lunch and would be back in two hours. No one moved. But the shoving suddenly stopped and people started to bond by cursing the callous, lazy bureaucrats. Like everyone else, I settled down on the steps to eat my sandwich. Now, businessmen began talking about the affairs and assets they had left behind; lawyers about their plans for the future; and women about their children and abandoned homes. These stories united them in a sort of agitated familiarity we now associate with American travelers whose planes have been grounded.

Too shy to ask questions lest I expose my ignorance, I just listened. Thus I learned that no one ever gets to see the consul; that even application forms were hard to come by; that Spanish citizens alone could get visas. Yet, all these French and Belgians, most of them Jewish, were determined to keep trying. No one seemed to know what was happening in Spain, and if anyone talked about the civil war that recently had ended, I missed it. Spain was perceived as a sunny haven, as Shangri La; and refugees didn't seem to know that most Spaniards were unemployed, that many of them were going hungry. Nor was it clear that the Spaniards had sealed off their frontiers: to the displaced in Toulouse, Spain was not yet Germany's ally (their collaboration was a well-kept secret) but the promised land. If the consul wasn't going to come across with a visa before they could show him that they had booked their transatlantic passage, some asserted, they would pass illegally over the Pyrenées. But they also told horror stories about the border police, about their loose triggers and vicious dogs. I was bathed in sweat, as I suddenly remembered the time in Pörtschach, at the age of four, when I couldn't stop weeping after having taken yet another bad fall: a local passerby had tried to stop me by threatening to set his German shepherd at me. Ever since then large dogs had terrified me. So I focused on means of charming the consul, to make him understand that my brother and I didn't want to stay in Spain, that we were on our way to America. Soon, I was rehearsing an entirely new speech—about children who wanted to join their desolate parents while their visa was still valid. That day, the consulate closed its doors before I got near them. I would have to arrive much earlier—by leaving Villefranche on the 5:00 A.M. milk train. Disappointed, yet determined, I gave Monsieur DeWaay a blow-by-blow account of my day—all the way to Seyre. On the following morning he cabled my parents for our tickets. By then, I already was on the train to Toulouse.

I had never gotten up at 3:00 A.M. or been outdoors before dawn. Nor had I walked through a misty, awakening country day. But skipping down bumpy dirt roads and cutting across dew-covered, burgeoning farmland and freshly plowed meadows, and circling around the fields of ripening corn, gave me a sense of abandon, as if I had become queen of the mountain. I did slow down every time I was startled by a crowing cock, or by the conjugal fencing of birds. And I cut a broad swath around farmhouses with barking dogs. But it was there, that I admired the rich clusters of lilacs, the array of yellow, purple and white violets, the rows of blue lupins and pink roses, behind white picket fences. When I reached the path lined with the tall, dark poplars that led to the railroad station, I knew I had arrived on time. I beamed when the ticket clerk in Villefranche kidded me as if I belonged, and when I joined the waiting workers whose toolboxes were glistening in the rising sunlight. However briefly, I presumed I was an insider. We stopped at every station, and wherever someone hailed us—waiting to load his heavy milk barrels, or cackling chickens. I listened attentively to the horsing around of the locals trying to get the hang of their dialect, which, although I then didn't know it, was heavily influenced by Basque and Spanish. If the mounting passengers came in threes, or in sevens, I kept assuring myself, I would get our visas at once. But not wanting to handicap myself, I reflected that even numbers might be equally lucky.

Upon reaching the consulate before 7:00 A.M., I was third in line, and inside the doors shortly after nine o'clock. The receptionist, a harassed, bulky, middle-aged woman whose rapid patois was almost unintelligible to a "Belgian" like myself, asked to see my French exit permit. I was bewildered. She impatiently told me to go home and tell my parents to come themselves, not to send a kid in their place. When I stammered that they were in America, she motioned me to sit down and explained, "Before you can even apply for transit through Spain, before I can even let you see one of the vice-consuls, you have to go to the French Préfecture."

"What is that?" I asked.

"*Ma chère petite*," she began, "you have a lot to learn before you're going to go anywhere. Why don't you go around the corner, where they help Jewish refugees from up north." She pointed me on my way. I sensed that I had made a friend.

The grand stone building I now entered, with potted palms in its foyer, was typical of the bombastic architecture of French regional administrations. The colorful mosaics on the high church-like ceilings, the shiny columns (Ionic, I thought), and the wide marble staircase, returned me to past sightseeing tours in Italian palaces. I felt as small and insignificant as I had inside Venice's San Marco. As soon as I had adjusted to the soothing coolness, and my eyes to the relative darkness, I noticed a yellow cardboard rectangle stuck to one of these marble pillars—with an arrow pointing up the stairs; subsequent arrows led me to room 345, where Jewish refugees were crowding in to receive help. That room's quadrangular space was lined with wooden benches, but there were too few of them, so that people seemed to be sitting and standing on top of each other. They all were fidgety, cooking up cockamamie schemes to get out of France, and of Europe. Their jabbering was deafening.

After a while, a slim, elegant man with a brisk walk and an air of authority entered. He was André Weill, a crackerjack lawyer from Strasbourg and, as I found out years later, a member of one of the oldest and most respected Jewish families in France. After a sudden moment of silence, everyone seemed to converge on him, trying to catch his attention. At the door to his office he stopped, looked around slowly, and pointed to me, the only kid in the crowd.

"Why are you here," he asked.

"My brother and I have to get to Lisbon and to my parents in America because our visa is expiring soon," I quickly stammered.

"Come into my office," he said as he held the door for me. Tongue-tied and astonished that he would pick me out, I nevertheless managed to explain our plight. When he had assured himself that we really had American visas, he mumbled something about being unable to do much for anyone else, though he was eager to do so, and said he would "handle" our case. He picked up the phone to call the Prefect.

"I have to bring you over there now," he said after putting down the receiver, "otherwise we'd have to wait until next week. So let's go."

I had trouble keeping up with Monsieur Weill's sure-footed stride across the cobble-stoned public square and through a long palm-lined courtyard. But after mounting another and even more elegant, pink marble staircase, we soon sat across from this all-powerful man, whose huge desk was stacked with mountains of important looking dossiers. Behind the prefect were two immense, paneled windows, on his left a French flag. He seemed to have an almost familial, relationship with Monsieur Weill. Instinctively, I trusted these men, slid back in my chair, and put our fate in their hands.

They deliberated about all sorts of contingencies, and lamented the general collapse of France and the prefect's impossible situation. This had to do with politics I didn't even try to grasp, and with the wisdom of issuing exit permits—at a moment when the Spaniards might be turning Jewish refugees over to the Gestapo now that Franco had won the war. He also said something about having to take the heat from both his constituency and the refugees.

"For the moment," he ended up declaring, "I'm living by my conscience." I didn't know what that meant, nor that he had just received orders to stop issuing exit visas altogether. But I did know that the only road out of France led through Spain ever since Italy had entered the war. The smugglers and bandits who had traveled the tricky paths over the mountains during the civil war, I gathered, now offered their know-how to potential escapees. Those who crossed illegally, and there were many, were thought to have reached freedom. Yet, as we found out years later, many of them had ended up in the hands of the Germans—and ultimately in Auschwitz.

In the end, the prefect and Monsieur Weill agreed that my brother and I were to leave by legal means, and that this could happen only with the cooperation of the Portuguese consul.

"Tell him to call me," the prefect said jocularly as he walked around his desk to shake hands. Since we were to leave from Lisbon, that visa, I assumed, should be no more than a formality. I returned to Seyre that Friday afternoon, reveling in the pink glow of the vibrant evening. As I passed the grazing cattle, the wooly lambs, and a few horses at their trough, I felt as cheered by the tranquility as by the prospect of being on my way to America in another week. By the time I got back, however, I found a cable from my parents: the tickets could not be sent to us directly, and we would have to wait for confirmation of passage from the American Joint Committee in Lisbon.

Undaunted, I again caught the early train the following Monday. The Portuguese consulate was located in a posh town house. It was mobbed. Babbling in many tongues, people were jostling and trying to get ahead of one another up the broad, stone steps while holding on to the wooden railing of the wrought-iron banister. The veterans among them told of their escapes to Toulouse, debated the means of being approved, of avoiding detection by the French sureté, and argued about the likelihood of getting caught while crossing into Spain. Again, I felt like an impostor, afraid to push, and yet nudging ahead steadily. I was becoming as expert at waiting on line as my mother had in Vienna; and I made friends while keeping my eye on the entrance door.

While cooling my heels, I heard how large families had fled from Paris, Antwerp, or Strasbourg; and how they and their relatives were faring in this limbo. For some, the line served as a source of information for vacant rooms, or for deals. Queuing up had become a way of life. At one point, on the steps of the Portuguese consulate, a pleasant, middle-aged lady, with soft dark eyes, turned to me: "And what is a child like you doing here?" I told her, and soon everyone listened. When I was done,

Madame Gruenberg introduced herself and declared: "You poor child. Where do you live now?" After I told her, she said, "You have enough trouble without walking twenty kilometers a day. You will stay with us, until you and your brother are setting out for Lisbon."

She had joined the exodus from Paris with her husband and her sister's family—including their three daughters—and they had rented a villa at the edge of town. I was hesitant to accept her offer, embarrassed by it, and certain that Monsieur DeWaay would object. At first, I even mistrusted her generosity, as afraid of imposing on this family as of white slavery.

Madame Gruenberg had the warm-hearted largesse of my "Omama Fischer" as well as her solid build, and she brushed aside my childish objections with a wave of her hand:

"I will clear everything with Monsieur DeWaay over the phone." He not only agreed, but offered to drop off my clothes, and to deliver my brother when we were ready to leave.

I telegraphed my new address to my parents and urged them to cable confirmation of paid passage. At the beginning of August, a week or so after I had moved in with the Gruenbergs, the American Export Lines notified me that we were booked on the *S. S. Excalibur* which was to leave Lisbon on August 31. I no longer recall the details of my endless rounds to Monsieur Weill, the Prefect, and the Spanish and Portuguese consulates. But I did become a familiar sight to the weary receptionists as well as to the people on the snaking queues; they now let me step ahead, or inquired whether I already had our pictures taken. In any event, I became something of a mascot among the refugees and almost stopped feeling like an alien.

Living with the kind Gruenbergs was a blessing. They fussed over me and I almost relaxed. I kidded around with the girls, the pixyish, enchanting, black-haired Odile who had just turned four, and the snickering eleven and twelve year olds, who had moved into one room to accommodate me. Only now did I realize that I had missed having a tablecloth on the dining table, a proper bathroom, and my own bed—with a mattress. I almost could make believe that I was the Gruenbergs' pampered guest instead of a displaced waif, as I responded to their questions about my progress with the authorities. (The family lived in Paris and was in textiles; they were hoping to join relatives in South America or would return home.) When I had encouraging news, they cheered me on, and when I was upset they assured me that they enjoyed my company or consoled me with an extra piece of cake.

Armed with the cable from the American Export Lines, I assumed my problems were over. However, for reasons I could not fathom, each of the authorities—French, Spanish, and Portuguese—insisted on being the last to issue its own permit. They wanted to have proof of the other two. To break the deadlock, I tried to persuade the Portuguese consulate to issue our visas first. Eventually, the consul's secretary informed me that Monsieur le Consul was out of town for two weeks, vacationing in Nice. I had heard that he took bribes, but didn't know how to go about offering one. Now, I burst out with what came to mind: could I pay for someone to travel to Nice and get his signature? The next day I was given the cost of such an arrangement and was told that I would have to wait until a trustworthy messenger was found. Anyway, I falteringly handed over our passports and 800 francs "for the trip." And I kept my fingers crossed while waiting suspiciously.

Finally, I could try for the Spanish transit visa. This time, the cordial receptionist introduced me to a vice-consul. He cross-examined me to make sure that we would not tarry in Spain. In the course of this interrogation it came out that my family was importing marble to America.

"That was my business before the civil war," he informed me while suddenly dropping his reserve, "and I knew your grandfather and dealt with his firm in the past. Maybe we could cooperate again." I took the clue: "Of course," I responded, "but I can't tell my father or my uncle to get in touch with you until I reach New York. So you have to give us our transit visas. We need at most five days to traverse Spain." He promised to put in a good word with his boss, and told me to come back the following week. When both Portuguese and Spanish visas finally came through, Monsieur Weill escorted me to the Préfecture for the last time.

My pseudo-sophistication did not fool Monsieur Weill. He was aware—as I was not—of the inordinate dangers we might encounter long before we got to the frontier. Thus he insisted I hire a trustworthy Frenchman to take us to Cerbère, via Perpignan, then the only legal route out of France. I also found out that I needed Spanish currency.

"You can get it only on the black market," I was informed, "in certain cafés." I was scared to enter these smoke-filled dungeons packed with sinister men who sat around bars drinking and making shady deals. Besides, I had no money. At that point, the benevolent Madame Gruenberg pressed 3.000 francs (about $50) into my palm. When I asked how and where I could repay her, she said, "I can spare the money. Hand it to someone who needs it, whenever you can afford to, and wherever you may be." I still feel strangely moved, and tears well up, when I think of Madame Gruenberg, and wish I had looked for her more strenuously after the war. Or that upon arriving in New York, before she left Toulouse, I had not found myself so totally paralyzed whenever I sat down to write to her.

Monsieur Weill found an experienced guide to escort us to Cerbère, "for a small fee." This to me dubious looking Frenchman, with his képi, round belly, and threadbare black briefcase, knew his way around. He confided that he had walked all sorts of refugees across the Pyrenées. And he procured pesos for me. I neither liked nor trusted him, and was afraid that he might abduct us. But I had no choice. When Monsieur DeWaay arrived at the Gruenbergs with my rather subdued brother, I was sad and upset about leaving them, yet eager to get going.

"God bless you, and be careful," said Madame Gruenberg as she hugged me with wet eyes. The Frenchman, who turned out to be decent though laconic and taciturn, in the meantime had gotten the necessary train tickets.

When we boarded that train, I had our money tucked in my bra, and a miniature Spanish-French dictionary in my pocket. My brother and the roly-poly, dour Frenchman carried my suitcases, and I the long loaves of white French bread, and soft cheese. Aboard the train, the Frenchman sat across from us and gave instructions. He advised me to answer questions but not to volunteer any unnecessary information; to carefully guard our passports—upon which our lives depended and which were worth a great deal of money. He told my brother not to open his mouth either in his broken French or in German.

"After I leave you in Cerbère," he ordered, "walk up to the French border patrol. They will inspect your passports. From then on, follow the other passengers to the train for Port-Bou. Do exactly what they do. And now repeat what I have told you."

"What will happen then," I wanted to know. He shrugged, pulled his képi a bit forward, and lit up another cigarette. As soon as the train stopped, he turned on his heel to catch the return train. Although everything he had said was helpful, he did not prepare us for the unnerving contingencies we were to face as soon as we were on our own.

6

Traversing the Iberian Peninsula

Walter Benjamin, the renowned scholar, reached Cerbère three weeks after me, and at the prospect of having to climb across the peak of the Pyrénées, gave up and killed himself. Marianne Loring,[3] who arrived there with her parents (her father was a top-level Socialist Party official) two weeks after Benjamin, notes that luckily for them, the frontier had just been reopened for twenty-five—randomly chosen—possessors of transit visas per day. But whereas she was full of nostalgia for the France she had known, I gladly left and focused only on forging ahead, on muddling my way through. I was as stunned by the beauty of the soaring rocks of this imposing mountain chain as she was, by the juxtaposition of their majesty on my right and the brilliant azure Mediterranean far below on my left. Our train seemed precariously suspended in-between. Fleeting comparisons to Viareggio, La Spezia, and Genoa came to mind, but I discarded them as my anxiety overwhelmed me—long before the train jerked to a halt.

Platoons of soldiers with menacing rifles and frontier patrols in military postures surrounded us and viscerally brought back my dread of Nazi discipline. Hansl and I grabbed for each other's hands. By the time we got off the train with our luggage, the passengers we were supposed to have followed had gotten far ahead of us, so that I beheld only their rounded backs. Moreover, I distrusted their rough ways and unrefined French, contaminated by Spanish and Basque.

Suppressing my fears and tears, we trailed them at a distance. We were last on the line that formed at the shack marked *contrôle des passports*. Like everyone else, I soon was being grilled about whether we were carrying any contraband. I had no idea what they might be looking for. Of course, we were being eyed most suspiciously—after handing in our brown, German passports with the huge, tell-tale "J."

With raised eyebrows, a burly border guard examined these documents, painstakingly turning them around and around, holding them up against the light and checking our visas—while looking from our faces to our pictures and back. Then, he repeated the many questions I already knew by heart—where we were going, why we weren't with our parents, and what we would live on while in Spain. After he disappeared into the shack behind him, one of his beefy buddies, while fingering the revolver on his belt, ordered me to open my luggage. I squirmed when he removed each item one by one, shook every piece of underwear, and dropped it onto a wooden bench—before scrutinizing the bottoms of the suitcases. What were they looking for? Hansl squeezed my hand more tightly, and forgetting his characteristic bravura, looked up at me beseechingly. I was too scared myself to reassure him. After I had repacked my meager possessions, another dignitary finally returned with our passports and with a flick of his wrist motioned us toward the frontier. We left slowly, again holding hands.

The ride on the ramshackle train we now boarded, that took us in an un-lit compartment through a pitch-black tunnel, was even more frightening. When we finally came out of the dark, I deciphered "Port-Bou" painted in faded white on the slate-gray rocks. We were in Spain. Unaccountably, my angst increased. On this late afternoon, as the long shadows of the roseate sunset enveloped the overhanging rocks in a mystical, somewhat eerie, iridescent glow, the armed guards on the narrow platform goose-stepped more stiffly than their French brethren. We were interrogated yet again, this time by a stern Spaniard. I had to consult my miniature dictionary before responding and thus was fumbling even more than usual for fear of saying something wrong. Feverishly turning its pages, I thought we were in more trouble when a heavyset, glowering giant with bushy eyebrows imperiously seized our passports and took them into his shack. Would he return them to us?

Another official pulled my brother into a lean-to at the right side of that shed, and a huge matron in what looked like a black school uniform grabbed me by the arm and started to walk me into a curtained cubicle on the left. She motioned me to hurry up and undress. I squirmed and, as was my habit, was ashamed to show my body. She ranted loudly in an incomprehensible mish-mash of languages, and impatiently urged me to get on with it. With the help of gestures, she made me understand that the procedure was routine. After frisking my clothes and looking into my mouth with her flashlight, she indicated in a conspiratorial tone that she wouldn't put this light up my anus, provided I didn't tell on her. While squeezing back into my clothes, my recurring fear of being sold into slavery to deep, dark Africa or Algeria resurged. Would Hansl be sent too? And if so, how would we manage to reconnect, and how would our parents find us? Why was this fat matron so intrusive? When she demanded to know how much money I was carrying, I proudly showed her my pesos and haltingly asked whether these would get us to Portugal. From yet another barrage I eventually comprehended that it was illegal to bring money into Spain. "Where did you get these pesos," she boomed. When she noticed that I was shaking uncontrollably, she came closer and murmured, while putting an index finger to her mouth:

"I will not tell anyone. But you have to buy pesos for at least a thousand francs at the desk across the yard, so they won't be suspicious." I complied. By the time I rejoined my brother, he was wiping his eyes with the back of his dirty fists:

"I was afraid you'd never come back. What would I have done if they had not let you go?" I never again would see him in such a panic. If I had been politically less naive, I might have known that so soon after a civil war paranoia may be normal, even justified. I was not one of the innocents I learned about much later, I was totally ignorant. In hindsight, I think my ignorance was bliss. Finally, the fat giant returned with our documents, grunted something I didn't get, hitched up his pants, and magnanimously waved us on our way. Relieved that we didn't have to run for the mountains after all, I nervously wondered about what to do next.

By now the sun had disappeared and night was falling. I hurried to inquire about the next train to Barcelona. But no one had any information. Nor could I find out how much the fare would be. Ultimately, the station supervisor said that the last train had left a few hours ago, and that we would have to wait until the following morning. Where would we sleep? (Loring describes the utter desolation of this village of ten houses, of which only one was left undamaged.) I got up the courage to accost a somewhat sleazy Frenchman with the tell-tale black beret, who seemed to know where he was heading, and asked him about a reasonable hotel. He motioned me to follow him. But why was he now walking us through this unlit, gloomy passageway hewn out of the rocky mountain? Don't let on you're alarmed, I told myself, while watching the Frenchman's elongated shadow dance on the pavement, and reaching for Hansl's hand. When, at the end of this tunnel-like corridor I saw a sign, "Hotel," I briefly relaxed.

Its lobby was dominated by a massive registration desk on my left. On the right there was an immense bar, which was surrounded by smoking and drinking males. From the center of the ceiling hung a huge but defunct electric fan. I barely understood what the desk clerk told me, but knew of no other place to spend the night. And the cost of our room was reasonable. Tired, and eager to settle in, we munched on some of our now stale bread, went to our room and immediately fell asleep.

During the night I woke up to the buzzing of flies and to loud snores. Only then did I discover to my horror that we were sharing our room with about a dozen men. No wonder the clerk had admonished us to close the dark, red velvet curtains around our beds: I had paid only for two adjoining lower bunks. Now, I was afraid to budge, to go back to sleep, or even to whisper to my brother lest someone were to notice my presence. Fortunately, we no longer owned pajamas and were sleeping in the clothes we had worn when we left Toulouse.

At dawn, we quietly sneaked out before our drunken roommates woke up. And we returned to the station, where I eventually was able to negotiate for two third-class tickets on the next train to Barcelona. It was scheduled to leave around noon. Because I was afraid of running out of money, I kept us on a diet of bananas and melon. That morning, Hansl, though sticking to me like glue, attacked me as stingy, bossy, and stupid. And just before our train was to leave, he refused to budge. Like a worker on strike, he sat on one of my battered suitcases, and threatened to leave it behind. I worried that we would miss our train. Still, after we were aboard, munching our bananas while seated on yet another narrow, uncomfortable bench, and watching the standees around us as much as we did our belongings, we were at one.

This endless ride was bumpier even than the cattle cars had been. We were surrounded by three generations of an impoverished peasant family—sad men in ragged, patched, dark suits; and women in frayed, shapeless black garments, with black kerchiefs tied around their heads. Their scraggly children wore black outfits that appeared to have been cut out of clothes their elders had worn out. All of them were nearly tooth-less, and whatever teeth they had left were gray, like those of witches in fairy tales. One after another, the grownups attempted to talk to us. I struggled to understand them, kept smiling, and consulted my diction-ary. Eventually, I grasped that they craved the remainder of our white bread and our soft cheese. In return, they offered us some of their heavy, unappetizing dark bread with thin slices of sticky sausage, which they had been kneading in their unwashed hands. We were as scared to refuse their victuals as we were reluctant to give them ours. They assumed we were rich, and we didn't know that they might be hungry. As Hansl and I looked at one another and tried to hide our disgust at this food, he said he felt sick. I was careful to disguise my revulsion. While feasting on our dried-out baguette and brie, our travel companions somehow got across that they had not tasted white bread in years.

I was eager to reach Lisbon, inventing one scenario after another of how we would survive were we to miss our boat. However, like a kewpie doll, I continued to grin at everyone who met my glance. I needed the good will of our fellow passengers to let me in on why the train was stopping amid arid fields and jutting rocks, and to guess at when we would reach Madrid. Exhausted and looking like the fugitives we were, we arrived there half an hour after the daily train to the Portuguese frontier had left.

*   *   *

By now I had learned to get my information from as high an authority as I could locate. Thus we headed straight for the office of the stationmaster. On the way, we nearly fell over people sitting on makeshift luggage—mostly cardboard boxes tied with string—and on the ground, or propped against the ornate walls of this imposing edifice. The lucky ones were stretched out on the marble benches. Madrid's central train station had become their home, their dormitory. Once again, I stumbled on a compassionate man. In a mixture of Spanish and French (probably Castillian, since I grasped what he said), the beleaguered stationmaster told us he would watch over our possessions, and warned against thieves. He handed us two huge pillows and led us to the first class waiting room. There, he freed up two adjoining benches and told us to go to sleep. When I woke up at around two in the morning, my brother was gone. I was petrified. But while I mulled over what to do, and was angry that he hadn't at least screamed at the kidnappers, or woken me up before going for a walk, or even to the bathroom, he reappeared. The stationmaster had given him a tour of his domain, and now he offered to take us for a stroll through Madrid. We brought our pillows to his office and went sightseeing.

I recall little of the city, except the unsettling calm of the steaming night, as we trod along unpaved roads atop hilly terrain. Our guide pointed to churches, the Prado, and other landmarks in the ghostly landscape below: it had been bombed out and was in shambles. Illuminated by a few neon signs and by the moon, Madrid appeared to have died. The stationmaster's war stories were over my head, since I knew nothing about the POUM, the Nationalists, the Republicans, the Communists, and every other political faction. But I liked being shown around, and being accorded the respect reserved for adults. Our escort, it turned out, had been with the Republicans. He cautioned us not to talk about his past while in Spain, but urged us to tell "the Americans" and "the brave people of the American Brigade" that they had "lost for now, but will rise soon again." I promised.

Back home at the station, we watched the hissing, puffing locomotives being checked by railroad workers who banged them with all sorts of hammer-like tools. Trains were being switched from track to track; electric sparks were flying. After we captured two seats on the bench with the best view, a strapping, laughing Spaniard in his early twenties, with tattoos on his arms, and who had been ogling me, sat down next to us. He soon confided that he was the lucky driver of one of the locomotives we were admiring. Gradually, he edged closer to me, and rested his arm on the back of the bench behind me. I was disturbed by the seductive look in his eyes, and inched away as he kept coming closer. When he offered to take me to his home, I was frightened but kept on grinning and hid my trepidation. To get to me, he explained that he lived on an embankment right off the tracks, nearby, and would take both of us there, on his locomotive: "My mother is a good cook," he said, "and after dinner, you will stay with me in my room, and your brother with my mother in hers." Hansl didn't grasp why I wanted to pass up such an exciting experience. But I finally wiggled my way out by insisting that we might miss our train, and that the stationmaster expected us to check in with him. After I got rid of this potential seducer, Hansl promised not to move from my side: he even waited for me in front of the ladies' room.

Uncomfortable in the excruciating heat, eating the sandwiches the stalwart stationmaster had bought for us, we anxiously waited for the ticket window to open. Our train was to leave some time that evening. Soon, we retrieved our suitcases and to my relief got out of Madrid—on the last leg to Portugal. During the following morning, the sweltering train stopped. We had to get off with all of our belongings in order to pass through Spanish customs. This inspection was uneventful, but I was offered the choice of spending or handing over my remaining pesos. Triumphantly, Hansl announced that I had been dumb, that we could have eaten appetizing food instead of bananas and melons. To atone for my caution, I spent every last peso in the canteen. After carrying our purchases across the tracks to the Portuguese side, and having to pass yet another customs check, we mounted the steep steps of our last train. All the way to Lisbon we greedily stuffed ourselves with the meat of two scrawny chickens, almost relishing that we had to use our fingers, munched the fresh, dark bread, and left the candy for dessert.

Finally, our ordeal would be over. But it was August 31, and our boat was leaving that day. I feared that we would miss it. Among the people in our compartment was a particularly sympathetic medical student who spoke fluent French. He introduced himself with his visiting card. (I had never received a visiting card and kept it for years.) When I told him about our predicament he talked to the conductor—who speedily got us off the train the moment we arrived in Lisbon. Then, our generous friend phoned the American Export Lines, rushed us into a taxi and brought us there. Apparently, the ship already had pulled up its anchor when he called. The official he spoke to, however, promised to intervene. After this young man handed us over to him, and he quickly had examined our passports, we were whisked off in yet another taxi: the *S. S. Excalibur* was waiting for us. All I remembered of Lisbon, until I got there again in 1980, was a speedy taxi ride, running along an unending pier, and the passengers' staring eyes aboard the ship watching our arrival. As soon as we had been hurried up the plank the sailors yanked it off, the sirens screamed, the foghorns tooted, and we were on our way to New York.

7

Transition at Sea

That gangplank transported us from destitution and poverty to luxury and wealth. Most of the passengers on deck—American expatriates and privileged French on "capitalists' affidavits"—were saying their wistful good-byes to the continent. I felt like Cinderella: my dreams of escape had come true. But I remained apprehensive: the Atlantic was peppered with highly explosive mines; England was suffering from the Blitz; and the purser was bemoaning his ship's bygone days of glitz.

As our fellow passengers watched Hansl and me walk aboard, they beheld stray fugitives, whom Louis B. Meyer could have cast in a Dickens story. We had slept in our clothes for over a week and were unwashed and unkempt. My brother no longer wore socks, and his hiking shoes and lederhosen were dusty; his once white shirt had turned a spotty, mottled gray, and most of the horn buttons on his loden jacket were missing. My scuffed navy shoes were as unappealing as my flowery blouse and its matching skirt—all of them belying their original shape and quality. Nevertheless, while the spiffy purser carried my suitcases, I sauntered aboard swinging my blue shoulder bag, while my brother skipped up taking two steps at a time. We had made it.

"The *S. S. Excalibur* was meant to be a floating ballroom, not a third-rate passenger liner," the amicable purser in his spiffy blue uniform lamented, "and it wasn't made to navigate in an ocean riddled with German mines. You're in for a dangerous voyage."

In fact, the ship was transporting about twice the number of persons it had been intended for. After handing my brother to one of his assistants, the purser escorted me to the stateroom the Duchess of Windsor had occupied on an earlier trip. A cot had been set up for me. Upon opening the door, my two American roommates jumped up from their twin beds to greet me. They held martinis in their hands. A jumble of colorful garments and an overabundance of baubles met my eyes. The portholes above their beds seemed to be the only vacant spaces. My cot was wedged between

71

a motley assortment of bulging suitcases, handmade shopping bags that doubled as souvenirs, and giant cabin trunks. As my roommates sized me up, bubbling over with indiscreet questions and well-meant advice, they exclaimed over and over how glad they were that I didn't have much to add to the clutter. I was moved by their compassion and warmth.

In the manner only Americans manage to form sudden friendships with fellow travelers, these two women already had exchanged their life stories and had become intimate. They appeared as thrilled to have been thrown together, as to have me along. I was blown away by their vivacity and regarded them as *fêmmes fatales*, much in the way I perceived movie stars. I was conscious of my own clumsiness, and of my tendency to bump into things—as most skinny girls who in their teens gain weight tend to be. In their early thirties, they both seemed old to me, and wise. I could not fathom why they insisted I call them by their first names. Jane, a dark-haired and stylish divorcée of medium build and height, moved with the elegance of a Siamese cat. She clearly never had had to consider working for her living. Emily, jolly, buxom, and blonde, with a snub nose and light freckles, kept laughing and telling jokes in a southern drawl, which even Jane had trouble understanding. She owned a boutique in St. Louis: "I should have left Europe last fall," she said, "but I wanted to stay around to buy merchandise for my store. There were so many bargains I couldn't resist, and so many unattached men." They giggled at that. I blushed.

Since my brother and I had been assigned to the early and less desirable shift in the dining room, my roommates urged me to have the first bath. They were too well bred to tell me that I needed it. Jane offered her shampoo and Emily her bath salts. They turned up their noses at the unseasonable fabric of the clothes I had brought: "You have nothing that's fit for a cruise in this abominable heat," Jane exclaimed in her passable French, "let's see what we can find. And your shoes are perfect for that awful Belgian drizzle, but not for promenading aboard the deck of a ship." Rummaging among her belongings while muttering that she was a sucker for bargains, especially for shoes, she fished out a pair of black and white, modish sandals with thick platforms of cork.

"Try these," she suggested. Emily, not to be outdone, dug out a sleeveless, black cotton shift sprinkled with bouquets of yellow daisies and red poppies she said she "didn't need." She pressed it on me over my coy objections, along with a small matching straw purse and daisy-shaped hairclips: "These things are not right for me, and on you they look absolutely perfect," she announced as Jane translated. (By the end of the trip they had showered other items on me, all of them in this discreet off-hand manner.) After my bath, both women outdid each other in showing me how to line my eyes, to accentuate my long lashes, and to rein in the unruly waves in my bushy hair. I was overcome with joy and gratitude.

As I strutted upstairs two hours later, the lights were dimmed and Europe began to recede. I wanted to impress my brother with my sleek appearance and with the Chanel 5 odor I exuded. Destitution and distress were behind me. My road to New York was paved with fairy tale luxury. "How come so many of the Americans on this ship," I reflected, "can be so blind to their good luck?"

Emily and Jane reminisced about prewar passages; complained about the blackout and the slowed-down speed; and were nostalgic for around-the-clock festivities. I still had twice the space I had had in Seyre, ten times the privacy, and no one expected me to do chores. Instead, a servile maid, in a black uniform and the customary starched white apron and matching headband, came in to turn down my bed. And yet, I felt humiliated, and squirmed at being the recipient of charity, while eagerly accepting with false modesty whatever my roommates offered.

That night before dinner, Hansl and I joyfully explored all the decks, discovering ping-pong tables and shuffleboards, deckchairs and a coffee shop—while jabbering away. Hansl said he had an upper bunk in a cabin in the bowels of the ship, which he shared with two dark-skinned Persians, who were "very rich and friendly," and with a German refugee, a "quiet old man" of about forty. The Persians had procured a pair of socks for him from a sailor. However, he was envious of my new finery: "Why do I have to wear my old clothes when you have fancy new ones? You have all the luck," he sulked. As I walked next to my cleanly scrubbed brother, I was not yet aware that my body had filled out, and that I looked womanly in my new attire.

As soon as the dining room doors opened, and we entered the splendor of that palatial setting, I forgot my recent deprivations and poverty. Tables set with welters of shining silver, sparkling crystal carafes and goblets, delicate china and artful flower arrangements on white, damask table cloths, beneath gleaming Lobmeyer chandeliers, topped even my fondest memories of the Südbahnhotel. (That was where I had spent All-Saints weekend, in November 1937, with my father and his parents—a luxurious outing my mother would trot out for the rest of her life to prove that my father preferred me to her.) Without missing a beat, my poverty and destitution had been replaced by almost obscene opulence and overstated elegance. While the black-clad *maître d'* in a starched white shirt and gleaming gloves was bending from the waist as deferentially as if we were royalty, he inquired: "What would you prefer to start with?" Overcome by gluttony, I wanted to sample every exotic delicacy on the menu. But I tried to hide my greed. Bowing and winking ever so slightly, the *maître d'* understood my dilemma and hastened to say that we could order as many dishes as we fancied. My pensionnat training kicked in. I advised Hansl on how to pack it in without appearing gluttonous. While starting on our *coquilles St. Jacques*, which he had never tasted, we figured out that the voyage would be long enough for us to work our way through the menu at least twice. Like most waiters in luxurious settings, ours loved catering to children. They knew we didn't like olives after we bit into them as if they were cherries and nearly choked to keep from spitting; and they offered to deliver extra desserts to our cabins, "in case you get hungry." Once, we decided to make dinner out of a succession of desserts, topped off with a chocolate soufflé.

Now that we were out of immediate danger, I looked forward to being taken care of. I was worn-out of being the responsible older sister, of having to be on the alert, and to anticipate and run from potential danger. I had been hiding my permanent state of anxiety beneath an almost equally permanent smile, and had expected Hansl to understand the menacing situations I often could not, or would not, articulate even to myself. I tended to act instinctively—much as my mother had with the Nazis. (In one of her letters to my mother, my grandmother imagined Hansl as crying for his Mutti and me as learning to cope.) I was increasingly impatient with our petty squabbles, and with being in charge of our lives.

When wrapped in soft, cozy blankets aboard deck while sipping my mid-morning soup or afternoon tea, I was at my apogee of bliss and imagined my future in poverty, though not without glamorizing the hardships of the poor. Ever more frequently, Hansl's roommate, a Persian version of Robert Taylor, would sit down on the deckchair next to me. I vaguely noticed that he was being seductive, that he was following me with his hungry eyes. And I found him amusing. Was he a fortune hunter, or a gigolo, given his enigmatic smile and savoir-faire? At times, his glances sort of aroused me sexually, and I felt an undefined discomfort. Inexplicably, at least to me, my mind drifted to the far away romantic nights in Viareggio, when we had been perched on top of a slippery toilet bowl, and Hansl almost had fallen in: we had taken to heart our father's half-serious admonition upon leaving Vienna to watch over our mother—who was dancing below.

I laughed at the thirty-two year old Persian's off-the-cuff remarks and jokes, which had as light a touch as my father's, and felt flattered that someone over twice my age treated me as a grownup. One evening, he casually invited me for a walk on deck. I was wearing my coveted platform sandals and halter-top dress. I felt full of myself for having reached the peak of sophistication and self-possession. As we stopped with our arms on the polished, wooden railing on this moon-flooded night, and looked at the star-studded sky above the calm ocean, while soft music was coming over from the quartet at the other end of the deck, he nonchalantly put his arm around my shoulder and squeezed it lightly. Bending nearer, he began to describe our impending and charmed life in America, and the far-away places in the mysterious Orient and the Middle East he knew so well, and which he looked forward to showing me some day. He seemed to take me into one of my fairy tales, and to promise me my most secret romantic desires. But the prospect of attaining them was as scary as it was tempting, especially after he pulled a huge, sparkling diamond ring out of his pocket. For a moment my mind floated in this enchanted space, but almost at once I recoiled with fear.

I solved my emotional dilemma by stammering that I first had to talk to my father, and in a flash found myself skipping to the other end of the deck. He slowly ambled after me. I not only was flustered, but wondered whether he really meant what he said or just wanted me to sneak the valuable diamond through customs. I avoided the answer to these questions, and to all my turbulent feelings, by making sure not to find myself alone with him again. But I couldn't get him off my mind. To protect myself, I stayed close to Hansl. Yet, I neither wanted my brother to laugh at me, nor did I trust his discretion. So I did not let on why I suddenly was so eagerly sticking to his side.

Yet I did not give up my fantasies of courtship, and created one scenario after another that might impress my father. Maybe he would invite this near-Eastern Romeo to his office and allow him to court me? He might even leave us alone long enough for him to embrace and kiss me. Of course, I was extraordinarily naive. But I hid this fact, mostly from myself. My father and his friends had been experienced roués, and I had overheard many of their stories—about marriage swindlers and suave seducers. In sum, I had been indoctrinated not to believe what men said. So I instinctively distrusted this oriental Lothario but found his cosmopolitan gallantry extremely enticing, almost irresistible.

When on the following day, his swarthier and less handsome side-kick took me aside and said he urgently had to talk to me in private, I was even more apprehensive. We met over tea. Sitting opposite me in the coffee lounge, he hemmed and hawed, took my hand in his, and then burst out: "I want you to know that you're better off with a Jewish man like me. My good-looking partner is Christian. As one Jew to another, I must warn you not to become engaged to him. I can give you just as big and good a diamond, and as a Jew, I will make a much better husband. Don't answer me, I can wait. I'm talking of the future."

Now, I squirmed even more, and didn't know how to extricate myself from this tête-à-tête. I vaguely murmured that I was too young to think of marriage and wasn't religious. Did they both have diamonds to get rid of? Did they really want to get to know my father as they kept saying, and if so could it be for reasons of business? I avoided being alone with either of them and evaded their all-knowing, inquisitive glances. But why was I running away at the moment when my childish fantasies were on the verge of being fulfilled? Why did my dreams have no relationship to flesh-and-blood males?

I never found out just what these two Middle Easterners did except collect large diamonds and valuable stamps, probably because I did not ask, or would not have been told anyway. But my unarticulated and uninformed suspicions were aroused further after I overheard one of my roommates wonder sotto-voce to the other one why these grown men were spending so much time with children rather than with passengers their own age. I never did figure out whether they were taken with my innocence, were not interested in any of the women on board, or were seeking to have me conceal a diamond from the American customs inspectors.

*   *   *

On our way, we made a quick stopover in Bermuda to pick up a few passengers. That was when the wheat was separated from the chaff, when the refugees were ordered to stay on board while American and British citizens could go for a walk on that green playground of an island. To a seasoned tourist like me, this was a humiliating restriction. I had imagined that setting foot on an American vessel would allow me the privileges of Americans.

I no longer recall much about the other passengers. Most of them seemed to be Europhiles who had been lulled into believing that the Allies would smash the Germans, and that the *drôle de guerre* would never erupt into a real war. The two hundred word English vocabulary I remembered from school in Vienna was insufficient to talk with the majority who, in turn, knew little French. German was out. The dark, winsome nineteen-year-old German refugee, whose experiences approximated ours, had gotten intensely involved with my brother's refugee roommate. They appeared totally wrapped up in each other. Still, I wasn't too outgoing myself. My floating apprehensions and feelings of inferiority extended to everything and everyone, and her sensuality unconsciously reminded me of what I was only faintly suppressing. I hopelessly intertwined our realistic problems of survival with my rapidly burgeoning sexuality: my secret dreams of romance were totally unconnected to live men—whom I perceived as the predatory males my grandmother and Madame had warned against. Moreover, while basking in my newly found comfort and pretensions of lightheartedness, I kept fretting whether we would pass muster with the American emigration authorities.

*   *   *

Our days aboard ship had passed quickly. I had spoken haltingly to some of the deck hands about the weather and the danger of mines, and had avoided a more immediate danger by resisting invitations to their sleeping quarters. I also hadn't trusted them when they told me that my pidgin English was adequate just because I could ask and thank them for their assistance. Although avoiding intimate conversations with the Persians, Hansl and I continued playing cards and ping-pong with them until we landed.

Upon approaching New York Harbor late in the afternoon of September 7, my thinking shifted to my dreams of family life. While anchored in its bay, I was overawed by the Statue of Liberty. Her raised arm made her look so commanding and yet so welcoming. True, I fleetingly had seen her in movie shots, but I had not known what she stood for, which one of the crew soon explained. Most of all, I was staggered by her Amazonian dimensions, and by the swarm of boats in the enormous harbor she presided over. That day, New York was suffering one of its sweltering heat waves. Since nightfall didn't bring any refreshing air, I decided to spend the night in my deck chair. Entranced by shadows of the alternating colors in the sky—of what I later found out were reflections of New York's neon lights—I spun out yet more visions for the happy future that finally was upon me. Relieved to have dodged all dangers of floating mines and flattering men, I was eager to be catered to by the devoted parents who were awaiting us.

Part II

8

In Dreams Begins America

During our last night in fairyland, I still imagined that a glamorous life was awaiting me—as a translator to a diplomat or a mogul, and in a pinch as a designer of evening gowns and Chanel-type suits. Eventually, I would become a famous painter and would write a book about my recent adventures. I hadn't yet read *Down and Out in London and Paris*, but my juvenile fantasies went along these lines.

My reveries stopped at daybreak. I was catapulted into reality by the army of border sleuths that had climbed aboard. They herded non-Americans into a roped-off section of the main deck. We lined up to be examined by a white-clad doctor with a magnifying mirror across his forehead, and who, with the help of an interpreter, wanted to know what diseases either Hansl or I might have had. He listened to our heartbeats and lungs, stuck a tongue depressor into our mouths, peered at our teeth and into our throats. After he filled out endless forms he made me sign, other meddlesome officials interrogated me, checked our passports, and filled out yet other forms. I was frightened, and congratulated myself for having refused that tempting diamond. Its owner was nearby, and whenever I met his glance and noticed his merry eyes fasten on me questioningly, my stomach cramped up, my heart beat in my throat, and I turned red as a beet. Was it true that in his country I would have been betrothed long before I was fourteen? But why was I so intimidated by the aggressive journalists with their fancy microphones and flashing cameras, and especially by the brash woman in a red blazer, who pranced about on high heels while moving her prominent horn rimmed glasses on and off her nose? Actually, the press had come aboard to interview the American ambassador, Myron Taylor, whom President Roosevelt had just recalled from the Vatican. When he successfully ducked them, they focused on the tall, strutting Dr. Voronoff, whose white mane and aquiline nose might have photographed well. But neither he, who with the help of monkey glands had invented a cure for male impotence, nor his much younger wife, who was a demure replica of Jean Harlow, gave them the time of day. That was why they wanted my story. For years I would regret not having given it to them. Who knows, I might have made as notable an entry as Katherine Hepburn or Greta Garbo. If a movie magnate had been interested in my tale, I fantasized that I too might have escaped refugee life.

After passing muster, Hansl and I gently pushed our way to the railing. Finally, we were able to scan the searching faces of the excited mob on the Hoboken pier. I had expected to see people with Claudette Colbert's chic, Clark Gable's elegance and charm, Bette Davis's allure, and stylishness, instead of the down-and-out, scruffy looking bunch that kept moving from one leg to the other: they were wiping perspiration off their moist faces, while waving welcome signs and handkerchiefs to attract the attention of the passengers they had come to meet. We couldn't spot our parents.

"Maybe they mixed up the days," Hansl remarked while shrugging his skinny shoulders with exaggerated indifference and squinting against the afternoon sun, "or maybe they got lost on the way. Don't you know that they can't speak English?" We had developed our own shorthand to face terror by "crying wolf."

Most of the nervously fidgeting passengers cheered their safe arrival. Faking insouciance, I noted that some looked solemn, that others were shedding tears or wiping their noses; that a few were hugging the railing, even hanging over it, and were waving to get their friends and relatives below to recognize them. Yet others signaled frantically to no one in particular.

I still expected a semblance of the glorious destiny on the gold-paved streets of New York, which Karl May so casually had taken for granted. Would I fare like Shirley Temple in Million Dollar Baby, or like Deanna Durbin in Three Smart Girls? As I kept wiping the dripping sweat off my face with my forearm, and Hansl displayed his most engaging smile, I was looking forward to challenging prospects. But where were our parents? We suddenly heard familiar voices: "*Hansl, Ditta, endlich seit Ihr da. Kommt schnell herunter. . .zu Hause warten Wiener Schnitzel und Apfelstrudel*" (Hansl, Ditta, finally you're here, come down quickly, Wiener schnitzel and apple-strudel are awaiting you at home). We tried to locate the nervous callers who, unmistakably, were our parents. But where were they? They couldn't possibly be these two agitated little people gesticulating so wildly, these two blue-eyed shrimps, she with tears pouring out of eager eyes in her glowing face, and he hiding his bursting pleasure behind the familiar, supercilious smile. We remembered our mother and father as large, imposing figures.

"How come they shrank so much," Hansl, who soon would be called Johnny, demanded to know. (In my mind, I was ashamed that they called out in German.)

"How should I know," I replied with relief, "maybe it's because they didn't get enough to eat on account of Hitler and the war." I could not yet take in that I had grown much taller, and chunkier. I immediately suppressed my misgivings. Though glad not to have to make it up the Hudson the way Huckleberry Finn had made it down the Mississippi, I did not want to respond in German. My fugitive antennae still were fully extended, functioning without my volition. So I yelled, "*Nous sommes ici, nous sommes ici.*" I guiltily banished my irreverent disapproval—overcome by the yearning for our immediate reunion, and by blissful expectations of being indulged by my doting parents. For the moment, we picked up our scant possessions and headed down the gangplank to Hoboken. The night before we had glimpsed the brilliant lights of New York harbor in the hazy distance—too far away for us to be dazzled by the city's look of artificial grandeur. But now, we were greeted by the nadir of squalor, the murky customs area. I was repelled by its stench and filth; by the remnants of cord, cardboard, and scraps of paper on the floor, while trying to avoid stepping on banana peels and apple cores, and into puddles of spittle. People seemed to be milling around the self-important customs inspectors who held on to clip boards and stalked around shaky benches and tables of rough wooden planks in this cavernous hall. While swatting an occasional fly, these men demanded answers to endless questions, poked into suitcases, asked that crates be pried open, waved some people off after stamping their papers, and detained others. They all ignored us, apparently assuming we were waiting for our parents who still were aboard. Finally, after I dared approach the most benign looking among these men, and got him to understand that we were alone, he quickly stamped us into legitimacy.

"Welcome to America," he boomed.

* * *

After proceeding through the turnstile, we fell into our parents' arms. My mother couldn't stop touching us to make sure we were really with her, and lived up to her reputation of crying on every sad and happy occasion. My father, who remembered that men don't cry, kept his brimming eyes from running and overcame his agitation by heckling Hansl

about his seasoned Lederhosen and me about my fancy hair style. At 5'
6" plus platform shoes, I was now a smidgen taller than he.

"*Du wirst mir nicht über den Kopf wachsn*," (you won't overtake or
best me), he teased in the typically Viennese manner of speaking, while
slowly looking me up and down, frowning and shaking his head sideways
as his eyes fastened on my sturdy figure. I still was unaware that my father
was self-conscious of his small stature, and that he was bothered that his
two younger brothers were taller than him. I suppressed the disrespectful
retort on the tip of my tongue.

To get to our new home, we eagerly trotted behind our parents in the
general direction of the Hudson tubes. They were unsure of the direc-
tion, each expecting the other to know the way. I felt nauseated by the
overpowering bodily odors in the dank, stuffy underground air. Had
I fantasized the details of my arrival, I would have made it via Times
Square rather than via its bowels. But I finally was on the magic train to
Manhattan—which I would not set foot on again until starting to teach at
Rutgers University in 1978, and which by then was called "the Path."

My virgin ride beneath the Hudson was a rude introduction to the
America I had not remembered from the movies. The placid, pudgy middle-aged men and women, whose brightness was in their ill-fitting clothes
rather than their gaze, looked tired and beaten. Some of their bodily shapes
were not so different from Omama Weisz's but, unlike them, her green eyes
had been as shining as her clothes were dull. I was overwhelmed, also,
by the deafening noise of the train, which a bunch of uproarious, shoving
kids tried to out-shout. Neither the white kids nor the black ones got up
to let adults sit down. They all hollered and jumped across the aisle; one
couple was kissing soulfully with closed eyes; a husky boy was feeling
the bottom of a buxom girl. I never had seen anyone chew gum, and was
entranced by the popping and sucking back of pink and green bubbles.
And I couldn't understand a single word of what they said.

My exposure to blacks had been limited to a sexually explicit movie
with Josephine Baker, and to the copper-colored student at the Lycée
d'Yxelles who had come from the Congo. I would have wanted to have
her small, even features, her quick, bouncy walk and her slender shape.
To me, dark-skinned people either were alluring actors, at least those
who had been liberated from slavery, were living courageously in the
unexplored regions of Africa, or in the American South. Or Joe Louis.
That was what I had gathered from school, from *The Jungle Book* and
from the *Tarzan* stories. Now, I stared at them. To them, we must have
looked like freaks.

In 1940, no one in New York wore short gray leather pants or unlaced hiking boots. Nor did mothers so intensely beam at—kvell some would say—and hug and kiss their grown children so uncontrollably. I held on to my battered leather suitcases, and carried my light brown winter coat.

"Where is your beautiful, beige camelhair topcoat," my mother asked.

"I thought it would get too dirty on the trip," I answered, "so I left it at Hansl's *home d'enfants*."

"How could you do such a thing," she said reproachfully. My father chimed in mockingly:

"When are you planning to pick it up?" We spoke in German, which to me was an unwanted throwback. My brother and I were interrupting each other, and firing questions at our parents without listening to their answers, just as we had done in Vienna. When my mother remarked that Hansl's Lederhosen vaguely smelled of urine, he informed her that he wore no underpants, that the pair he had on when leaving Brussels had been tattered to shreds. She was shocked, yet strangely pleased to be catapulted so soon into motherly action. Then and there, she resolved to make up for the two years of mothering we had missed. She had no set program of reeducation but felt duty-bound to straighten us out. So she inspected me more closely: "You know, Ditterl, don't you, that you are wearing too much make-up, and too much perfume. And why do you put up your hair in such a prominent pompadour?" she went on. I did not take kindly to her reprimand, and bristled when she continued: "Look at me, I never put anything on my skin and I'm so much older than you. You will be sorry later on."

"My cheeks aren't as rosy as yours. And the Americans aboard the ship said that everybody looks better with a bit of color," I responded. To me, my upswept hairdo and black eye make-up were proof of French sophistication. And I vaguely sensed that my mother was challenging my independence.

*   *   *

As soon as Hansl and I had skipped through the spacious lobby at 260 West 72nd Street, to the elevator in the rear, we fell into our earlier sibling rivalry. In the subleased furnished apartment, we quickly ascertained that neither of us had a preferable setup: that my side view of 72nd Street and the threadbare convertible easy chair in the tiny bedroom, was no worse than Hansl's sagging sofa in the combined entrance and dining area with its narrow window into an airshaft, and its direct access to the kitchen. (Our parents slept on the cheap metal pull-out bed in the living room that doubled as day-time couch.)

My mother's festive meal transported me back to the best of my childhood memories, to the countless schnitzels and strudels eaten with grandparents and a bevy of other family members. But I soon became more withdrawn: I was appalled that Hansl, by means of his natural and ingratiating charm, gave the story of our escape his own slant. He complained that I had made him carry my suitcases, and had him eat bananas and melons from one end of Spain to the other. He stole the show and I suppressed my displeasure. To the end of her days, my mother would tell new friends of her truly horrendous flight from Vienna, and that Hansl had protected me on our trip through Spain.

Already that evening, my father teasingly contended—just as he had in Vienna— that whatever either of us accomplished was due to his superior genes, while my mother maintained that her child rearing methods were bearing fruit. They both had learned from their own families that children ought to be grateful to their parents for having been born; that they must obey; that parental wisdom is fated to be correct; and that "*Wie man sich's einführt so hat man's*" (things will be as you establish them). During their separation, they both had been forced into dangerous and unexpected experiences. They had been humiliated over and over again, and had questioned whether or not they would ever be reunited. My father was bound to have faced his frustrations with the aid of a few romantic interludes, to which he could not admit. My mother still corresponded with the architect she had befriended before her departure from Vienna—at Cilly Ettinger's address. They both were determined to stick together and build a new life in America.

"I am a dutiful man, and I have never shirked my responsibilities," my father would reassert whenever his wife brought up his past flings and flirtations. I don't think he ever found out about the architect, the secret my mother confided to me only in her old age. "He wanted me to come to England with him," she said, "but I couldn't bear giving up my children."

These separate pasts and "what ifs" they speculated about, could not but add to the difficulties and frustrations of their refugee existence. My own expectations of being pampered by my parents did not help. I had totally forgotten my mother's unpredictable emotional outbursts, her adulation of my brother, and my mostly unsuccessful attempts to please her. My father, who liked bantering with me, had a way of flipping into remoteness. I was distressed whenever he turned aside my bids for attention or intimacy with a sardonic or joshing remark. While on my own, I also didn't remember my parents' Saturday fights over the size of my mother's household allowance; and that money always had loomed large, because my father was both wealthy and stingy. And it didn't occur to me that without his business and status he had lost his moorings and his dashing spirit. Or that much of his bravado was covering up his feelings of inferiority: he was a foreigner who now perceived himself as a nobody, and who expected to become a somebody—on the double.

I desperately held on to my own fabrications of the future. On that first night in New York, I went to sleep dreaming of romance and adventure. Pollyanna had nothing on me.

9

Our New York: Vienna on the Hudson

My parents couldn't possibly have lived up to my lofty dreams. They were in a hurry to reestablish our former lifestyle. That was why, on my first morning in New York, my mother left for her job at a dressmaker's, and my father took us to meet our uncle, Felix, at the offices of the International Marble and Granite Company on Columbus Circle. As we ambled down Broadway, he pointed to the architectural feats and gargoyles on some of the tallest buildings I had ever beheld, and especially to their occasional marble façades.

"Most of the stone here is grey and comes from Vermont, but as soon as the war is over, we will bring in marble from Italy, Portugal, and elsewhere, and you'll begin to see white and pink façades as well," he stated. I listened obediently, not wanting to let on that I was more interested in the lives of the oldsters who were lounging on the metal fire escapes and stoops of their low-slung brownstones; and in the Chinese men and women who were ironing so diligently behind the transparent curtains that hung inside the windows of their laundries. I gaped at shoemakers and their barefoot clients who waited for their sandals while sitting on straight-backed chairs. I gladly smelled the coffee, frying fat, and waves of hot steam that wafted from the dingy diners we passed. And I suffered silently from the excruciatingly moist heat. When my father noticed that I didn't much share his interest in marble, he stated, "Everything that glitters isn't gold. You'll find out soon enough. As long as the war in Europe will last, the import business is dead, and we have to go out to earn money."

I thought of poverty as an interesting condition that I would sail over blithely. Unlike my father, I had not lived through rampant inflation, and could not grasp what it meant for a man whose reputation rested on his business savvy to be without a business. Just then, a red-and-white open-sided tram, with clanging bells, and that was driven by overhead and sparking electrical lines, caught my attention.

"Before taking any tram, you will have to earn your keep," said my father somewhat mockingly, "until that time, you'll have to walk."

I happily skipped along and doubled back, until we reached Columbus Circle. What little motor traffic there was made a wide swath around Columbus's statue. We stopped to listen to some of the agitated, gesticulating men on soapboxes. They bellowed through enormous megaphones, and impressed me with their passionate, high-pitched diatribes. I did not understand a word. Frantic listeners argued and waved their arms, and an angry heckler threw a tomato that splashed on the ground. My father commented, "Stop and listen to these speakers whenever you have a chance, that's how you'll learn English. And make sure you pay attention to their pronunciation." I nodded agreement. Neither of us as yet grasped that their speeches were on the lowest level, full of lurid invectives, and that their vernacular was meant to incite rather than educate. I was entranced by these demagogues' fiery gestures, and by the honky-tonk atmosphere, and the tumult.

Of course, we spoke German. But I was self-conscious of using the language of the Viennese *haute bourgeoisie*, which had become somewhat rusty. I occasionally lapsed into French, because I was more fluent in it, and because my father made fun of any Pieffke words I might utter. But more than anything else, I wanted to pick up English in a hurry, if only not to stick out in, and adapt to, my new surroundings. I had no idea that this was part of what my father had in mind for me. After my mother's death, I found a letter he had written to her before embarking in Le Havre:

> Ditta's French is superb, she sent me, for example, a beautifully illustrated poem for my birthday. Since she is perfect in two languages, it should be easy enough for her to learn a third one, so she could start to earn some money soon. Hansl wrote too, it was a short note and full of errors. You should inquire about a good school for him; I'm told they don't cost anything over there. . .

1819 Broadway was an elegant commercial building, which was torn down a few years later to make room for the Coliseum. (In 2004, the Time-Warner complex took its place.) I admired the friendly doormen in blue and gold-braided uniforms, whose brass buttons sparkled so brilliantly. One of them pointed us to the elevator that instantly whisked us up to the tenth floor. The office of International Granite & Marble was a grungy cubicle. The empty desk in the tiny entrance seemed to be my father's, and behind it, separated by a translucent glass pane was my uncle's huge *écritoire*. Before I could utter a word, the portly Felix walked towards us with open arms.

"How come he has grown into Opapa Weisz," I silently noted. He had the same stooped shoulders, the same gray complexion, upturned nose and double chin. Felix greeted us effusively: "I almost don't recognize you, you've grown so much," he kept marveling over and over. Through the large window, he proudly pointed to some of the landmarks of the exciting metropolis below, to the Empire State Building, the Chrysler Building, Central Park—as if he had invented them.

"Don't forget to give your uncle the message from the Spanish consul in Toulouse," my father now urged me.

"When I told him that you were in the marble business, he said that he knew Opapa Weisz long ago, and that he wants to export Spanish marble to America," I dutifully summarized, "and when I said to him that we needed our visas so I could tell you to get in touch with him, he saw to it that we received them." I expected to be congratulated for my smart ruse. Instead, Felix and my father said almost in unison: "Imagine, the children were saved by the good reputation of our firm. How extraordinary." They both were less interested in the rest of our odyssey and in the other and much closer calls. Before we left, Felix handed each of us twenty-five cents to buy lunch at Horn and Hardardt's, at the southern end of Columbus circle, where years later Huntington Hartford would build his controversial museum.

I was goggle-eyed upon entering the Automat's enormous semicircular space, and admired the lit-up glass walls lined with chrome-encased cubicles whose contents made my mouth water. An endless array of tempting, delectable foods were waiting for our nickels and dimes. After getting change and carefully inspecting every compartment, both Hansl and I ended up with a sandwich, a piece of cake, and a glass of milk. But I did not let on, for fear of being ridiculed, that I had been so enamored by the automat on rue Neuve in Brussels, that I had planned to convince my family to open up a similar one in New York. Now, I found myself seated in an automat ten times its size, while my father sagely informed us that all technical inventions get started in America—where everything is bigger and better, "for frugal individuals who study hard and work even harder." On the way to Macy's, on 34th Street, I again was careful not to let on that I was less interested in the building façades my father pointed to, than in the showy hats and clothes women wore, and in the miens of the people we passed. What would I say to the handsome Persian if we were to run into him? My father kept asserting that Macy's was much larger than Bon Marché in Brussels; and that we didn't have the means to buy anything until we would "earn some money."

*   *   *

I was aware that my father and his brother were distrustful of one another, but they were too guarded for me to suspect the depth of their wariness. Although in Vienna I once had overheard one of their fights while hiding behind a door, I had no clue of the dynamics between the brothers. I was too young to know how deep sibling rivalries may run, and how long they may last. In Europe, my father had been the driving force in the family business, but now had to play second fiddle to Felix. They no longer yelled at one another: good manners, sarcasm, and bantering tones covered their jealousies—and those between their wives. Circumstances had gotten Felix to hold the purse strings to the scant capital left over from the family enterprise. On that hot September day, I took note of the brothers' *sotto voce* altercation, but was too immersed in my new impressions and old fantasies, to pay it much heed.

"How did Felix greet the children," my mother asked the moment we got home. Her tone was proprietary and superior, since her sister-in-law, Franzi, was childless.

"He seemed pleased to see them, what else could he have said or done," my father replied impatiently and announced that Felix and Franzi were going to visit us the following afternoon. The sisters-in-law never had liked or trusted each other. Nevertheless, my father had suggested in his letter from Le Havre that we all share a large apartment "in order to save money and accumulate the necessary working capital more quickly. After all," he had elaborated, "thanks to Felix, our financial future in America will be facilitated." By the time my father had crossed the Atlantic the sisters-in-law had had a major set-to. Now, they kept their hostility under control. But when she thought I couldn't hear, my mother whispered, "Franzi is manipulating Felix because she's as lazy as ever, and she is pretentious by telling us about American ways." Nevertheless, my mother added that she didn't "want to set the children against their uncle."

Since Felix claimed that by paying for our transatlantic tickets almost none of the original capital was left, the impending rift could not have been avoided. During that tea time, the grownups did no more than exchange gossip. While balancing a chipped, blue and white onion-patterned cup on her lap, the affected, elegant Franzi—who had donated some of this china to us—instructed: "Americans mean well, but they don't understand us. They follow their whims. Still, it's a fantastic country. You can be a dishwasher one day, and an elevator operator the next one. For example, Joshi Singer, after jumping from a job as a bus boy in a Greek restaurant to an Italian one, and then operating an elevator, by now has learned enough English to be a (door-to-door) salesman of silverware, not real silver, of course." Other such tales followed. After they left, my mother remarked, "She does all the talking, did you notice that he doesn't open his mouth when she is around? And who is she to give us lessons?"

On that evening, my parents were to take us to the Éclair, to meet some of their friends for coffee and *Sachertorte*. I looked forward to this treat. The heat had not abated, and I did not expect to wear stockings. Moreover, the only pair I possessed had a run. I had no intention of mending it.

"No daughter of mine," stated my mother, "either wears torn stockings or goes outdoors bare-legged." I looked out of the window, and pointed to the many women below who displayed their nude legs.

"You are not just anyone," my mother responded severely, "in our family we wear stockings. We may have no money, but we will hold on to our good upbringing."

"We're in America now," I shot back. I tried to appeal to my father as I so often had in Vienna, fully expecting him to support me. He seemed to be wavering and tried to sidetrack my mother by converting the crisis into a joke. But she didn't bite and just got angrier, refusing to be countermanded: "*Du bist aus einer guten Kinderstube, und Du wirst mir nicht über den Kopf wachsen*" (you're from a decent family and you're not going to contradict me), she insisted. She did not even heed my brother's half-hearted plea to lay off.

"We have to get you straightened out once and for all," she continued, "you might as well realize that in my house I am the boss."

"You always have taken her side against me," she continued while turning on my father, "even though you never had any idea of what it takes to raise children. That will have to stop."

Suddenly, we had arrived at an impasse and were locked in battle. I lost. Nevertheless, I did not think that my family could possibly leave me behind, that my mother could be so cruel. After they closed the door behind them, I was seething. I rushed to the window, unable to comprehend that my mother would not relent and motion me to join them. But when I saw my family emerge onto the street, they never even turned to look back. They were chatting animatedly as they moved in the direction of Broadway, apparently without giving me another thought. I was infuriated and overcome by helpless rage. What had happened to the Mutti who had entrusted Hansl to me, and who used to side with me against unfair teachers and feckless classmates? Why did she not appreciate what I had done to save us? More and more enraged, I seriously contemplated revenge, and thought of jumping from our seventh floor window: it would show my mother how wrong and nasty she had been, and she would forever have to blame herself for my death. But I soon noticed the narrow, fausse balcony and realized that falling was impractical, and that I would have to climb over the ledge and leap from there.

By the time I wondered how to heave myself over this obstacle, and whether I would really be dead, the impulse had passed and I looked around for another and less final means of revenge. Now, I resolved never to mend my stockings. I was going to get even by looking for a job in order to be independent. With the help of the dictionary on the coffee table, I deciphered the want ads in the *New York Times* and the *Daily News* to follow up on my decision. Sadly, I had to pass over the more glamorous job offers, such as receptionist and model, for which I needed to slim down and learn English. However, I found a perfect one: Chez Chapeau needed a milliner's helper. Certain that my afternoons at the École Professionelle had been well spent, and that I would be able to talk to the owner in French, I decided to lie about my age, which Franzi had said Americans do, and to set out for Chez Chapeau on Monday morning.

This millinery shop was on East 36th Street, off Lexington Avenue. I consulted the New York subway map, which was also on the coffee table, and figured out how to get there. That done, I went into the kitchen, searching for something sweet to console myself. All I could locate was a bottle of raspberry syrup on a top shelf. I moved the stepladder to reach it. Then, I deftly poured a few tablespoons of the sticky liquid into a tall glass and added water from the tap. This concoction tasted better than the cake I was missing at the Éclair, I said to myself while topping off the syrup in the bottle, again from the tap. Having developed my strategy, I calmly sipped my drink, while feverishly looking through the rest of the newspaper all the while consulting the dictionary. To become self-supporting I would have to master the English language in a hurry.

*   *   *

Exactly one week later, I too was introduced to the Éclair, the restaurant and *Konditorei* at the center of Vienna-on-the-Hudson. That was where newcomers were being initiated into America. Hans Selinger, a lawyer from Prague, and my uncle Felix's old friend, had opened this establishment on 72nd Street, between Broadway and Columbus Avenue. He employed former colleagues, most of them lawyers and their wives as waiters, bakers and cooks. Their flirtatious ways among themselves, and with the customers, made me feel I was back in Vienna, in the homey, and erotic, atmosphere of the post-Austro-Hungarian empire. The occasional faux service and clumsiness of the staff added a special panache to that saucy spirit.

The Éclair's regular clientele lived on the West Side, between 70th and 96th Streets. Their German was Austrian. It included the allusions and sayings they had grown up with; and they kidded each other about their many miseries. They called it *häkeln* (literally crocheting, but meaning to pull each others' legs). They commiserated about uncouth Americans, dead end jobs, and their lost prestige and fortunes. They bragged about a raise, a better job, or a deal. By the time I arrived, some had been around for as long as two years, spoke passable English, and were considered experts on America. When they dished out advice to me, as they did to all other new arrivals, they made me feel I was one of the grownups.

Americans who frequented the Éclair came in for the pastries and for the show: they gaped at the display of sensuality; gawked at the women who like peacocks had preened to impress one another, reemerging into the bourgeoisie for the evening; and at the Viennese finery—silks, cashmeres, and handmade shoes and pocketbooks—that had been acquired to last a lifetime. Viennese women exhibited the most cultivated manners, outstretching their pinkies and delicately wiping their lips while slowly sipping their coffee and picking at their strudel. And were quick to smile and lead on every half-way attractive man. Their husbands addressed each other, somewhat laconically, by their last names and were referred to by their former occupations: my father and uncle were the "Marble Weisses"; Fritz Spielmann was the "Kravatten (tie) Spielmann"; Leon Kraemer, was "Herr Kommerzialrat"; David Goldmann was "Herr Finanzrat." The place was swarming with men addressed as Herr Rechtsanwalt, Herr Bankdirektor, Herr Hofrat, Herr Advokat, Herr Doktor, Herr Regierungsrat, and more. Even the waiters were summoned as "Herr Ober." None of these newcomers were employed or employable in their former occupations, so they knowingly would raise their eyebrows and shrug their shoulders in gestures expressing resignation. My parents were on a first name basis only with friends from their early youth, with whom they had swum, played hockey or soccer for Hakoah. (Eventually, they all would be judged by what they had accomplished in America, by the jobs they had landed, the success of their businesses or professional practices.) They did not readily talk to strangers, and that included Germans, but waited to be introduced. Over time, cliques developed.

The refugees at the Éclair judged Americans by the ones they saw eating their dinners of goulash with dumplings and of Wiener Schnitzel with cucumber salad. To them, they appeared "rich" just because they could afford to eat a meal out. The Viennese slyly would make fun of the women's garish outfits, gaudy color combinations, and excessive makeup, feeling superior to what they considered lower class taste and bad form. They had no clue that some of these natives were former ex-patriates who imagined themselves back in Vienna or Paris; that others came for the tasty food and the rich desserts; that yet others sustained this refugee enterprise because it was the liberal thing to do. Selinger, who couldn't afford to encourage the insiders to linger all evening over their cups of coffee and the single piece of cake, which couples often split, kept saying, "Do you think this place could survive on what you eat here? Without these Americans I couldn't pay the rent, and where would you go then?"

Even the former Viennese who were hell-bent on melting into main-stream America, such as Karl Ettinger whose family moved into a tiny apartment not far from Gramercy Park, and the lucky few who had the financial means to buy homes upon arrival—in Scarsdale, Riverdale, or Great Neck—kept in touch. As did those who wanted more space for less money and had settled in Washington Heights, Brooklyn, or the Bronx. (I envied them.) But old habits die hard: all former Viennese judged one another harshly, just as they had at the Kaffee Zentral, the Opernkaffe, the Kaffee Bristol, or the Herrenhof, found fault with the quality of the Sachertorte or cherry cake when comparing it to the one they used to consume, and rated everyone by the way they looked and dressed. (Until the end of her long life, my mother asked me whenever I visited her, "how do I look?", and when I gave her news about someone she used to know, she would ask "how did he [or she] look?")

Viennese men's instinctive need to seduce women just for the fun of it, and the women's propensity for beguiling gestures and seductive gazes—calculated to make their mates jealous—were never far from the surface. Coquettish banter aside, the Éclair did serve as the site for a number of lasting encounters. I was as yet unable to distinguish the serious from the jocular, but refrained from asking questions that might have unveiled my ignorance in the ways of the world. Before making friends of my own age, I joined my parents whenever I could. I relished *Doboshtorte, Indianer Krapfen, Sachertorte*, and all the other gooey desserts. And as family tensions were mounting, I kept looking to their friends for support. (Dr. Eva Farber and Hedi Wertheimer were especially helpful in defending me against my father's ironic antagonism.)

When not dwelling on the immediate problems of making ends meet, on Americans' idiosyncrasies, or on the difficulties of mastering English, the former Viennese relived the good old days. And they worried about the possible means of bringing over their relatives—whose efforts at leaving Europe were being thwarted at every turn. They often read aloud their families' letters, trying to interpret what they couldn't find out from the American press. They never fully trusted what was printed in the *Aufbau*—the German language publication that brought news and comments about their former homeland, and that addressed the refugees' concerns. (Hannah Arendt, who still was unknown, had a weekly column.) To the extent that they understood American politics, they refracted them through their newcomers' lenses. Many of them read the *New York Times*, mostly to improve their broken English. I don't recall whether they bothered learning anything about national or local politics, but they thoroughly perused whatever referred to the war in Europe, were alarmed by Hitler's military victories, by Americans' relative unconcern, and were disturbed by the naïveté of our press. (When some years ago I first looked into the 1942 archives for reports about the extermination camps, I discovered a column of no more than ten inches, on page 10.) However, like me, all the refugees seemed to adore President Roosevelt and rarely blamed him for enforcing the strict quotas on immigration. Whether fearful of criticizing America or covering up worries by changing the topic, they tended to retreat with comments such as "who knows what's really going on," or "so and so always exaggerates to feel important," or dismissed bad news by calling the messenger an *Aufschneider* (self-promoter or exaggerator).

Ultimately, Vienna-on-the-Hudson was the prism through which I, and many of my contemporaries, learned to assess America—oblivious to the fact that that view was skewed. Still, even imperfect information was beneficial—about a reasonably priced apartment, a possible job one was bound to detest, or how to approach a potential employer. Joking at one's own and one's friends' expense, translating one's greenhorn stupidity and misunderstanding of English into an entertaining story, helped us deal with unending indignities and embarrassment. By overplaying our victories and underplaying our setbacks we could endure.

I automatically forgave our friends for their pretenses. But I was critical of my parents when they were stretching the truth, when as another Viennese proverb had it, they *schmücked* (adorned) themselves with others' feathers. Then, my father had not yet slipped off the pedestal I had erected for him, and I did not dare call him to account. Instead, I excused him by forgetting shameful incidents. This happened, for instance, when I visited Madame de Becker, one of our Belgian benefactors.

Monsieur DeWaay, who had rescued me and the other ninety-some children by getting us to southern France in May 1940, had made me promise upon my departure from Toulouse, to contact Madame de Becker the moment I arrived in New York, in order to ask her to "do something" for the "orphans" she originally had saved. My father recalled that a fellow inmate at his detention camp in Lisieux, a former Budapest lawyer, who briefly had been her cousin's chauffeur in Paris, had told him that Madame de Becker was an attractive woman. On a late afternoon, soon after my arrival, he accompanied me to see her at the Waldorf Towers, where she resided.

We had a bit of trouble finding the hotel's side entrance. A liveried concierge guarded the elegant yet discreet lobby of this residence. He blocked our way, saying that we had to be announced before entering the elevator. After many tries he understood the name, Weiss (we no longer spelled it Weisz). Over the house phone, Madame de Becker declared that she neither knew a Mister nor a Miss Weiss. When I eventually managed to explain that I was one of the children from the *home d'enfants*, and that I was bringing a message from Monsieur DeWaay, she instructed the concierge to send me up but not my father; that she was sick, and expected another visitor within fifteen minutes.

I was intimidated by the beige-clad elevator man in his fancy gold and beige cage, who waited until the French maid in her black dress, embroidered white cap and matching apron received me on a high floor. She repeated that Madame did not have time to spare, had a cold, and was expecting a guest. I recall only the soft, green carpet, its matching upholstery and heavy draperies of the sitting room, while being whisked into to the adjoining, pink bedroom. Sniffling, while propped up in her huge pink bed, Madame wore a delicate lacey negligee, which blended into the bedding and coverlet. While delicately dabbing at her nose, she urged me to tell her all about the children. When I started to recount our flight from Brussels, she interrupted to tell me that she had little time, but wanted to know whether there was anything she could do for them. She ended up saying that it was beyond her powers to get anyone out of France, and asked me who the man was with whom I had come. Before I could say more than that he was my father, her guest was being announced. She reached for the silver mirror and comb at her bedside, while the maid started to rush me out the door. (Sixty-five years later, I was sent the copy of a letter she had written to another committee member, Madame Goldschmidt, in Switzerland: "I was touched to see Edith Weiss and to hear the descriptions of your plight," and urged that "something be done for these children.")

My father had been cooling his heels downstairs. He was visibly annoyed at having been kept out and wanted to have a minute description of Madame de Becker, and of her apartment. I didn't have much to report.

"Why didn't you set up another appointment," he chided, and added, "You should have known that one must keep up with someone like her."

The experience had been upsetting not only for my father but for me as well. I had gotten a glimpse into another world, and vaguely realized that not all newcomers hung out at the Éclair, or had to take unskilled jobs in factories and restaurants, as elevator men, or as night watchmen. Although I then had no idea that only the elite of the elite congregated at the Waldorf Towers, I knew that Madame de Becker was an exile rather than a refugee.

I was even more perturbed by the way my father reported this incident to his buddies. He didn't spell out that I alone had been upstairs, vaguely implying that he had an entrée to that world. I felt ashamed for him, and was glad when the conversation shifted to someone else's boasts. But I immediately suppressed this insight by precipitating myself even more eagerly into what I perceived to be America.

*   *   *

Still, nearly all Viennese refugees were apt to make wild generalizations from their limited experiences just to impress, and were superimposing their native prejudices on American ones. Given their abysmal command of English, and their total deafness to American vernacular, they tended to misconstrue and over-generalize from their limited contacts with shopkeepers and workers to all Americans. They tried to master the language, but where could they have picked up proper English? The doctors and psychoanalysts, and the handful preparing for professions, did learn more rapidly. But even though they might from time to time come to the Éclair, they soon entered middle-class culture. Actually, most of the regulars were trying to make it into the America of money. It didn't occur to me then, that they all were trying to make sense of a milieu they didn't comprehend. Even the doctors' wives were slaving in garment and millinery shops while their husbands studied for their state exams.

My father marveled, "In America even millionaires work, look at John D. Rockefeller and J. P. Morgan." He forgot to note, however, that their occupations differed substantially from those of the refugees.

"The harder you work," he would go on, "the sooner you'll be established. You can't begin too early. Think of how much my father accomplished without going to high school; and none of the big shots in the marble business went to college."

His cronies would nod in agreement. But he also commented on the fact that Americans spend every nickel they make; and dollars they had yet to earn. How, I then wanted to know, does going into debt allow them to get rich?

"Money," my father emphatically declared over and over again, "is the root of all success—money makes money."

It seemed to me that the beginning of every sentence that didn't start with *bei uns* was: "You don't get ahead by remaining loyal to a job, or to a boss, the way you do in Europe. Loyalty is considered stupid. You have to keep moving from one job to another, that's how you advance—from floor sweeper to stock clerk, from stock clerk to salesgirl, from salesgirl to floor manager, from buyer to President of Lord & Taylor's."

All one had to do, I was led to believe, was to get into the swing of things, to be clever enough to sell oneself to a prospective boss. To prove his point, my uncle hinted that he might accept a sales position in an American marble enterprise, and that my aunt might run a bridge salon, or sell stationary at Macy's.

The habitués at the Éclair had worked out a sort of "advice to the jobless" they proffered to newcomers. It was similar to the one for "the lovelorn" in the Daily News. Lesson number one: "To get in, you must lie and say you have experience." Lesson number two: "Never admit that you don't already know how to operate a sewing or any other kind of machine, even if you've never seen it before; or that you never held a job in your life." Lesson number three: "If you want to be hired you have to say 'yes' to whatever a prospective employer asks, even if you don't understand a word of what he's saying." How else can you get "experience," and a "foot in the door?" "After you're inside a shop," according to lesson number four, "keep your eyes open, and look at what the person at the next machine or workbench is doing. And if you're fired at the end of the day or the week chalk it up to experience: you've probably picked up enough to hang on to the next job and you're ahead a few dollars."

Notwithstanding all that wisdom, my mother kept admonishing us to be honest, insisting that liars always are found out. Since I was sure I wouldn't be able to lie without being caught, I wanted to know whether lying on the job was different from lying at home. She blew up, and ordered me to stop being so *übergescheit* (smart-alecky). My mother, who had her own frustrations to cope with, was increasingly stumped by my wisecracks, and I didn't know how to back off. We frequently quarreled.

* * *

My father alone would not have to work for a boss. Around December 1940, on a typical evening at the Éclair, one of the cronies arranged for him and Felix to meet Heinz Keller, a loose-limbed blond, clean-shaven German-Jewish artist. Keller had heard that the marble Weiss's were looking to get into a new business and hoped to interest them in financing his fanciful venture. He was privy to a magic formula that could turn cheap prints into antique masterpieces. The process, he was certain, lent itself to the manufacture of a novel type of Christmas card.

"You know that Americans go for every new-fangled gadget, especially if it's handmade," Keller said, while showing them samples of 3 x 5 wooden plaques with antiqued pictures of saints, and stating, "You can mail this greeting card to a friend and he can put it up on his wall. And the following Christmas, when he's sick of it, he can send it to someone else. You must admit it's an ideal gift for spoiled Americans who have everything." Keller's own paintings didn't sell, and he was broke. To get this enterprise off the ground, he needed money for rent, and for supplies—plywood, run-of-the-mill reproductions of Madonnas and Christmas scenes, glue, assorted lacquers and huge tubes of sepia oil paint. My father and Felix agreed to back him.

Felix put five hundred dollars into Artistica. The brothers rented two dingy rooms on the top floor of 1919 Broadway, a six story tenement at 65th Street and Broadway that had been converted into lofts: its hexagonal black and white floor tiles were cracked; its rickety elevator groaned; the gashes in the sticky windows remained unrepaired; and even when overheated the place felt damp. My father located an old desk, and a few beat-up tables and chairs at the Salvation Army; and he installed a phone. Keller designed the showy stationery which he was certain would sell the "eternal" cards all by itself. Franzi was to peddle these Christmas greetings to department and stationary stores; Felix was to write business letters; my father was in charge of purchasing and running the office; and he was to assist Keller with production—until they could afford paid help.

After a month Keller's interest flagged. He explained that artists get their inspiration at night and that he was unable to show up before mid-afternoon. For a while he continued to "*schmeer* away" for a few hours after my father left for home. But then he didn't show up at all, explaining that artists, unlike businessmen, had to be in the proper mood for work. After another month, he no longer came around except to pick up his weekly check. My father increasingly resented doing all this artistic work without having the privileges of an artist. However, when he realized that Keller didn't appear because he had a new (rich?) girlfriend he got more and more incensed and jealous: "What are they doing before 2:00 P.M., when they finally pull up the Venetian blinds," he wondered in annoyance. (Keller lived diagonally across the street, on the East side of Broadway, where the Mormon Church would be built twenty years later). A month after that, Keller no longer came to collect his salary. When he resurfaced, my father bought him out for fifty dollars. Now, he expanded Artistica's scope and counted on it to make our family's fortune. And, referring to my thwarted artistic ambitions, he turned to me with a condescending smile: "Here is your chance to put your creative talents to use, after all, you're free on Saturdays." Since my other option was to help my mother clean our apartment, I gladly—though somewhat sporadically—took him up on that offer. By then, I already was sick of manual labor.

10

Father Knows Best?

Even in Vienna parents had been aware that adolescents are subject to mood swings. But they expected them to suppress their instincts, and to fall in line. After all, didn't they know that moping must be fought with willpower, and that father is bound to know best? In America, these fathers were floundering, but were hell-bent on hiding their insecurities from their offspring. This made them even more controlling than they had been brought up to be. Their children, however, expected to keep up with their most loose-hanging American contemporaries. Because they all were, as the French would put it, *dépaysé*, clashes were inevitable between traditional, old-fashioned principles and progressive customs and morals.

In the early 1940s, psychoanalysis had not yet made its inroads, and, with rare exceptions, my parents' generation of Viennese was nearly as critical of Freud as they were of Mussolini. Or they made fun of his teachings. They did not want to believe that there was such a thing as an unconscious, or childhood sexuality. Assuming that sexuality unexpectedly overcomes pubescent daughters, one had to "protect" them. This could be done only by keeping them close to home, by supervising them. But what teenager doesn't resent being watched? We have come to write off such rebellion as part of normal development. Still, what could be normal for a former industrialist who had dropped into the proletariat?

My father compared how things had been done *bei uns* and in America, and inevitably favored the comfortable past. I disdained his judgment, wanted to break loose, but was unable to do so. I also loved and admired him. Didn't my mother keep saying that he was out to protect me, his favorite child? She understood that I yearned for day school, although she resented that I did all I could to avoid housework; and I didn't want to be controlled. My father, a business genius, had no clue to what motivated his fairly intelligent daughter. His scathing put-downs devastated me.

He did not perceive that I was as fearful of every boy I dated as I was of him. And that he was bound to win every argument.

Our clashes started the Monday after my arrival, after I had safely navigated my way to East 36th Street, and had landed the job at Chez Chapeau; and while I still imagined that I could continue to remain as independent as I had been on my flight from Europe. When I arrived home that evening, bragging that I would be earning eleven dollars per week, my father countered, "Only one dollar less than the minimum wage."

That Friday, I was fired because I did not have a social security card. When I proudly showed the ten dollars and eighty-nine cents to my parents, my mother said, "I don't keep my earnings, so why should you?" My father added, "We need all the money we can scrape together to get on our feet. We have to build up the family capital. And why should you be better off than we are? You may keep one dollar—50 cents for your weekly carfare, 25 cents to buy something to drink with your daily lunch, and 25 cents allowance. And on Monday morning, go to the Council of Jewish Women. They will tell you how to apply for your papers." I cried, begged and argued to no avail. What was I going to do about new stockings?

The pleasant lady who manned the desk at the Counsel for Jewish Women wrote to Baltimore for my social security card, told me that anyone under eighteen needed a work permit, and that my mother had to accompany me to a designated health official for a physical exam. During her lunch break, we went to see a busy doctor, a black man in a white coat and a mirror across his forehead. He diagnosed a heart murmur and refused to sign the permit. My shocked mother immediately dragged me to a family friend, Dr. Eva Farber, who was studying for her medical license. She confirmed the murmur but pooh-poohed the handicap. Only then did I vaguely recall my bout with rheumatic fever in the *home d'enfants*. My mother was upset by my affliction, but relieved that her child-rearing methods could not be blamed for it. She stated, "If the Nazis hadn't come to Vienna, you would not have gotten sick," and ended up saying, "what's done is done. From now on, you will eat lots of vegetables and fruit, and get plenty of sleep."

"When will she be able to look for work," asked my father.

Home alone and bored, I filled my days with homework—stuffing leather animals for women's lapels—putting saddles of silver sequence and eyes of red pearls on white elephants; brown and pink trimmings on green donkeys, and so on. I yearned to go to day school, to meet my prince charming, and to escape from the parents I had been longing for.

"You can learn English by listening to the radio and reading the news-papers the way I do," my father opined. Luckily, my mother had kept in touch with Regina Bieber, the assistant principal of the High School of Commerce, whom she had met in Vienna. Since she was a typically straight-laced schoolteacher, and physically unattractive, my father didn't take to her. But she had managed to shame him into allowing me to attend New York Evening High School—after work. My mother handed me my Viennese school certificates, and encouraged me on the sly.

When my working papers came through, I was advised to attend Continuation School every Monday morning. In a huge classroom, way east on 86th or 96th Street, students loudly kept up private conversations while the teacher and two huge girls were demonstrating how to bathe an enormous doll. I didn't understand why I had to be there. So, after a month or two, and with much hesitation, I haltingly approached this teacher.

"Why can't I take up mathematics or history? My evening school is much more interesting. We are reading *King Lear*, and the American constitution."

"Then why are you here," she responded. "Since you are already going to school, you don't have to come any more." It didn't dawn on me that I was probably the first girl in her class interested in academics, and who had not dropped out of school because she was pregnant.

For what seemed to me an eternity, I hunted for jobs in the millinery district—east of Broadway between 35th and 40th Streets. There were plenty of Help Wanted signs, but after checking the safety of elevators in run-down buildings, of rickety staircases, and listening for rodents in squalid hallways, I skipped most of them—thereby escaping the drunkards that seemed to live in these passageways. I bestowed friendly smiles on many an unfriendly receptionist; and tried to ignore the leering once-overs by foremen. If I lasted more than a day I went on automatic pilot and dreamt myself into the life of the heroine or waif of the novel I had been devouring the previous night. In this underbelly of America I espied fire inspectors who received hush money, and truant officers who stayed away from grimy establishments. I was fired as a designer's assistant because I was too slow at stitching hatbands into hats, or, maybe, because I was too fascinated by the abundance of flashy flowers and grosgrain ribbons, and by the stacks of gaudy feathers and veils, tropical birds and multicolored blooms, male workers in loose zoot-suits wheeled past me on loaded trolleys; or by the parallel rows of chattering women who sewed birds' nests and waxed berries onto wide-brimmed hats.

Hemming neckties at Bergmann Brothers was almost worse. Here, refugee women handed me stiff taffeta ties and gave the soft silk ones to their friends. Since I was doing piecework, I earned considerably less than the minimum wage. And more put-downs from my father. When feeling sorry for myself, as I did much of the time, and lamented at home, I would be told, "You have to steel yourself, and we need the money," or, "you're a refugee now, and the sooner you get used to it, the better." Sometimes, I "got even" by walking to 42nd Street and spending my daily subway fare on the movies—and, uneasily, inventing a botched job interview.

My mother caught on to my fibs, but she was torn: she knew at first-hand what I had to cope with—sweaty men, demanding foreladies, foul language, unwelcome advances, squalor—but was eager to prove her loyalty to her husband, and to reestablish our former lifestyle. She was resigned at being cramped into three small rooms, and to forego household help. But she was adamant that we live as if such help were still around. She chased the indestructible roaches—slimy, disgusting creatures I never before had encountered— wherever we were living or were about to move to. "Can't you stop watching that cockroach walk up the wall while we're eating," she would snap during some of my bouts of detached reverie. She made sure that our sheets, dishtowels and hand-kerchiefs were ironed; that our small, fake Persian rugs be spotless; that pots were scrubbed to shine. And she assumed that any daughter worth her salt would cheerfully share in these tasks. For her, every shortcut was a step into the proletariat. For me, it was a step into America, and I was a bit of a slob. I desired to see everything, experience everything, and to discover every nook and cranny of American life—on the double. But not the sweatshops.

Things looked up when Kohner Brothers hired me as an "artist," to paint thousands of tri-faceted, red-dyed beads white on one side and blue on another: America was not yet at war, but some alert entrepreneur already had come to think that patriotism might become good business. When I had speeded up the process and produced my allotment in half a day, I was put in charge of the button orders. Making out work slips and overseeing "my" orders in the factory, I imagined myself an executive. My pay was raised to fourteen dollars.

"Why not more," baited my father. I liked using the mail meter; typing labels and invoices; organizing my own work; assisting in the office; and initiating new "artists." But I was crestfallen when after typing a letter for Paul Kohner, he told me to learn how to type on my own time. When raised to fifteen dollars, I wanted the extra dollar for myself, but my father remained true to form. Of course, he realized that, money-wise, Kohner Brothers was a dead end, and challenged me to find another job. So I became the "chief chemist" at Reflecto Letters, where I gilded mushroom-shaped glasses for house signs that would gleam in the dark—by shaking them in a variety of acid solutions. The odor gave me headaches. Again, I was rewarded by helping out in the office, but refused extra pay.

By 1943, I qualified as stock clerk and "contingent" sales lady at McCreary's department store, at seventeen dollars. Subsequently, I became the bookkeeper in the illiterate Mr. Rappaport's millinery supply business. He was impressed by the work sheets for my accounting class I happened to carry with me. But I had to give up my treasured and tranquil office when more money beckoned in diamond cutting.

* * *

Between 1940 and 1945 the diamond industry had moved from Antwerp to New York. My father's friend's, Leon Kraemer's son, Heinz—a somewhat arrogant, tow-headed boy—allegedly was earning "a fortune" by polishing diamonds. Now, his boss was looking for girls to replace the boys who were going into the services. Pushed by my father, I applied.

When the boss, Mr. Schenker, opened the door to his shop, I beheld row upon row of males on high stools, who faced each other across workbenches fitted with massive steel spinning wheels—which were fastened to thick crossbars above these worktables. The steady, grinding noise occasionally was interrupted by gnashing screeches of a diamond on metal, and by loud curses. I was informed that it would be difficult to get the hang of the demanding skills: I had to be strong enough to lift the heavy implement that had to be fitted firmly with the proper "dop" (the gadget to hold the diamond); that I had to learn "working in" my wheel; and was to polish my stones to perfection. If I could do all that, I would receive fourteen dollars per week during the first six months of apprenticeship. Thereafter, with piecework, I might net as much as $150 a week. Union regulations mandated an 8:30 A.M. to 4:00 P.M. workday.

On the following Monday, I met the three other girl apprentices: Anne, the boss's niece—who proved inept—was promoted to be his secretary. Ilse, a few years my senior and the daughter of Kraemer's partner in their insurance agency, was the spitting image of her blonde and blue-eyed, non-Jewish Gretchen-type mother; and Shirley, a bleached blonde—who wasn't fazed by that all-male milieu. I was assigned to the foreman John's, wheel.

"This wheel rotates 2,000 times per minute," he solemnly said, as I was hunched over it across from him, "and if you don't keep your hands off, you can easily lose a finger." He then taught me how to "balance our wheel," to saturate it with oil and diamond dust, and to avoid scratching it: "The better you work it in, the faster you cut your diamonds, the more money you make." With a magnanimous gesture, he handed me a brand-new magnifying loupe and a metal gage, taught me how to create a flat "table" and isometric sides—bordered by a 45-degree edge; to line up and polish the "bottom," and so on.

I liked John even though his ribald language made me blush and squirm. But I was discomfited by the vulgar jokes of about forty ill-bred and lewd males. Their come-ons were crude, and yet not always unwelcome when we were at a safe distance. They looked away from their diamonds only to leer at and provoke us, and to assess our sexual potential. They also resented us as possible competition, but relaxed when they realized that we were entrusted only the smallest and least valuable, raw stones—which paid the least.

Even if I then had heard of degradation ceremonies, or had been familiar with working-class mores, I would not have been able to avoid feeling perpetually embarrassed by the street talk. Or by Nate, the twenty-two-year-old cheap imitation of Johnny Weissmuller with tattoos up and down his arms. When he yelled from the other end of the large L-shaped room that John had better send me over with his screwdriver, I obediently brought it to him. But I did not know why the entire room resounded with laughter and guffaws, as the men followed me with lascivious eyes and lecherous comments. I self-consciously stumbled back to my bench—wondering whether my blouse had slipped out of my work pants or my seat was torn. Nor did I want to accept a date with the hunch-backed Joe, who offered to protect me.

After two months Shirley and I figured out that each of us produced between $80 and $100 worth of "merchandise" per week while receiving $14. So, we asked Mr. Schenker to pay us what we deserved. He refused and double-talked about having to stick to union rules. Our union representative, a big Irishman, pretended to be on our side, even though he tolerated girls only as (temporary) intruders he had to represent because they were paying dues. (At City College, I already had learned in my economics class that capitalism exploits, but not yet that labor leaders may be corrupt.) Now, Shirley and I threatened to slow up and cut half as many stones as we were able to, through the rest of our apprenticeship. After much haggling, we agreed to work full speed and be paid twenty-five dollars per week.

While negotiating at the union offices, a brownstone in Brooklyn Heights, John joined us, and then gallantly invited us to dinner. A decent man in his mid-forties and devoted to his wife and grown sons who were in the army, he never made a pass. But he liked to present himself as a ladies' man, as a bon vivant, a big spender. So even after we had settled our grievance, he continued to ask us for drinks and dinner at the nearby steak house, or at his favorite restaurant, Cavanaugh's, on 23rd Street. He would beam proudly when entering with two young girls—a blonde on his right and a brunette on his left— sparking the other men's fantasies and envy. I was confounded by the frantic table-hopping, and the "hail-fellow" ambience of these expensive establishments. I did not dare ask about what was going on in the curtained booths, where mostly dark fat men with slicked hair entered with sexy blondes. I knew that I didn't belong but was thrilled to be there, and to eat soft steaks. Of course, I kept these outings from my parents. In case of trouble, I trusted Shirley to get us out of it. (I did not figure out, not even after she took me to her Bronx home—a dingy apartment with unmade beds and closed blinds facing the Third Avenue El—that her father was permanently absent and her mother a drunk; and that she must have learned to fend for herself at an early age.) Actually, she turned out to be a true friend, by rescuing me from the boss, Mr. Schenker. He had told me to come in on a Saturday morning to recuperate the two diamonds that had jumped out of my dop and off my wheel. Instead of entering the shop, he ushered me into his office and, without any fuss, started to shove his short, pudgy body against mine, saying that he was sexually deprived because his wife was expecting their third child. When Shirley rang the bell from downstairs, he speedily buttoned his pants and begged me not to tell her. Of course, I did. Apparently, he had played the same trick on her a few weeks before.

11

Floundering About

Now that multiculturalism and women's liberation have captured our culture, it is difficult to convey what it meant to a greenhorn like me to flounder in New York's to me undefined social strata—that I pretended, not too successfully, to master. Did I move from pillar to post to find my own niche? Was I curious or just unhappy? How long would it take me to stop trying to please parents who seemed unaware of their shortcomings? Was I hoping to find the perfect man to save me? Where was my Persian Romeo?

I expected to know all about America at once, to pass as American on the double. When would people no longer wonder where I came from? When would I know that I was "girl," rather than a "goil," or a "goial," or to "ask" or "aks" questions? In the 1940s, ethnic origins were not being flaunted with pride. Instead, they were a hindrance, the mark of outsiders. I carried a German passport, whose red "J" branded me as Jewish—a religion I didn't practice. Austria no longer existed, and when I was referred to as German-Jewish, my Viennese soul recoiled. I was without a country, without a religion; and I dreamt in three languages. Where did I belong? Why was I in love with romance and afraid of sex?

* * *

My parents tended to blame the friends I hung out with for my obstreperous behavior. They sort of approved of Marta Marx. She had come to work at Kohner Brothers. We started by visiting museums together, but soon ventured further. By the time she was dating Frank Kohner, we tended to "accidentally" run into him in nightclubs. Marta rebelled against her Orthodox Jewish parents, and was brazen enough walk into any village nightspot while puffing on a cigarette. I would trail behind her—afraid that we might be turned away, or that our parents might find out where we were.

Annemarie Ettinger's father had been my family's lawyer in Vienna. He occasionally shamed my father into allowing their daughters to celebrate their birthdays at Asti's on 8th Street, or at the Jumble Shop; and he got us tickets to a few—to me unforgettable—concerts at Carnegie Hall.

At a get-together of former Hakoah swimmers, my father had taken a shine to the flighty Marietta, who had married her best friend's boyfriend at the age of seventeen. By 1943, he occasionally invited her to join us at the Tip-Toe Inn. Not much older than me, she was light years ahead of me in the ways of the world. She knew how to talk to boys and men, and even dared ordering the most expensive items on the menu. When reprimanded, she told my father that he could afford to pay for it. I was in awe of her stunning looks, her nerve, and her snappy ways.

*   *   *

Few of my parents' friends had children. When any of them praised me, and wished they had as enterprising a daughter as they did, my mother would put her forefinger to her lips, saying: "*Die Ditta ist sowieso schon zu eingebildet*" (Ditta [diminutive for Edith] is already too conceited). My father would make a deprecating gesture, or a crack about my voracious appetite. Still, their friends' company kept parental "lessons" within bounds. In any event, when my parents ran into Trude and Charles Kolish, they arranged for me to meet their daughter, Dorly. As soon as she opened the door to their spacious apartment, she told me that she was bored at Julia Richmond High School, and said that she envied me my independence. I immediately set her straight. Dorly recently had been dropped by her boyfriend. I envied her for her lack of inhibitions, and her easy way with boys. We agreed to become best friends.

My parents also believed that the spunky Maria, the daughter of one of my father's Éclair confrères, David Goldmann would be the right type of company. She had graduated from Brearley and now was at Finch Junior College. Maria put much of her energy into opposing her elderly, overprotective parents. She, too, longed to acquire my seemingly autonomous working life.

The Kolishes and the Goldmanns were wealthy enough to avoid the squalor of refugee life. They liked me, and hoped that my academic ambitions and work habits would rub off on their daughters. As did Dorly's mother's boyfriend. I warmed to their comfortable homes, and to the ready-made chickens, patés, and pastries that always seemed to be waiting in their refrigerators. None of them were aware of their daughters' fairly free ways.

"Thank God that Dorly has taken her to meet others of her age in the Austrian-American youth club," my parents kept repeating with relief. Its meetings took place at Dorly's apartment. The twenty-one-year-old Otto presided over " Kreis 2." I don't recall what we talked about, except that he urged us to read the news in order to get ready to help free Austria from fascism after Hitler's demise. On weekends, we met at New York's free tennis courts in Central Park and under the George Washington Bridge, and took trips to Pelham Park, Staten Island, and to the other freebies New York offers. But trouble brewed when I wanted to spend the Fourth of July weekend at the Workmen's Circle's (a socialist organization for members of labor unions) Camp Midvale, in New Jersey—for a total of two dollars. My father declared, "We cannot afford such extravagances. No one in our family has as yet taken a vacation, so why should you?" However, it soon transpired that he thought I couldn't be trusted to spend the night under one roof with boys. (My mother did suspect that I found myself freezing whenever an attractive boy came too near.) In solidarity, Mr. Kolish now rescinded Dorly's permission. He consoled us, by letting me sleep over at their apartment. We set off at dawn, to spend the day at camp. And we never told our parents that we had gotten into more danger than we could ever have experienced during a night at Midvale. Since we would have had a long wait for the bus to Patterson, we hitched a ride from the ferry with four rowdies in a shiny green Plymouth. Only kicking, scratching, and pinching helped us escape them.

At the beginning of September, Otto announced that our group had gotten too large and would be split into two. He assigned me to "Kreis 3," and ruled out that I stay with Dorly. In protest, I dropped out altogether. Had I not been so politically naïve, I might have figured out that Otto was obeying party orders; that, unlike me, he had not mourned for Austria's chancellor, Dollfuss, after his assassination in 1934; and never had worn the *Seid einig*! insignia or chanted *Rot-weiss-rot bis in den Tod* (red-white-red until death), as I had. Why else, did he do an about-face from his fierce pro-peace position on the day Hitler attacked the Soviet Union, to write in the "Young Austro-American" newsletter:

"We are waiting for the Japs. Let them come—we will give it to them—for Pearl Harbor and Stalingrad, for Coventry and Lidice, for all the misery the fascists have brought upon mankind. We are here to revenge."

In the mid-1950s, we read in the New York Times that the four mainstays of the Austrian-American Youth organization had reenlisted in the army after 1945, had been stationed in Vienna as operatives of the OSS and then of the CIA, and, all along, had been double agents for Moscow.

*   *   *

My parents did not object to the Viennese girls and German boys I met at New York Evening High School. However, they were truly pleased when Maria asked me to a party with her Finch College classmates and the blind dates she invited from the Yale officers club. My father even went with me to buy a dress for the occasion. Some of our former closeness resurged, until he began to lecture about my vulgar taste and bulging hips. I agreed to look for a garment that would hide them.

After dragging along Broadway for three or four agonizing hours, we settled on a light blue number with a loose sprinkling of pink strawberries, and an elongated "V" neck. Its sash across the hips—higher on the left side than the right one—was tied into a knot, from which the soft fabric cascaded elegantly to the hemline. I liked the silken swish of the rich material, and the semi-circular swirl around my knees when I walked. My mother, however, tried to hide her misgivings by declaring that the dress made me look too old. Since that was the effect I tried to create, I was pleased with my choice.

"Still, the most important thing is that you like it," she conceded, and offered to lend me her string of pearls for the evening of the party.

I rehearsed my dramatic entrance and expected to camouflage my foreign accent. I knew no one would want to hear about my life as a diamond cutter; that boys needed state-side memories, and letters from girls after they shipped out. And that they were looking for a girl to go to bed with. I had not realized that Maria's classmates and the neophyte officers shared a common past, such as Harvard-Yale games; and that none of these brand-new officers—homogenized by crew-cuts, clean shaves, shiny boots, and made-to-order khaki uniforms—were Jewish. Maria, who too was Catholic, like her mother, had said that none of her friends cared about religion. And her friend Lonny, who was Jewish, and whose black dress was trimmed with white lace, almost mimicking the Franz Hals portrait above the exquisite Louis XIV desk, had come down from Radcliffe. She exemplified what my father deemed impossible—to be both intelligent and beautiful. All the other girls also wore black sheaths—decorated with discreet round or oval pearl lapel pins, and matching bracelets and earrings. I ignored that Maria's classmates—daughters of a Southern congressman and of high-level corporate executives—were being rude: they didn't talk to me in their eagerness to capture these officers' attention. I was devastated.

Maria's devoted mother expected to make everyone feel at home, and assisted the hired help in the kitchen. Her solicitous father, who already was a minor player in the financial world, assumed he was acting American by walking about with a dishtowel. I tried to pretend that I enjoyed myself. In desperation, I imagined that I was gathering material for a story I would write—even though I had not even kept a diary since leaving Brussels.

When Maria rolled up the living room rug, turned on the music, clapped her hands, and invited everyone to dance, I suddenly developed one of my excruciating headaches. Mrs. Goldmann hugged me, and handed me two aspirins. Not long after that, I made a feeble excuse, tripped over the Persian rug at the threshold, and rushed home.

My mother, who had looked forward to vicariously enjoying this party, was disappointed, and didn't have much patience with my recurring headaches. She knew that they were psychosomatic, but assumed I brought them on at will. I clammed up, and did not tell her about the delicious meal, or about my feelings of despair. I wanted to be alone. The last thing I could admit was that she had been correct about my dress, that the only thing about me that had not been off-key had been her pearls.

*   *   *

My parents approved of Ronald, an intense nineteen-year-old, whom I had met at Annemarie's party, soon after America had entered World War II. He just had enlisted in the army and had invited me to meet his German-Jewish family at their home in Great Neck. As I was about to leave, my father could not help saying: "You would look very pretty, if only you could lose a few pounds." My fleeting self-confidence was punctured. Ronald gave me his army pin, and then was all over me in one of the bedrooms of his elegant house and in the train back to the city. I withdrew. We almost stopped writing to each other already before he suddenly died of meningitis while at boot camp. Might he still be alive if I had understood that he needed me to love him, I kept asking myself foolishly.

Clearly, my parents were as befuddled as I was. Moving from class-bound Vienna into what I still thought of as unbound American mobility unhinged us all. Years later, I would study overt and covert class distinctions. At the time, however, I only blamed myself for my ineptitude, and for feeling so distraught over my petty personal wounds. Why couldn't I just be thankful for having escaped the Nazis, or focus on feeling sorry for the boys who were about to risk their lives? Or, as my mother kept telling me, think more of what was happening to my grandparents. Actually, I did that, too, after my bedtime. For I was sure that they would have seen to it that I could attend day school, and would not have wanted me to work in filthy factories.

* * *

I almost escaped. For soon after entering the evening division of City College, in 1942, during my mandated appointment with the Dean of Women, I inadvertently told her about my dismal home life. She listened, asked a few pointed questions, and then suggested that I go away to college.

"But I have no money," was all I could stammer.

"Don't you know about the College Blue Book? It lists all sorts of scholarships. I'm sure you would qualify for a number of them." Encouraged by her confidence in me, and guilty about having badmouthed my parents, I spent the following Saturday at the Public Library on 42nd Street, and sent out fourteen letters.

That April, I received acceptances from Kent State, the universities of Colorado and Wisconsin, Alabama State Teachers College, and Radcliffe. I chose Radcliffe, not because I knew of its superior quality and prestige, but because Boston was closest to New York and I was certain that I could scrape together the money for bus fare, and maintain a "B" average while earning my spending money with half-time work in the registrar's office. Elated, I showed the letter to my parents.

"You are free to go," said my father, "but don't count on coming back once you cross this threshold." I argued and cried, but he remained adamant. It never entered my mind that he might be ignorant of the extraordinary chance I was being offered. My mother, while dabbing at her eyes, reminded me that my friend, Susi Ronay, to whose boardinghouse I had been packed up to move a few months before, had died of an undiagnosed intestinal ailment. When she said that I might get another attack of rheumatic fever, brought up her anguish while we had been apart, and that we needed money to bring the grandparents over, I gave up.

My father did not state that going away might leave me prey to white slavery, but I could not completely disregard his declaration that "no one gives you anything for free, and if you're looking for an education rather than entertainment, you can get it just as easily by spending your evenings at City College." Around then, I started to neglect school. Neither Shirley nor the other diamond cutters cared for learning, or couldn't manage it, and I didn't have the strength of character to refuse the delectable meals John kept offering, and which neither I, nor the City College boys I was dating, could afford.

I thought and talked about boys as often as my loosest girlfriends. But I did wonder why, while dating Fred Meyer, whom I truly liked, I pushed him off whenever closeness closed in. After meeting Harold, a gangly, square-faced engineering major with sandy-colored hair and acne, who initiated me into the house-plan, a fraternity on Convent Avenue, full of heavy smoke and girl-crazy boys, I hung out with him and his friends Derek and Henry. The four of us, who soon were joined by a Dutch girl, went on picnics, and to concerts at Lewisohn Stadium—where we sat on the stone steps for ten cents. We heard, for instance, the first American performance of Shostakovich's Fifth Symphony. We argued about the merits of his and other composers' music, about art and biology. When Harold and the Dutch girl became a twosome, I dated Henry, who was Viennese and an aspiring veterinarian. After they all were in the services I went out with a string of boys—all of whom my father found "unworthy of his daughter," "a gigolo in the making," an "unattractive nobody," or an "awkward and gangly snot-nose."

"She eats too much, spends too much money, runs around too much; she doesn't listen; and she doesn't know how to judge people," said my father. "She'll get sick because she doesn't get enough sleep," said my mother. Sometimes she added, "Had we stayed in Vienna, she would have gone to dancing school and met the right kind of boys, from respectable families. Here, we don't know whom she's with, and where they come from."

They had a point. But I continued to be sucked into the whirlwind that was New York. The more people I tried to keep up with, the more my parents berated me for my lack of judgment, and the guiltier I felt towards those I was dropping. Sometimes, I imagined myself dating out of patriotism or out of a need to prove that I was attractive. Other times, I made dates I didn't plan to keep. But every time I did so, I got depressed and stayed at home for a few Saturday nights—reading the books I borrowed from the St. Agnes Public Library. At that librarian's advice, I immersed myself, alphabetically, in every book on their shelves, beginning with Jane Austen, going on to the Brontë sisters, and so on. I have no idea whether I read Theodor Dreiser's *An American Tragedy* twice because I so thoroughly identified (and cried) alternately with Clyde, Roberta, and Angela, or was just sorry for myself. This might not have been the best way to appreciate literature, but it shut out my surroundings, to the point of not hearing my mother's calls from the kitchen. (She resented that she no longer had the time for such frills.) That after a Seder at Marta's house I wanted my parents to observe religious holidays was yet another way of rejecting them.

As the war went on I increasingly burst with egalitarianism, and became rather casual about how I met servicemen. How else could I have been introduced to Benny Goodman's band, and to Roseland's—by the Irish-American corporal who didn't believe that the parents of a girl living on West End Avenue were sleeping in the living room of a tiny apartment. Needless to add that none of these boys could measure up to my idols, Clark Gable, Jean Gabin, James Stewart, or Joseph Cotten.

When boys weren't foremost in my mind, and when talking to the more serious among them, I clued in to American politics. So, remembering my father's advice to learn English from the men on soapboxes on Columbus Circle, I listened. As I began to understand what they were saying, I was shocked by shrill America Firsters, Bundists and Fifth Columnist—who claimed that Hitler was a great Führer; that stories of his persecution of the Jews were untrue; that the Jews were too powerful; that Mussolini was the first person ever to have Italian trains run on time; and that the French were dissolute cowards who didn't wash and the English not much better. I was afraid to open my mouth, but wondered guiltily how grownups could be so stupid and not know what even I knew.

* * *

On Sunday December 7, 1941, while Marta was over for coffee, we heard President Roosevelt tell the nation that Japan had bombed Pearl Harbor. My mother, Marta, and I, convinced that the fascists would win, began to sniffle. My father however stated that, finally, the Allies had a chance at beating them. We worried about our relatives in Vienna and Shanghai, from whom we now would be cut off. Would all Jews end up being "resettled in Poland," as had been rumored? We feared that our relatives might go hungry and freeze to death.[4] Increasingly, my mother was near tears when opening our empty mailbox.

Sometime in 1943, after yet another fight, I convinced my father to let me buy the grayish-blue uniform—for $10.99—to sell war stamps in front of the 72nd Street Newsreel Theater. This allowed me to see the news for free. Although the war stories scared me, I often sat through them twice. (I still watch every Holocaust film. And felt driven to publish and annotate my grandmother's letters to my mother.[5])

* * *

Altogether, I did not have as hard a time fighting off the boys my father disdained as the old roués. There was the upper class WASP dentist to whom the ladies at the HIAS had referred me, who, with shaky hands inserted his saliva ejector and drills. While I was strapped in his dental chair, he slowly would bend over me and put his lips to my forehead.

The Czech refugee dentist who was a sort of younger and brown-eyed replica of my father at his most enticing, offered to save me—apparently for himself—from his partner's penchant for Lolitas. When I told my mother about it, she cautioned that I keep such things from my father, because he would intimate that I had provoked them. Thus I no longer mentioned the unknown who, in a crowded subway car, had masturbated into my slip, or the one who brutally attacked me on my way to work in Williamsburg. (A couple of hard-hats heard me scream for help, and got the police.) In defense, I increasingly turned into myself, but not without developing my own snappy ways. I was determined not to become as submissive as my mother, who was getting more and more deferential to her husband. She guessed at some of my internal chaos by innuendos that were meant to keep the lid on explosions.

Robert, an intense and conventionally handsome Bronx boy was the would-be rapist I found nearly irresistible. He already had his engineering degree and now was reading the *New Masses* and *Partisan Review*: he was a conscientious objector. On a clear, frosty winter evening, as we were sauntering under the triumphal arch in Washington Square Park, I was enchanted by the quiet snowscape, the flickering lights on the north end of the square and the far-away notes of "Oh, Christmas Tree." Suddenly, I found myself pulled onto a snow-covered park bench, with Robert's legs between mine.

"You know that I can take you now, don't you," he stated matter-of-factly while holding me in a vise and slowly unbuttoning his pants. I froze, appealed to his better nature and eventually convinced him to desist. But I didn't believe him when he gave me until New Years Eve: at his friend's party on Sherman Avenue, we would either go to bed or never see each other again. "He can't mean that," I told myself. But he did. He failed to appreciate my virtue and dropped me.

That evening had more serious consequences. I had been dragging with a cold and sore throat for some time. The long, chilly New Year's night had aggravated it. I started to run a low-grade fever and developed pains in my wrists. Eva Farber, who by now had her medical license, diagnosed rheumatic fever. She ordered me to bed. My mother was worried. She cooked fresh vegetables and other appropriate foods, and even took a trip to Convent Avenue to register me for spring semester classes. To prepare me for my course in psychology, she bought A. A. Brill's Modern Library Edition of Freud, and his Introductory Lectures. I not only immersed myself in Freud's ideas, but, like so many kids before me and since, "analyzed" my dreams, thoughts, and emotions. For the first time since leaving Vienna I did not feel pressured. I stayed in bed, took my aspirin every four hours, ate my meals, and relaxed.

After five weeks my father had gotten impatient with a blood count that kept registering too high a sedimentation rate, and with Eva Farber who could not predict when it would drop to normal. So, one afternoon, he came home early: "I feel ill too," he fumed, "and I can't afford to lounge around. You'd better stop playing sick and get up and go to work." Livid, and weakened by my bed rest, I barely managed to drag myself into the kitchen, to serve him the soup he demanded. My mother couldn't decide whether to be more upset by my illness or by my father's tantrum. Eventually, her foreman, Charlie Brown, spoke to the boss, who was on the board of Beth Israel Hospital. He arranged an appointment at its clinic. I squirmed when placed naked behind a fluoroscope while a senior physician demonstrated the onset of an enlarged heart to a bunch of medical students who, I thought, made allusive jokes.

When my mother revealed to this doctor that we were poor refugees, he declared that I might as well get out of bed, regain my strength and go to work, saying:

"But be sure to have her take it easy. And have her tonsils removed."

Now, Eva Farber's earlier, socialist convictions resurfaced: she asserted that if we had not pleaded poverty he would have ordered bed rest—to keep the damage to my heart at a minimum. I soon resumed my former routine, and when I returned to City College, looked around corners afraid of running into that Robert.

*   *   *

Already the year before, my father and uncle had gone to an arbitrator, who had decided that my father keep Artistica and Felix all other assets. Now, my father engaged a shrewd and to me a bit unsavory middle-aged salesman who wore green, checkered suits. Upon America's entry into the war wood was rationed, and the Christmas cards began to be made of cardboard, and prints of flowers and maps were added to the crêches and the Rubens, Leonardo, and Caravaggio Madonnas. Artistica's creations began to be displayed at bi-yearly gift shows. A Viennese matron was hired to antique an increasing diversity of products, such as stamp and cigarette boxes, desk and wastebaskets of papier maché, and to paint glassware. Soon after investing in a spray booth, a male emigrant replaced my father. Nevertheless, my father kept complaining that he had been reduced to a manual laborer, and had dropped from the major league to the sandlot. (It never entered his mind that my mother and I were exposed to more than the stench of turpentine and the squalor of cast-iron decay.) Gradually, he hired more women, moved to larger quarters on East 19th Street, and Artistica took its place among New York's small manufacturing enterprises. By the time its balance sheet showed a net worth of $30,000, my father's cronies at the Éclair ranked him among America's millionaires.

By then, I was earning between $100 and $150 per week, and managed to withhold some of my pay. Being able to buy a few frills made me less belligerent, and my father seemed less bossy. Still, after I was accepted at the Art Students League, we found out that the classes and supplies cost money, that, once again, "we could not afford."

"You don't need a live model to become a fashion illustrator," my father declared while suggesting that I learn by copying ads from The New York Times. So, I whiled away many a Sunday, sprawled on our living room floor, inundated by newspapers. I copied endless drawings, reproducing the strong strokes and soft washes used in rendering the swooping styles the models wore in the beguiling Lord & Taylor spreads. I bought myself a book, *Anyone Can Draw*, to learn about human anatomy, and another one on the use of oil and water colors. But before long I had seen enough art on my countless visits to museums, to judge that my homemade sketches were amateurish.

To turn myself into a draftsman seemed a perfect compromise. Thus I attended a "free trial lesson" in a spacious studio on West 42nd Street. On that sultry evening, I was perched in front of a large easel, while heavy steam drifted up from the hot pavement. A radio played a soulful version of "*Stardust*," and a sexy, black-eyed South American girl in a flowing halter dress of black cotton with red roses, and a red rose in her hair, was swinging her shapely legs from the high stool. The instructor's lesson consisted of some sort of combination of elementary geometry and of drawing lines with a ruler. No sweat. I soon was convinced that drafting was a challenging profession. I was ready to sign up. But neither my parents nor I had been aware that this free lesson was the come-on for a very expensive course.

I reluctantly admitted that my father's perseverance was paying off, but found the interminable dinner talk about customers, employees, orders, collections, and what to bring to upcoming gift shows, ever more grating. I kept saying that I was tired of cutting diamonds and wanted to go to college.

"Stop being sappy, America is a country of conmen and swindlers, one can't be too careful," my father would pronounce from time to time. But I already had learned that "in America all people are born equal." My father didn't want to be equal. He wanted to be rich. And my mother dreamt of once again living in clover, and spending her afternoons with her friends in coffee houses. Nevertheless, when Charlie Brown, her good-natured foreman, who lived with his wife in a semi-attached brownstone where Bensonhurst meets Brownsville, kept inviting my parents to come out on a Sunday, she persuaded me to come with her. (My father balked at such a friendship.)

I never had been in a tree-lined street in suburbia, or watched people sip tea on their stoops, tend their flowers and mow minuscule lawns. The young Alfred Kazin had perceived this neighborhood as the end of the world. I took to the Browns' gaudy but homey place, assuming that it provided the privacy I craved. Mrs. Brown, a jolly and obese woman, overfed us from the moment we arrived, pulling tray after tray of kasha, potato kugel, gefilte fish, latkes, various hashes, and a huge pot roast, out of the depths of an enormous oven. On a subsequent visit, I did observe that she was the prototype of the "Jewish Mama," good-natured, helpful and interfering constantly in her numerous sons' and daughters' lives. They all were in their late twenties and early thirties and lived within a few blocks. I opened up to their freewheeling ways and their generosity, especially to the comely, dark-haired daughter-in-law who gave me the Modern Library edition of *The Works of George Eliot*—which I still have on my shelves.

$$* \quad * \quad *$$

I had learned in my economics class about rugged individualism, principles of anarchy, working class solidarity, capitalist exploitation, and other Marxist-inspired theories. But it didn't occur to me that the eventual unification and victory of the working class might affect my life. In philosophy I had been plunged into Dewey and Santayana. I excelled in psychology because I read every book the instructor—Leopold Bellak, a second lieutenant and a resident at Flower-Fifth Avenue hospital—mentioned. I had managed to get a B- average by taking notes during lectures and relying on my nearly photographic memory during exams. My mother insisted that I could learn without studying, and I chose to believe her. Like other students, I wanted good grades without cracking a book. In the French club, I was among the kids who had stopped over in a French speaking country on their way to New York, and who pretended that French was our mother tongue, preferring to be thought of as Parisian exiles rather than as Viennese or German refugees.

In the psychology club, we argued about Fromm's ideas of human freedom, and Horney's critiques of Freud's views of femininity. On Friday nights, a bunch of us took the subway to Jacob Moreno's psychodrama, on 41st Street, where some of my fellow students would enact family conflicts. I was too timid to be more than a spectator. However, I was confident that ultimately I would be able to apply Freud's prescription for enjoying both work and love—although I couldn't fathom how long that would take. Would I ever learn to separate problems stemming from my budding sexuality from those posed by my family, or teenage rebellion from being a refugee? My father was sure that I would get married in a few years, and that "men don't like smart women." If he were correct, I would have to think of marriage, and if not, I would have to get married to get out from under.

* * *

As America kept revealing more and more intriguing facets, Vienna was dissolving into New York and Brussels was forgotten. The chameleon-like qualities I had acquired during my flight made me adjust, however anxiously, to whomever and whatever I encountered. That may well be why by then, all of New York had become my backyard. I danced at the Claremont Inn—a romantic outdoor spot that overlooked the Hudson, and whose "booths" were framed by potted palms and well-kept shrubbery, or at the equally romantic Tavern-on-the-Green in Central Park. There was hardly a play or a movie I missed. Like any American teenager, I hummed the opening words to popular tunes, such as "*Begin the Beguine*," "*I'm Gonna Buy a Paper Doll*," "*When Johnny Comes Marching Home*," "*It's a Long Way to Tipperary*." While drifting from date to date, I lapped up a popularity I knew I didn't deserve. Sometimes I believed that I would live in eternal bliss after the war, while singing "*Night and Day*," "*The Lullaby of Broadway*" or "*Always*" with the man of my choice. But despite my frenzied activities and multiple inroads into American society, I rarely could forget that I was a greenhorn.

12

Falling into Marriage

In June 1944, I again I bumped into Dorly. She caught me up on who was going with whom, on the boys who had gone into the armed services, and on the couples that had gotten married. She let on that she was as disinterested in her classes at New York University as she had been in High School. That summer I was enrolled at City College's from 8:00 A.M. to 10:00 A.M., thereby cutting down on diamond cutting, and was learning to type on two nights a week. Once again, Dorly urged me to come with her to Camp Midvale over the Fourth of July weekend.

By now my father anticipated the Allied victory and his return to the marble business. And he was less focused on my doings. My mother fretted that I got too little sleep, while saying, "You're still the way you were as a little girl, always afraid to miss something." But she had mellowed, now that Johnny's activities helped divert attention from me. He stayed out late, allegedly practicing soccer or attending a ball game. He got along at school, earned his spending money, and didn't care for clothes—as he evolved into a typical American teenager. At meal times, my mother looked at him lovingly while he was packing it in. He smoked on the sly. When the smoke from his friend's, Tommy Bishof's, cigarette rose behind him as he stood near our entrance door, she remained silent. But she was offended by my sloppiness.

"Why can't you ignore your mother's stupid prattle the way I do," my father occasionally suggested, "she means no harm." I rarely could. He ostensibly was tired of playing umpire between us and yet kept setting us up and egging us on—whether it was about my turning the radio on to Frank Sinatra or Louis Armstrong, ignoring dirty dishes in the sink, or withdrawing into my cocoon. Was I unreasonable by wanting a telephone?

"There is nothing wrong with being called to the phone in the lobby," my father kept insisting, "and I am perfectly willing to take messages for you at my office." I accused him of keeping away my dream idol, though I really just wanted to lounge on my bed and chat with my girl friends, to jabber. If my parents realized that even under the best of circumstances four people in two cramped rooms had to go on each other's nerves, they did not admit it.

When on that Fourth of July weekend, I again arrived at Camp Midvale, I was stunned that my former pals also had become American; and that their younger siblings had grown up and had joined. Dorly and I suddenly felt we were turning into old maids, and that our future was passing us by. So we threw ourselves into the social flurry—with upswept hair, heavy lipstick, and mascara. On that Friday night, a handsome second lieutenant, who was studying medicine, sat at the piano.

"He's already going with two girls," whispered Dorly when he welcomed me with a broad smile. Until that moment, I didn't know that I had gotten nostalgic for the waltzes I had grown up with, and whose beat the gracious pianist somehow managed to impose on whatever he played. Everyone was swaying to these soulful melodies, or hopping to the popular tunes emanating from the jukebox. Trying to appear urbane, Dorly and I pursed our lips, gestured self-consciously, and joined in. Most of the boys were in khaki. Stationed near New York, or on their way overseas, they had come out for a weekend of fun.

At one of Annemarie's parties, I had met an "older" boy from Berlin, Paul Rosen. I had made a date with him but had stood him up. "What is he doing among the Austrians," I wondered panic-stricken as he confidently strode in. He casually ambled over and asked me to dance. Tall, with thinning sandy hair, and unflappable, Paul wore his selfishness and insincerity as if they were cherished emblems. He was the image of the aggressive yet cajoling male, the type I most feared and found most tempting—Berlin's version of the Viennese *Schlürferl*. As he threw me in and out in a fancy jitterbug, or squeezed me too intimately in a slow foxtrot, he made believe we never had met. Soon, he asked me to go for a drive. I didn't trust him at such close range and suggested we take a stroll instead. Like every other "4F" in those days, Paul immediately explained that he wasn't in the service because he had to support his aging parents. (He was a floor manager in the garment district.) While lighting his cigarette, he pretended I was the girl he had been waiting for, with Peter Lorre's accent but in the manner Humphrey Bogart used when talking to Ingrid Bergman. His seduction scenario, full of sweet talk and lies he proffered as confidences, was not very original. As he kept searching for the most appropriate, secluded spot in the woods, I kept pushing us toward the lit-up and well-trodden paths. It was a sweltering night, ideal for romance and passion. I felt myself yielding to Paul's caresses—while taking in what he was doing as I would a mesmerizing movie scene. Before long, I disentangled myself and told him, uncertainly, that I didn't yet know him sufficiently to go all the way, and retreated into the girls' dorm. I half-regretted my victory, and looked forward to explaining my "prudish nature" over the communal breakfast. Paul, however, avoided me. He refused even to make eye contact when we bumped into one another at the coffee urn. Instead, he started to court Dorly. When they came back from their extended walk, Dorly confided that she was in love, that she had found Paul irresistible. Hiding my distress and embarrassment, I begrudged Dorly her courage.

Dorly was a loyal friend and insisted that she absolutely would not drive back with Paul, Charlie and Nora unless I came along. By then, Charlie Schmidt, a stocky man in his early thirties, and a national ping-pong champion, had invited me for a walk. He had just broken off with Nora, he said. He too was "4F," not because he wore glasses, but because his two younger brothers were in the army and his parents needed him in the business. (They were selling dental supplies, which allowed him to obtain gasoline coupons.) I was flattered that a "mature man" took me so seriously, wanted to see me in the city and wasn't pressuring me.

That fall, we often double-dated with Dorly and Paul, going to the races and to secluded restaurants along Sunrise Highway or near Jones Beach.

"It's no more expensive to go to the trotters than to a nightclub," Charlie repeatedly said. That had been his father's view as well, to his mother's lasting chagrin. But Charlie went only for the fun of it, while saying: "I never bet more than I can afford." It didn't occur to Dorly or me to suggest that we much preferred dancing to betting, and found the races rather tedious.

One day, Dorly swore me to silence, hemmed and hawed, and then confessed that she might be pregnant.

"What will Paul say? Will he want to get married," she wondered. He definitely did not. In fact, he blamed her for not having taken the proper precautions.

"She knows I don't like condoms," he answered defensively when I broached the subject, "and I told her it was her business to protect herself."

He tried to extricate himself from the relationship altogether while Dorly kept pretending to herself that he was in love with her. She didn't know how to go about getting an abortion and was afraid to tell her parents.

"You must help me," she begged, "there is no one else I can turn to." So I called on the Czech dentist. He not only refused to believe that I was still a virgin but was convinced that I was the one in trouble. With a supercilious smile, he suggested I talk to my doctor, as he excused himself to answer a telephone call. I made an appointment with Eva Farber.

"Who sent you to me?" she kept asking over and over. When she finally believed that I had not been recommended by a satisfied patient, she told me to send Dorly (with whose mother her husband regularly played bridge) to her, so that she could recommend her to someone she knew of.

Two weeks later, on a Saturday morning, I took off from West End Avenue to the dingy Hotel Endicott, across the street from the Museum of Natural History. I carried myself like an accessory to a crime, looking around me as furtively as a bank robber carrying his ill-gotten loot. I wondered whether the few people walking up 88th Street were suspicious of me. At the hotel's registration desk, I plunked down two dollars "for my friend Mrs. Smith from out of town." The abortion was performed in Eva Farber's office, five blocks away, with the assistance of her husband. When it was over, Dorly walked to the hotel "to save money," and on the way stopped at Woolworth's to acquire a fake wedding ring. I stayed with Dorly until Paul arrived, after 7:00 P.M. He was put out at having to "spend an uncomfortable night." Years later, long after she was married and the mother of two boys, Dorly let on that he had ended up in the double bed, and she on the chaise-lounge. But at the time, she was shattered only because he was "angry at her carelessness" and never wanted to sleep with her again.

Dorly scraped together a part of the two hundred dollars for her abortion by buying a few dresses on her parents' charge accounts and returning them for cash. Paul, after much coaxing, contributed thirty or thirty-five dollars. She borrowed the rest of the money from Charlie.

If Dorly hadn't gotten pregnant, would I have married Charlie? He appeared so generous and so discreet compared to the callous Paul. And he was so respectful of my virginity that I relaxed more and more. He must care for me a lot, I told myself, to spend the night with me without going all the way. One evening, however, he did, and I accidentally lost the virginity I had cherished for so long. I was surprised only that nothing had changed.

That I had allowed myself to get carried away to me was proof of my love for Charlie. At the time, it didn't consciously dawn on me that by marrying him I would be escaping from home and gain the breathing space I craved. When I told Charlie that Henry, who still was in dental school, wrote that he looked forward to seeing a lot of me on his forthcoming furlough, he started to speak of marriage. His parents didn't like the idea any more than mine.

"How can you marry into such a petit bourgeois milieu?" my father protested, pointing to the smelly, shedding German shepherd who permanently occupied the sagging couch in the Schmidt's front porch, to his mother's screechy voice, and to his father's slovenly manners. He further objected to Charlie's age, rigidity, and narrowness. He said he had the mind of a greengrocer.

"You are pretty and desirable, and come from a different kind of family," my mother now told me, "and even if you should have gone too far with him, don't worry about it." This was an about-face to her former cautionary tales. So, I didn't believe her. I chose to ignore all my parents' well-meant warnings, along with my own not inconsiderable fears, apprehensions, and reservations.

I nearly broke off with Charlie a week before the wedding. This is what happened. Since we had to take Wasserman tests before receiving the marriage license, Charlie suggested we go together to his doctor rather than to Eva Farber. Because he offered to pay, I agreed. After that doctor had given me a complete physical exam, he said that due to my heart murmur, it might be hazardous for me to have children. When I questioned Charlie about this examination, he conceded that his mother had worried that he might be marrying a woman who could become a burden.

"I'll marry you in spite of your handicap," he now said magnanimously, "and I don't mind that we might not have children." I certainly did mind and was outraged by his underhanded behavior. While crossing Dyckman Street in his car, I demanded that he stop. In anger, I pulled off my engagement ring and threw it at him. He was stunned, but ended up by persuading me that he only had wanted to pacify his mother. Since I was almost as reluctant to cancel the wedding arrangements as Charlie, who worried about what people might say, we got married.

We had a small wedding—at Joshi Gruenfeld's restaurant in the Hotel Fulton on West 71st Street, which by then had become the former Viennese's restaurant of choice—fewer than five years after I got to America. It all seemed so "normal," even American: I wore a short light blue dress which I would be able to use later on; my mother gave me her mother's gold filigree bracelet; my father gave me away. The place was crawling with the enormous Schmidt clan—my new relatives. Still, I felt curiously alone. I suppressed tears while thinking of my own aunts, uncles, and cousins, and I especially missed my grandmothers. My people consisted of my parents, my brother, the estranged Felix and Franzi, of Dorly and Marta.

We drove to Atlantic City for our honeymoon. While moseying along the East Coast, Charlie casually said that a few days before the wedding he had signed a partnership agreement with his parents that, among other things, stipulated that I would continue to cut diamonds and would put my earnings into the till.

"Why didn't you discuss this with me," I asked. He answered evasively, and I didn't dare pursue the issue. I vaguely sensed that I had gone blindly into this marriage. But I focused on its compensations: I now would have privacy, more space than I needed, and a telephone. I would be master over my spare time. The first "frill" I bought was a console radio and record player, along with Beethoven's sonatas and a few Mozart symphonies: I played them from the moment I arrived home after work until Charlie returned a few hours later. My second frill was a relatively expensive gray Prince de Galles, hounds-tooth suit with a thin, smart leather belt I found on Saks Fifth Avenue's designer floor. At no point did it dawn on me that I was doing what I had thrown up to my mother: her fear of fights, her tendency to overvalue expensive clothes, and her inability to face unpleasant truths; and that I too had dropped my intellectual ambitions.

I then had no inkling that, like so many of these teenage refugees' unions, this one too was doomed. Or that I had gone into a marriage with a man who, like myself, then was unable to fall in love. Roland Barthes might have called it a simulacrum of a marriage. Nor did I know that at some point I would have to face all the nerve-wracking realities I had suppressed while running from the Nazis; that I had gotten married to prove to myself that I was an adult; that I still cared how my parents were judging me; and that I would have to mature a great deal more before I would be able to stop running.

13

My "Starter" Marriage

In 1945, the west side of Riverdale Avenue still had mostly gated, secluded mansions. Our side of one- and two-family homes also was exceedingly quiet. When home alone, I drowned out the ominous silence by listening to my new records, while lounging on my comfortable off-white striped sofa, and glorying in my own apartment, nearly twice the size of the parental one. Charlie's mother had found this place on Tyndall Avenue, off 261st Street, just two blocks from hers, on Liebig Avenue.

I assumed that marriage had emancipated me—even while I was preoccupied by my mother-in-law's petty bourgeois concerns: she was filling Charlie's ears with stories about my "extravagances." Kurt, Charlie's brother-in-law, who lived with his wife and two children in his in-laws' front bedroom, kept telling me about them while driving me to work. Charlie, who had breakfast with his mother every weekday morning, was exceedingly secretive by nature.

During family get-togethers we exchanged emerging information about the death camps. All of my father-in-law's large family was in the United States, but my mother-in-law's wealthy brother had not been heard from. I kept imagining that at least my plucky Omama Fischer, who by then would have been sixty-three years old, had escaped into the woods and would turn up unexpectedly—even after my mother had been notified that the Fischers had been shot in Riga on December 3, 1941. In my nightmares, they were burning just like the ships the "Japs" had bombed at Pearl Harbor, or had been shot while pleading for their lives with Nazis who looked like Erich von Stroheim. When Kurt's sister Ruth and her husband arrived in New York, sometime in 1947, she told of atrocities she had witnessed, and that she had been saved only because she was a ballerina and had performed—naked—for her Nazi keepers.

*   *   *

After the war, the diamond industry was on its move back to Europe. Charlie worked long hours, visiting his dentists and delivering their orders. When I suggested that he might want to use United Parcel Service at twenty cents a package, so that he could visit twice as many dentists, and that dental mirrors and drills, syringes and dentifrice, ought to be shelved rather than rummaged for in cartons on the floor, his parents foresaw bankruptcy. (His father spent his days on the office couch, and his mother preferred him there rather than at the racetrack.) As tensions increased, my in-laws asked us to buy them out. Neither Charlie nor I realized that, like helpless marionettes, we were dancing to our parents' tunes. So, we turned over my savings, signed a few promissory notes, and I reorganized Schmidt Dental Supplies. It started to flourish.

Before long, I wanted to have children. Eva Farber and the cardiologist we consulted declared that my heart murmur ought not be a deterrent to a normal pregnancy, but the sooner I was to give birth, the better. I said "now," Charlie said "later." When he began to waver, I conceived my first child, Ronald. He was born on January 26, 1948. Now, our landlord kept reminding us that he did not expect to have "the patter of little feet" above his head. So, we spent two years of Sundays looking for a place of our own. I don't think we missed any of the countless model homes in the developments that were mushrooming in Westchester, Queens, and Nassau. Whatever I liked, Charlie found to be beyond our means.

Twenty-two months after Ronnie, Vivien arrived. I was busy taking care of two babies, and keeping the company books. The Korean War made me uneasy, but it didn't take my mind off preparing meals and changing diapers, and worrying whether my brother, who had been recalled, would be sent there. (I then was oblivious to the political concerns of intellectuals, such as the communist-run Waldorf Conference, and its protest by Mary McCarthy and Dwight Macdonald, that I would hear about many years later.)

In 1952, we finally settled on a house—one block outside Jamaica Estates, which Silvie Murray [6] notes, was "one of the oldest and wealthiest neighborhoods in Queens." 186th Street off Union Turnpike was included in its school district, P.S. 178—which was set up as a model school.

I gloried in my eight rooms, my enclosed backyard, flowering shrubbery, back and front porches. For the first time I got to know my neighbors—most of them Jewish—their children and their dogs. Their husbands' occupations ranged from a taxi driver and small businessmen to corporate managers and lawyers.

In my spare time, I read bestsellers, such as *Mister Blandings Builds His Dream House* and *Marjorie Morningstar*, and whatever my friend, the lady in the lending library, recommended. I was among the alienated people C. Wright Mills [7] wrote about, who were little more than spectators of their own lives; and whom David Reisman, in *The Lonely Crowd*, [8] had described as other-directed. Still, I neither considered myself alienated nor other-directed. My life revolved around the children, as did that of most young mothers. And I was as engrossed in shopping as the rest of them, acquiring household goods and clothes, but would have taken offense at being called a consumer.

We have come to think of the 1950s as the Eisenhower or the McCarthy era, and as a quiet and reactionary period. However, I only recall that for me each year seemed to have its own rhythm and significance, geared to the children's growth, which I anxiously and carefully checked against Dr. Spock's "bible." Accordingly, I was fairly permissive.

By 1953, the children already preferred to play with our neighbors' children on the sidewalk. So, on lazy afternoons I befriended their mothers. On weekday mornings, I pushed the baby carriage to the shops on Union Turnpike, or to Bloomingdale's at Fresh Meadows; or romped with them in Alley Pond Park.

In 1954, both children went to Shirley Greene's nursery school, and I again devoted myself to the dental business. Soon I felt that I had to be there and at home at the same time—a conflict every working mother still tries to resolve. That spring I acquired a flashy second hand Studebaker, and an *au pair* girl from Germany. Since it was an excruciatingly hot summer, I drove us to Lake Placid, where I rented an apartment for a month. Charlie came up for a week.

*   *   *

From the moment we moved to Queens, my parents came to see us on Sunday afternoons for coffee and conversation. My mother relished the children's progress, and cuddled them. My father, who all of his life praised his wife as a perfect mother, sat in the comfortable easy chair next to the baby grand and faulted my child rearing methods: that I was too easy on Ronnie; that both children were turning into spoiled American brats; and that it was my duty to keep a tighter rein. As time went on, I dreaded Sunday afternoons, being caught between a young son who argued with his grandfather about what television station to watch, a husband who immersed himself in his silences and his sales slips, and a mother who complained about having had to bring the coffee cake. I was utterly exhausted, almost dozed off, but kept pretending that all was well.

That year, I found a tenement building on Flushing's 164th Street, supervised its extensive renovation, and moved the business from the Bronx. Now, I was forever rushing back and forth, depending on the children's schedules. In my spare time, I repainted or wallpapered one room or another, arranged for our porch to be enclosed, became the den mother of Ronnie's boy scout troupe, and drove Vivien to piano and ballet lessons. I joined the women who fought to improve the conditions of the school playground; worried myself sick about polio, and about what to do in case of an atomic attack. If it was as boring a period as it seems from later perspectives, I didn't have time to notice.

I grew restless. Charlie used to come home after the lights in the children's bedrooms were extinguished, and was too tired to talk. He kept reading the label on the ketchup bottle while he ate. (Only much later did he let on that he purposely had waited in the driveway until the children had been put to sleep; and that he had left home early in the morning for bacon and eggs at the corner diner, in order to escape the inescapable commotion young children are bound to make.)

Unlike Betty Friedan, in *The Feminine Mystique*,[9] I felt at home with my suburban neighbors. I did not perceive myself as passive, or as conforming. Even though I did live up to what Charlie expected of me, I was not chomping at the bit. I was rather exemplary of the middle class Queens housewives Sylvie Murray interviewed, who recalled that the 1950s had not been as stultifying as Friedan had found. A good number of them had been involved in community action and aware of the larger political forces.[10] I don't recall my suburb as a Mecca of enlightenment nor as the nadir of hell. My neighbors and I had given birth to the babies we had wished for, and had arranged our lives in order to take care of them—in the best houses and surroundings we could afford. After they were in school from 9:00 A.M. to 3:00 P.M., some mothers resumed doing whatever it was that they had done before motherhood; others decided to have yet more children and volunteered in community work; still others returned to continue their college education, or take art classes.

In 1955, William H. Whyte,[11] focused on their husbands, on the organization man who spent most of his days away from home, in order to make it up the corporate ladder. Charlie had no ladder to climb, but marched to his own demons. Apart from his ambivalence to his mother, whom he kept indulging, he was irrationally worried about making ends meet: after receiving an order, he jotted down what profit it brought, and was certain every Sunday that during the following week he would not break even. (Usually he did by Tuesday evening or Wednesday morning.) I tuned in to this neurosis, and agreed that he was working too much.

*   *   *

Unless I don't recall correctly, my politics were swayed by my past: thankful to have escaped the Nazis, I did not worry much about presidential or local elections, although I was an enthusiastic Stevenson fan. If there was any radicalism on 186th Street, I was unaware of it. (By the time I attended the children's school assemblies, and watched them ceremoniously walk down the aisle, saluting or even carrying the American flag, my eyes began to flood.) That may well be why I perceived the McCarthy hearings as a fascinating example of democracy in action. I then did not yet know any professors and intellectuals who were affected. And I recoiled at anything that might have damaged our democratic institutions, such as fascism or communism. On our bridge evenings with other Austro-Americans we were more likely to discuss European events, to compare our children's development, and to gossip.

The longer Ronnie and Vivien were at school, the more time I spent at the office—contacting wholesalers and customers, streamlining the system, and so on. Charlie appreciated my help, but needed to control me—while pronouncing that I was "the boss." For example, when we needed a new car, he announced to everyone who would listen that he trusted me to make the choice. I then was enamored of bright convertibles, but he made me promise to get dark four-door sedans. I complied. I also shuddered when he addressed both Vivien and our pug as *girlsiekind*—while petting them on their backsides. In sum, I knew what bothered me, but was unable to put it together.

*   *   *

Like most industrious people in that decade, we were thriving financially. So were my parents. In 1948, my father had convinced my brother to take out a G. I. loan, in order to start importing marble. My father's brother had ceded his European interests. But when on a brief trip to Europe, my father had sued for the return of his Cologne enterprise, the judge, a former Nazi, had ruled against him—on a technicality. (Until 1955, our Austrian properties still were in the Russian zone.) He was determined to overthrow that verdict. My mother sympathized, until the summer of 1955. Together, we had rented a house on Lake Mahopac. As soon as we had moved in, my father announced that he had to leave for Vienna—by himself. His wife was angry for the rest of the season—mostly at me. She not only wanted to get a look at postwar Europe, but assumed that, like the proverbial leopard, her husband wasn't about to change his spots, and again would stray.

I too was eager to revisit my childhood, but Charlie was afraid of ocean liners and planes. So, for once, the husbands were at one, and suggested that "the two women" take a grand tour the following summer. In preparation, I registered for Italian as well as art and music appreciation classes at Queens College. One dusky evening on my way to class, I espied a young couple in an intense embrace. Suddenly, I knew that I never had felt that way about Charlie, nor about any other of my many dates.

* * *

When my mother and I walked up the gangplank of the *Liberté*, on a steamy day in July 1956, we expected our trip to be the cure-all for everything that ailed us. I had put the children on their camp bus two days before, and they already had new friends. As we clicked our champagne glasses with Charlie and my father aboard deck, I began to feel like the young Ditta I had left behind nearly sixteen years before—ready for whatever unfathomable adventure might be in the offing. The stormy sea kept most people out of the dining room, but neither my mother nor I missed a meal. We focused on the luxury we were enjoying, on our meals at the captain's table, and fussed only about what to wear. Exploring new vistas was in my blood. Or was I fleeing from the tedium of routines?

Indeed, Paris was as exciting for me as for anyone who gets to see the Mona Lisa, the Eiffel Tower and Notre Dame, the Panthéon and Montmartre for the first time, and to walk on the same cobblestones that Flaubert, Dumas, and so many other writers had described. Touring Versailles, Fontainebleau, and night clubs such as the Moulin Rouge and the Follies Bergères, and visiting the galleries of the rue Faubourg St. Honoré, and so on, were as rewarding as were the marvels of Florence and Rome. In none of these cities was I reminded of the war as I was in Naples, where no one as yet was trying to fill the bullet holes in the walls of damaged buildings, and where kids were begging on street corners.

When we got to Vienna, I was surprised that it seemed so small, so quaint and provincial. In my eyes the Kärntnerstrasse had shrunk, and I kept marveling that the mail chute inside the Hotel Astoria still was marked: *Kaiserliche und königliche Post*. True, the Russians had just left, which might have explained why all the buildings were grey with soot, and the people suspicious of us. To me, only the rich pastries and the waltz music seemed authentic. We did connect with a former friend, Hedy Bischitz, who had a fancy dress salon, and now lived in the building next to the Schloss Schönbrunn—the former home of the Kaiser's mistress. And we were inhibited enough by our memories not to enter even the lobby of Gaudenzdorfergürtel 47—the stately building of my early childhood. I had remembered our apartment at Wiednerhauptstrasse 139 as elegant, but now did not dare go beyond its shabby lobby. The ice cream parlor and furniture store were gone. Had I really loved sledding in that tiny courtyard? Frau Meier still was the concierge, and seemed not to have taken off her red and white checkered apron since we had left in December 1938. She pretended to be friendly, but was truly worried only about what would happen to the people who now occupied our former apartment. Why did she assume that we had come to take it back? We were most appalled at her not-too-hidden anti-Semitism. But I was even more put off during our tour of the Vienna Staatsoper that just had been rebuilt and reopened. During our German-speaking tour the snotty guide, while showing off the most up-to-date stage equipment, informed us that "the Americans paid for it, but that was only right, since they bombed it on purpose." We were glad to leave Vienna—with many fewer illusions than we had had upon arriving.

* * *

In Germany, we were worried that the rapid rebuilding of Frankfurt and Munich again would produce German hegemony. Most of the time, my mother and I got along. But by the end of the trip, in Brussels, we had a drag-out fight. Neither one of us then grasped that we were carrying our emotional baggage with us, and that we were reliving some of the despair we had felt during the Nazi days. Then, my mother had ignored my complaints, and we both had mistaken my growing competence as maturity. Now that some men her age were trying to get my attention rather than hers, that my French was fluent while hers was poor, she was upset by my seeming superiority. She also overestimated my ability to get around Brussels where, after sixteen years, I too had to regain my bearings. While trying to find the pensionnat at 51, Chaussée de Vleurgat, I relived my misery. The dour-looking woman who was scrubbing the sidewalk in front of the structure that now occupied its space said that the *pensionnat* had been hit by a bomb, and that Madame never had returned. As memories washed over me, I felt relieved that she could not have come upon my diary. Nevertheless, my former frustrations, with what Balzac called the *odeur de pension*, with Madame's minute supervision, and with my loneliness, resurged, yet sounded exaggerated to my mother.

"You were lucky to be here, and you didn't have to worry about being arrested and tortured, so what are you complaining about," she began, "and you and your father could learn French, and have a good time." I still was too self-involved to realize that she was upset at traveling with me rather than with her husband.

*   *   *

After the *Liberté* docked in New York, I was bursting to tell Charlie about Europe. But he only wanted to know whether or not the house he had inhabited in Munich still was standing. By the time we reached the Lincoln Tunnel, our conversation was exhausted. Charlie's disinterest in nearly everything but dental supplies—and routine sexual intercourse— became ever more palpable.

Now, I often went to luncheons and parties with "real" Americans— those who had grown up on pot roast, latkes and gefilte fish rather than goulash, strudel, and schnitzel. With them, we attended the reform synagogue a few blocks down on Union Turnpike. I did not become religious, though I tried, went through the motions, and sent the children to Sunday school. I made sure not to let on that every time a plane passed overhead, on its way to or from Idlewild (now JFK) or La Guardia airport, I was reliving the panic I had felt after the Nazis' arrival in Vienna and in Brussels. I turned into a master at adaptation.

I attributed my restiveness to my surfeit of activities, to worries about the children's friendships, their progress at reading or sports, and so on. At the same time, my interests in the larger world increased. As these unfolded, I was ever more aware of Charlie's need for a restricted horizon. And if, as Marx suggested, the urge for revolution occurs under situations of rising expectations, that trip to Europe had alerted me to vistas and ideas Charlie needed to shut out. I no longer was satisfied to confine myself to his little world.

When that fall I again registered at Queens College, I had to cope with Charlie's disapproval of my "highfaluting" ambitions. Although psychological testing and statistics certainly did not grab me as much as the insights provided by clinical psychology, some of what I read, and my courses in literature, opened my mind. But whenever I tried to involve Charlie in my more esoteric quests, he would shrug and say: "That's not so important." Increasingly, I was irked by this recurring phrase and by having my life center around dental supplies—just like my own family's revolved around marble. Nevertheless, I still kept myself from knowing that my marriage was falling apart.

Determined to turn marital relations around, I assumed we could change them by togetherness on Sunday mornings, now that both children went to Sunday school. But Charlie preferred to spend that time at our office. So, on the first of these Sundays, I sat up in bed and free-associated on twelve pages of a yellow pad—and ended up stating that we needed family therapy. He procrastinated for a few months and then consented, provided he would see the therapist without me. I said yes. He soon reported that she agreed that he had a crazy wife. Only after two months did he allow her to see me in order to recommend someone who might set me straight. After my own first session, I realized that Charlie and I could not stay together in the way we had up to then.

Now that half of all marriages end in divorce, and that some refer, retrospectively, to a first marriage as a "starter marriage," it is difficult to believe that Charlie expected me "to be a simple woman like his mother," or that I truly shocked my cohorts when we split up. My father, who routinely had been dismissive of Charlie, now told me that "there is trouble in every marriage," but that "in our family one does not divorce." My mother attributed her frequent headaches to my willfulness. To help her unwind, she left for Florida. That evening, my father invited me to dinner at the Café de la Paix, on Central Park South, to convince me that I would be wise to save my marriage by having casual affairs.

For over ten years, Charlie and I had pretended, to ourselves and everyone else that we were happy. In fact, we never really fought. But we both had been damaged by circumstances and by parents who were continuing to (successfully) pull emotional strings—in opposite directions; and by our unfulfilled ambitions: he had wanted to be a physician, and I had aspired to intellectual life ever since my paternal grandmother had read classical poetry to me. Moreover, I once again was exploring some of Freud's teachings.

"Why are you always dissatisfied?" my mother kept asking. "After all Charlie is a faithful husband and a good provider; and you have two healthy children, and no financial worries."

She implied that this was a condition I was about to change at will; or that it was an aspect of the (bad) character traits I had inherited from her mother-in-law.

"I have stayed with your mother in spite of the scenes she makes, because I am dutiful. Why can't you do the same?" my father kept saying.

It didn't take long for me to realize that none of us could shed our skins. With much difficulty and recriminations Charlie and I eventually separated. As has become customary in such situations, he held on to most of our assets and "allowed" me to keep the children. He was a relentless bargainer, and I was in financial straits. He played on my guilt about "depriving" the children of their father, and suddenly wanted to spend time with them. I too had to come to terms with some of my emotional hang-ups.

There were fewer divorces then, and dating and mating had not yet turned into what it has become—on the singles scene and on the Internet. Neither was it acceptable to have dinner out with a woman friend on Saturday nights. I spent much time at home, playing with the children, reading, and dreaming about future bliss. Or I went on one-night-stands with good-looking guys, whom before the end of the evening I found too dull or too pushy. In sum, however shrewd I was about business matters, my naiveté extended not only to my own marriage, but to the rest of the people I then knew: when it came to questions of personal relations, I tended to believe what met the eye, and what people told me.

14

Robert Enters My Life

To make up for lost time, I crammed at college. I read in bed, standing over the kitchen stove and while the children had their various lessons—from assigned texts to child psychology, from Freud to Nietzsche. But how would I learn about love? I knew enough not to get involved with guys I found boring. Still, did I think them tiresome because I was fearful of commitment? I identified with Ingrid Bergman and Greta Garbo, and dreamt of true love and sexual fulfillment. It's what I talked about endlessly to my therapist. I had a casual affair with a married physician, and soon realized that clandestine relations were not for me. My new friend, Hannah Kurzweil, the wife of my music professor, Frederic Kurzweil, pronounced, "You have to get around." We had met, after I brought Vivien to Fred for piano lessons: Vivien was a would-be Clara Schumann, as well as a ballerina. While waiting for her lessons to end, Ronnie and their son, Ray, also hit it off, and I soon found myself chauffeuring them for swimming lessons at the YMCA in Jamaica. Moreover, there was a Viennese connection: Hannah's father and my aunt, Helene, had been good friends, how good we do not know. Under the circumstances, it was almost a given that Hannah and I would become confidantes.

A few months after Charlie had moved out, Hannah thought I had been "moping long enough," and insisted I join them for dinner that evening, because her brother-in-law, Robert, was coming over. I reluctantly accepted. She had spoken of him, not always favorably. She had disapproved of his divorce. But she admired (and envied?) him for his footloose manner, and exciting work in Italy. That evening, I found him charming, and was intrigued by his sparkling gaze that seemed to soak up everything. How could he manage to be so affable and distanced all at once? Was it because his mind was on his upcoming trip to Milan two days hence? Or because he carefully avoided answering Hannah's indiscreet questions? He told amusing anecdotes about trying to bring the Italian machine tool industry into the twentieth century. In 1952, he had gone to Italy for the Marshall Plan and then had redesigned the machine tools of a number of enterprises. A smidgen below six feet tall, somewhat overweight, and seemingly unaware of his good looks, Robert was an enigma. When before the evening was over he asked for my address, I sensed it was pro forma.

*   *   *

Robert and Fred were born in Vienna, in the twentieth district, on Passettistrasse 24. Their father, who had been an engineer for the Austrian forestry service, had died soon after he returned from World War I. Robert then was nine years old, and Fred was eight. By the time they went to their *gymnasium*, Robert helped support the family by giving math lessons to failing students, and Fred by teaching the piano. That was in the 1920s, when their widowed mother had to live on a minimal pension. They both were bright and enthusiastic *Rote Falken*—the Austrian Socialists' youth group. By 1935, Robert had earned his engineering degree from the Technical University of Vienna. Fred received his doctorate in musicology just as the Germans were marching in. He was of medium height, and his dreamy darkness drew his listeners to him—whether he played the piano or conducted. Among his fans was an American woman from Philadelphia, who immediately after the *Anschluss* sent him an affidavit. By then, Robert had been rescued by his former girlfriend, Ruth: she had left for London after he had broken up with her the year before. Because she had arranged his exodus, he married her out of gratitude the week after his arrival. Fred soon managed to get them both to New York.

When Robert and I accidentally ran into each other, in December 1957, he started to court me. Of course, I still was dreaming about love in the most abstract way, but my recent forays beyond the ordinary run of things, intellectually if not yet emotionally, had helped me grow, and had loosened me up. As we were sitting next to each other on our first date, on a soft bench in a romantic Viennese restaurant, Robert began by asking me why I was getting a separation. Not accustomed to such directness, I asked whether he wanted to know the lawyer's reasons or the real ones.

"The real ones, of course," he answered. Apparently, as I began to talk, my honesty touched a nerve in him. He confided that he still was smarting from his own divorce, mostly because his ex-wife did everything she could to keep him from seeing his two sons. As the evening progressed, I babbled as freely as I did to my therapist. Robert seemed ever more attuned to me and I fell under his spell. We were getting to know one another, laughed at some of the Viennese expressions we shared, and talked seriously of the guilt one feels when being the one who wants to leave a seemingly contented spouse, a decent person. I fell in love and, afraid to let on, thought of what I could say to make sure to see him again. Because I spoke a bit of Italian, he asked me to the upcoming Christmas party at his office: he was training four Italian engineers for the huge project he was about to initiate for Sant' Eustacchio, in Brescia.

"Please come and help entertain them. They refuse to learn English, and don't like the food in our Italian restaurants. Not that I blame them," he said.

Robert had invited his American and Viennese friends and business contacts, as well as a number of current, and former, girlfriends. It was what I sensed from the languid glances a trim airline hostess directed at him, from the well-known socialite who eyed him somewhat quizzically, and from the good-natured and slightly sturdy nurse. The elegant model, while talking to one of the Italians, kept following Robert with eager eyes, as did the woman who flitted about on shoes with glittering diamond-studded heels. I was overcome with anxiety, and reacted as I had to every attractive guy while in my teens: I kept smiling while turning into an icicle. Because I had glimpsed Robert give the one with the glittering heels a long good-bye kiss, I confided to Hannah that I would not date Robert again. She convinced me that good manners required me to call him and thank him for the invitation. I did, and we had another date the following Tuesday.

Robert not only was thirteen years older and more educated than I, but he too had been in a fog during his marriage, and had come out of it after the initial session with his analyst. Consequently, he understood some of my mood changes, and clued in to my swaying behavior—whether due to my impending divorce, to anxieties springing from our relationship, or to friends' disapproval. Luckily, I was working through some of my uncertainties, so that my flights into coldness became less frequent, and less automatic. And we could talk about them.

That Tuesday evening, after getting into his car, I had dared to ask Robert how come that, unlike most men, he had not gotten involved with one type of girlfriend, but with such different sorts of women.

"I was wondering about that myself," he replied, astonished that I had caught on, and saying that each of them had "something," such as excellent legs, a sense of humor, caring manner or savoir faire, and that he was looking for the "perfect" one. I burst out laughing while saying that such a woman could not possibly exist. One thing led to another, and we were into a whirlwind relationship.

In That Touch of Mink, Doris Day (Kathy) broke out in hives after Cary Grant had softened her up by dangling a trip to Paris, and then took her to a luxurious hotel in Bermuda. I had pooh-poohed (and withdrawn at) the suggestion of traveling with Robert into the Italian hill towns, but soon accepted a weekend in Atlantic City. And I too was direct and sincere—qualities which, according to Cary Grant, bring out a man's conscience. This farce, which was filmed in 1962, five years after I met Robert, might well have been a take-off from our courtship.

Robert was a mature and experienced ladies' man. I was immature, frightened and conflicted. Still, for the first time after his divorce, he brought his boys, Lenny and Peter, to meet me, his current "flame." They joined my children and me during our ski vacation in Fleischman's, in the Catskills. I was apprehensive, worried that Ronnie and Vivien might misbehave, and that his boys might not like me. But as soon as we sat down to lunch after their arrival, I was stunned that we all interacted as if we had known each other forever, as if we were a family. Vivien, who just had turned eight, appreciated getting attention from good looking twelve and fifteen year old boys, and ten-year-old Ronnie joined them by teasing her. Robert and I beamed and relaxed. Later in the day, he elicited my support in refusing to buy the Swiss Army knife for which Lenny kept pestering him; he jokingly got Ronnie to stop annoying his sister; and we had as much fun as could be had on a ski vacation without snow.

After I confided to my friend, Lisa, that we had had such an unstrained and wonderful time, and that with Robert and his boys the easy banter I had been unable to achieve with Charlie in over ten years of marriage had come about without trying, she told Charlie—who now started to act as his own private detective. As yet, there was nothing to detect. Against my urges, I remained chaste for about two months, and Robert appeared to be wondering why he put up with it.

I first was alerted to Charlie's sleuthing when Robert and I left a play on 43rd Street, and I spotted his car. I had told Lisa what we were going to see, and she had informed Charlie. Now, Robert decided we were "going to have some fun." Since at the time, the only ground for divorce in New York State was adultery, I was scared when thinking about the cockamamie story Charlie might cook up in a courtroom. So, I begged Robert to drive me straight home to Queens. He refused, saying that one does not buckle under to fear, and that one had to fight fire with fire. He too had read Sherlock Holmes and Raymond Chandler. He led Charlie on a wild chase, from Times Square to the Upper East Side. We lost him, and ended up having drinks at one of the old-time Irish bars on Third Avenue. A bit later, Charlie checked on the ski resort in the Berkshires we had been to with all four children on a previous weekend. Since we each had had our own room, he came back empty-handed. Being stalked made me nervous, but Robert always found "just the right" restaurant to "enjoy" the cops and robber games.

While our courtship progressed, negotiations with Charlie became increasingly bitter, especially when at a meeting with our attorneys he didn't show up, and his lawyer announced that he was cutting his weekly payments to eighty dollars, and was about to move back in.

"If he tries to do so," my lawyer countered while dramatically walking up and down the room, "I order you to call the police." By then, I trusted Robert as much as I trusted my analyst. And Charlie enlisted my father to try talking some sense into me. He tried. He agreed with Charlie that I was under the influence of my therapist, and they assumed I was having an affair with this newly married man. Charlie even insisted on seeing him—I didn't object—and accused him of this "fact." To my father, anyone seeing an analyst was deemed crazy, and my resentment of him—due to some of what came up from my unconscious, to his recriminations, and to my mounting sense of self—proved his point. In any event, I soon realized that Charlie's aim was to squeeze me financially, even though he also had major problems about impending changes in his life. He kept repeating, whenever he picked up the children: "You'll soon come to me on your knees begging for money, you'll see." My mother might have sided with me, but began to attribute her recurrent headaches to my stubbornness. And she already had learned to get her husband to think for her—as an act of loyalty. It took a long time for me to understand these dynamics.

When, that April, Robert had to spend a week in Italy, I needed to get into his apartment. I experienced its emptiness as abandonment. I was disconsolate, sat on the couch and cried as bitterly as Doris Day did whenever she had left Cary Grant. Upon his return, Robert showered me with the gifts he had bought on Paris's rue Faubourg St. Honoré. Among other things, he unpacked a sleek, strawberry colored sheath, a stylish, silken housecoat and matching nightgown, and a few belts and scarves. It took some time for my therapist to make me realize that receiving gifts did not necessarily turn me into a kept woman, and that there were men who enjoyed being generous. With the help of my therapy, I learned that falling in love is easier than living with it. What would I do after Robert moved to Italy, I wondered in desperation. My emotional ups and downs, my parents' disapproval, feelings of guilt and panic attacks, were hard to deal with. I still could not believe that as desirable a man as Robert preferred me to all other women, or that I was as attractive as he said. I somehow learned to cope with it. I was helped by the casual and bemused manner Robert responded to me, and by his easy way with my children.

Before Robert left for Italy, he asked me to pick up his new car and drive it to the pier. He had bought the vehicle of my dreams: a white Chevrolet Impala convertible with red leather seats. Long before we had met, Robert had arranged for his boys to join him that summer, and I too had promised us a European trip. We planned to meet in Milan. Since Italy then produced only small cars—Fiats or fancy sports vehicles—Robert had concluded that he needed a roomy and dependable automobile.

For two months, we wrote to each other nearly every other day. Robert's letters were loving, supportive, but far from gushy. Mine were free floating epistles, recounting daily events, worries, crises and feelings. When he referred to a honeymoon at the Château d'Ouchy, in Lausanne, I asked whether he was thinking of marriage. He responded that one could have a honeymoon with or without marriage.

After the children finished school we flew to Italy. In our propeller plane, Vivien already vomited before we landed in Boston. Ronnie waited until Iceland. From Reykjavik to Dublin one of the plane's two engines conked out, and we missed our connection in Amsterdam. Tired and bedraggled, my smelly children and I arrived at Milan's Malpensa—where Robert picked us up. He had made reservations at the Grand Hotel in Gardone, on Lake Garda, which was a convenient commute to his job in Brescia. Ronnie spent his days catching salamanders. Vivien cheered him on and picked flowers in the enormous gardens of the hotel. I relaxed. That was where we decided, after yet another one of my major withdrawals, to get married.

Soon, we found out that we had to scramble for documents, and that divorcés could not marry in Italy. Even in Switzerland, bans had to be posted for a week—after papers, including original documents of our births, weddings and divorces, were submitted. (These had to be procured from a perennially angry ex-wife, laid-back Austrian authorities, and my empty house.)

It was a hectic summer, with drives to Geneva to pick up the boys, chauffeuring the children to their three different summer camps in the

Rhône valley, spending weekends with them, and to do so while Robert was commuting to Brescia and occasionally to Turin. (That September, the waitress in the restaurant atop the Simplon Pass, while hemming and hawing, wanted to know what we were doing with all these children.) After many cliffhangers, everything worked out. On the eve of the wedding, on August 2, 1958, we took the boys to explore the Château de Chillon, whose dungeons were immortalized in Byron's poem, "The Prisoner of Chillon." Over dinner at the intimate, châlet-style restaurant across the road, we feasted on filet mignon and crème brûlée, Peter confided that he wasn't supposed to like me, but did. Robert and I were thrilled. That afternoon, Robert's two aunts, Marta and Paula, had arrived from England, and my mother had come from Vienna. My father, allegedly because I had made my decision without asking him, and was making "yet another mistake," claimed he had to keep a business appointment in Vienna.

* * *

Our wedding ceremony took place in Lausanne's ancient City Hall: Ronnie was my escort and Vivien my bridesmaid; Lenny was Robert's best man, and Peter his ring bearer. Afterwards, we consumed yet another festive meal in the gardens of the Château d'Ouchy—which then opened up to its manicured park and to a magnificent vista of Lac Leman. (Later on, it would be turned into an amusement park.) Aunts Marta and Paula and my mother got along famously; Lenny gorged himself on countless bottles of Coca Cola; Peter and Ronnie fooled around; and Vivien was beside herself with joy, as the recipient of both the bridesmaid's and the bride's bouquet. After we drove our offspring back to their respective camps, we retired to our suite in this former castle's tower. We divided our honeymoon into a leisurely trip through Switzerland and Austria, a sightseeing tour of Italy with "the boys," and a visit to the Brussels World's Fair with all four children, before settling down in Milan.

During the drive through Austria, childhood experiences I previously had forgotten resurfaced, and many of the fears connected to them evaporated. It is immaterial whether this was attributable to post-analysis, or to the fact that I trusted Robert and could rely on him. While resting my head on his shoulder, we broke into songs we happened to remember from our Austrian past; stopped whenever we felt thirsty; or when Robert took his (professional?) photographs. Among other treats, I recall shopping in Zurich for the picnic we then consumed on a shady lawn in the Alps of Vorarlberg; a *Magic Flute* in Salzburg's Felsenreitschule, a number of concerts in the Konzerthaushalle, and a *Jederman* on that city's Domplatz.

With difficulty, I convinced Robert to accept my parents' invitation to join them in Bad Gastein. The two days we spent with them were laden with—mostly unacknowledged —conflicts. I hoped to have everyone get along. But I was not yet able to see that my father expected to dominate Robert. The battle of wills erupted during our first lunch. Robert ordered wine, and my father said one didn't drink wine with lunch—implying that only alcoholics did so. Robert responded that as good a meal as we were ordering had to be consumed with wine, and that he would be happy to pay for it. But my father didn't want that either, and thereby lost this round. I was overcome by free-floating anxiety.

After that, we moseyed along to Vienna. We both had been there since our immigration. But now that we were together, we could laugh about the predictable habits of the city's burghers, decry their anti-Semitism and their anti-intellectualism, and comment on their clichéd lives. When Robert went to see some of his erstwhile radical buddies he reported that they now held high governmental positions, were ensconced in posh offices, and were complaining of ennui. We took Julie, my nanny and my uncle Albin with whom she now was living, to dinner and visited our former homes and haunts. That was when I first learned about Austrian politics—including Robert's allegiance to the Socialists, his street fights against the Communists and Fascists—which, among other things, had caused his nose to be broken. Mostly, we kept saying how lucky we were to have been forced to escape the city's inevitable stultification.

Even after having seen Vienna with my mother, I had held on to my fantasies of grown-up life, such as dancing to Strauss waltzes at the Kursalon on Sundays, and drives up the Kahlenberg or the Kobenzl for afternoon tea. These were treats I had enjoyed with both sets of grandparents. Robert, however, felt increasingly nervous. Reluctantly, he recalled having demonstrated against the construction of the very road we were on—as spoiling the environment by the bourgeoisie. What has become of me, he kept asking, as he took one steep curve after another. And what has happened to my ideals?

We kept discussing them all the way back to Lausanne, where we dined with the children and picked up the boys—who might well have preferred to continue playing tennis at their camp rather than look at "boring monuments." Robert, who so carefully had planned this Italian tour for them, was disappointed. But I convinced him to give in by extending our stay in Portofino, where the boys enjoyed swimming, sailing and motor-boating; and to drop our reservations in Rome and Naples for a stay in Viareggio. Still, Robert had to leave us for a few days in order to see a client in Naples.

That was when Peter and Lenny tested me—pestering for lire to feed the pinball machines, ordering the most expensive foods, and not even wanting to visit the leaning tower of Pisa, or nearby Florence. But by the time we drove to Milan over the Furla pass, and the brakes of our car were giving out, and Lenny cooperated with me to work the handbrakes as I steered us up and down this treacherous ride to safety, and Peter—unaware of the danger—told jokes, we had become a family.

On the last legs of that summer, after I had picked up the children, we flew to the Brussels world's fair. There were treats galore for all six of us, as we covered one pavilion after another, commenting on the strange architecture of the French one, playing games in the American one, and kidding and arguing about all kinds of things I no longer remember. During our meals, Vivien was thrilled that Lenny and Peter maneuvered to sit next to her—not because she was cute, which she was, but because she never could finish what was on her plate, and they were eager to gobble up her leftovers. One evening, as we lined up on the way into the dining room of the Hotel Metropole, we overheard one guest say to another: "Finally, they had a girl."

We all felt sad when we saw the boys off on their plane to New York. Robert, of course, was wondering whether their mother would allow them to join us the following summer: we were planning to stay in Italy until the completion of his project. But whereas the Viennese might have said: *Der Mensch denkt und Gott lenkt* (man thinks and God guides), our gods were the owners of the Italian machine tool industry. Robert was hailed as their savior, the man whose designs were bound to make them rich. Because he was offered consulting jobs he could not refuse, we ended up staying nearly eight years. *La dolce vita* had its ups and downs, but we made the best of it. In line with Robert's resolve to live every day to its hilt, we enjoyed traveling around and learning Italian, and to manage taking the many and inevitable frustrations in our stride. During that time we saw the boys whenever we came to New York, but their mother never again allowed them to visit us.

15

La Vita Italiana and Back to New York

"Der Zweck des Lebens ist das Leben selbst."
("The object of life is life itself.")
—*Heinrich Heine*

In August 1958, I married Robert because I had fallen in love with him. I moved to Italy because that was where he was working. And because I had fond childhood memories of sightseeing in Florence and Venice, and beach life in Cesenatico and Viareggio, it did not occur to me that "this land where lemons bloom" might not be paradise. Nor was I aware that my arrival coincided with the so-called *miracolo italiana*. With Robert, the foremost consultant and designer of machine tools, I was about to meet the most enterprising Italians who—ambitiously and haphazardly—were moving their country from artisan to industrial production. I learned to keep my eyes wide open to their never-ending ingenuity. My take on life expanded, as I encountered Italians of all classes and regions, American expatriates, executives and diplomats.

Robert had alerted me about Italians' *furbismo*, their ingenious subterfuges and deceptions, brilliant improvisations and beaux gestes. He had warned me about pickpockets' and street vendors' scams. But he also had told me how most of the natives managed to turn mishaps into adventures, with a savoir-vivre that can turn everyday tragedies into fun and games. In my mind, I anticipated a *dolce far niente* full of glorious sunsets—while recalling Goethe's travels and Freud's dreams of Rome. (Luigi Barzini had not yet published *The Italians*,[12] his "full length portrait featuring their manners and [dubious] morals.") Expecting a continuation of my touristy experiences, I anticipated a fulfilling and carefree existence, being courted by obsequious shopkeepers and handsome Don Giovannis—as an American with a supposedly unlimited supply of dollars.

Occasionally, even Robert became a victim of *furbismo*. So, when he didn't pin down the details of our lease on the charming Baronessa von Frauenberg's fabulous penthouse apartment, she ended up supplying us with a lumpy couch and armchair, a bookcase that collapsed when burdened with more than six books, and claimed that the owners of the building's other apartments didn't allow her to put lattice and ivy onto the glass enclosed terrace— as we had stipulated. She had assured us that "our wishes were her commands." But we ended up living with the optical illusion that stepping out onto our terrace would land us in an abyss. Still, in the nearby center of town we cheered up: the children savored their ice cream in the coffee houses on Piazza Duomo and in the *galleria*; we relished our excursions to the surrounding lakes; we ate dinners in posh restaurants and country-type bistros—whenever we met Robert at the *Stazione Centrale* after his return from Brescia, and on weekends.

Our first *donna di servizio*, Louisella, was a fabulous cook and an excellent cleaner. She also taught me that my daily baths were bound to have my skin peel off; that one had to shop in at least four stores before every meal; and that wine rather than San Pellegrino was the way to good health. Some of her successors, who primarily descended upon Milan to find husbands, were less satisfactory: one flirted with every delivery boy, another picked up guys while shaking out her mop from our balcony, yet another sneaked out by the backdoor after our evening meal, leaving the baby unattended if we were out. Still another absconded after two days because in Sicily she "could breathe," while in Milan she "would suffocate." And when, in the early 1960s, houses of prostitution were closed down, one had to carefully check references of one's potential help. This, too, was an aspect of progress.

To begin with, I had to concentrate on my Italian, and had to get the children registered in school. In my naïveté, I had assumed that Ronnie and Vivien would attend public schools and, as the bright children they were, would pick up Italian by immersion—just as I had English after getting to New York. However, during afternoon tea with the outspoken Helen Scott, whose husband was a management consultant, and whose ancestors had come to Boston on the Mayflower, I was told that foreign children, automatically, were being placed two years back. Two of the Scotts three strapping girls were at boarding school in Switzerland. Because the youngest one was six years old when they first arrived, she started first grade, "with the nuns," Helen noted with a bit of disdain.

Two days later, Marjorie Harlepp, who had fled Cleveland for journalism, and now was the spunky freelance Milan reporter for the Rome Daily American, added that Italian children habitually make fun of foreigners, whose Italian was bound to be defective; and that they called them "stupid." Her daughter, Hilary, who was a few years older than Vivien, attended the American School of Lugano; six-year old Christopher went to the nearby public school.

Around then, Charlie had learned of our marriage and stopped paying child support. He claimed that he expected to see the children every Saturday afternoon, and that unless they attended P.S 178 I was neglecting their education. With worries and heavy hearts, we enrolled them where they had spent the summer—Ronnie at Beaulieu outside Vevey, and Vivien at Bleu Leman in Villeneuve. There, they would pursue both English and French curricula.

Nearly every Friday evening, we ran for the Trans-Europe Express to Lausanne, rented a car, and spent two glorious days in the Rhône valley and the Swiss Alps—in Leysin, Gsteig, Crans-sur-Sierre, Zermatt, and in countless hamlets in between. But when, after three weeks, Madame Failletaz, the owner and director of Bleu Leman, had moved Vivien to her ancestors' farm outside Nyon, we felt that that was no place for her: we did not want her to live without electricity, to lug wood from the shed, and to walk through snow to a one-room schoolhouse—a situation that truly was inferior to P.S. 178. Determined to take her away from there, and full of apprehension, I rather than Robert, confronted Madame. She argued, but to my delight and astonishment ended up giving me a refund. After Vivien was packed up, we ate her birthday cake—with candles—at breakfast in our hotel room. We spent the rest of that day inspecting half a dozen boarding schools. For some of their directors she was too young; others we rejected as too snooty or authoritarian. Finally, we took her back to Milan and sent for books to New York. Schooling Vivien at home was fun for both of us. That Christmas we picked up Ronnie, who impressed us with his knowledge of curse words in twelve languages rather than with his French, and went on to ski in Gstaad. There, their father visited and accused me of neglecting Vivien's education. So we enrolled her at Bergsonne, a *home d'enfants*, where Vivien perfected her skiing, her skating, and her French. (She now claims that as a result her horizons expanded, so that she never found the time to learn her times tables.)

* * *

Up to then, I had not closely followed Italian politics. Like most Americans, I had sort of generalized from my suburban perch to the world at large. Now, while Italian Maoists were advocating a permanent revolution, and we watched the Communists' jolly May Day parade from our windows, I began taking our daily crises in stride—sudden transportation strikes, telephone outages, garage mechanics' ignorance of the innards of our Chevrolet, shopkeepers' shortages, and doctors' antiquated advice. But as chaos turned into routine, I too focused on the Italians' good humor, and on their ability to *arrangiarsi*—the flexibility to make the best of the worst calamities, and to laugh at these. Gradually, we got used to emergencies and even enjoyed some.

In 1958, northern Italians were in the midst of modernization. *Milanese* and *Torinese* family enterprises were in the lead, leaving their southern peers far behind. (The historical and cultural gaps were real, and accentuated by the northerners' disdain for the southern "*terrone*," and for the hold by the Mafia.) New industries were being started in haylofts and garages to satisfy the needs of consumers, who had been impoverished during World War II. But they all were handicapped by a banking system that dated back to the one the Medicis had set up in Florence in 1397, unless Francesco Sforza, had improved it when starting his own bank in Milan, in 1447. Because foreigners were not allowed to open bank accounts, Robert's monthly pay came in cash—in a bulging briefcase. Only because he had a "friend" at the Banca Populare, could we buy the Swiss francs and dollars we needed. The rows upon rows of women in black aprons, who sat over their thick ledgers, armed with ink pens and square inkbottles, reminded me of my grueling days in garment factories. They entered every transaction by hand.

Time and again, Robert told me of yet another man who had approached him to employ a son, or a neighbor, and who was annoyed because Robert had had to explain that industrialization banked on skills rather than friendship. Still, thanks to these personalized ways, the saleslady at Buccelatti's told us to take home the ring I liked, to see whether I "wanted to live with it"—without having to pay or sign; the *couturière*, Lea Livoli, made an elaborate dress for me and said that we didn't have to take it unless we found it *assolutamente perfetto*; and the founder of Gucci's—in his tiny store in via Montenapoleone—refused to sell me shoes that did not fit "like gloves."

In sum, the *miracolo* was a slow process. Rapid industrialization and nepotism didn't mix well. Every American involved in setting up the Italian branches of, among others, U.S. Steel, Amoco, General Electric, Dow Chemical, Arthur Anderson, McCann Erickson and Merrill Lynch, told amusing stories, many of these at the British American Club. There, we met them all, along with the Fulbright scholars and artists who occasionally lectured, the contessa who introduced us to the finer aspects of Italian cuisine, and the British contingent, many of whom had been long-time residents. This club was the information center for newcomers, among whom Robert was an old-timer—who already knew how to navigate in this pell-mell thrust to modernize.

Twice a week, Mara Mosca came around to teach Italian to the women who wanted to learn, although not all of them cared to go much beyond asking: *"quanta costa"* and answering *"tropo caro."* However, many lasting friendships ensued, often replacing the extended families we had left back home. We organized picnics, Christmas and Halloween parties, and Fourth of July and Thanksgiving celebrations. Whether nostalgic or depressed, sick or well, English-speaking women supported each other. They shared the frustrations of having to get along in a foreign country. Not the least of their distress had to do with the more or less Puritan attitudes they brought with them. For, Italian men of all classes—from delivery boys to doctors, from bakers to bankers, and from train conductors to telephone repairmen—felt that in order to assure women of their charm, they had to make sexual innuendos or advances. Their routines varied from pinching bottoms to invitations for an *apperitivo* or a weekend, from lewd remarks to seductive gazes. Some of our women felt flattered, others felt insulted. But they soon learned to avoid such opportunities, and to respond gracefully when pressed.

American men were less shocked when their secretaries fell in love with them, and often enough succumbed. Some of their wives suffered silently, while others clamored to get transferred back home, and a few asked for divorce. Given my Viennese background, I was less upset by office hanky-panky. Some of my Italian women friends confided their own peccadilloes to me. Since Italian law didn't allow for divorce, there was a certain amount of open tolerance, and all wives and a very few husbands closed their eyes to their spouses' indiscretions—as long as these were discreet. Whenever Robert and I met between five and seven o'clock at, for instance, Sant'Ambroes in Corso Matteotti, we recognized some of these illicit couples. By eight o'clock they all were home for dinner with their families.

* * *

Gradually, ambitious shopkeepers and artisans, small entrepreneurs and factory owners got on the bandwagon, bankers loosened their purse strings, and new buildings went up. In retrospect, that was what stimulated *il miracolo*. However, that process also upset the workers. Their unions—whether Communist, Christian-Democrat or independent—enrolled more members, whose rising expectations engendered what Marx had called a pre-revolutionary climate. Robert told me of restless machine operators he spoke to on his rounds. I only encountered entrepreneurs, bankers, politicians, and directors of industry, none of whom ever spoke seriously with any woman—even the most educated and unattractive ones. At the proliferating receptions the "weaker sex" was around to tease and flirt with. Italians found these occasions instructive, and quickly caught on to "working the room." Later on, they too began to drink whiskey and bourbon, just as our Americans started to fancy themselves connoisseurs of wines.

*   *   *

To truly break into the Italian *haute volée* was difficult. I was initiated at a dinner party, at the home of Signor Barbieri, a manufacturer of pasta machinery. Robert's colleague, the dapper Silvio Simonatti, whose wife was said to be intimate with the host, met us at a bar on Piazza San Babila. After escorting us to the penthouse of a new office building, the door opened onto a terrace where waiters in white gloves offered drinks and hors d'ouevres. In the entrance to the apartment proper hung a few Degas ballerinas, in its living room a number of old masters, among them some Rembrandt hands and an exquisite Caravaggio. After an hour of chit-chat, the twelve guests were shown into the round dining room, whose enormous circular table appeared to be laden with more sparkling silver, crystal goblets and delicate china than Vienna's Lobmeyer and Augarten stores. Even though my Italian still was rather primitive, I caught on that our hosts wanted to amuse themselves at the expense of that "milkmaid from Switzerland" Robert, their favorite American bachelor about town, had married in Lausanne. As luck would have it, one of the guests' relatives owned a few marble quarries outside Carrara. When I mentioned that my grandfather had bought marble there, he recalled that he had met him as a little boy. Suddenly, they gave up joking at my expense, and I became *persona grata*.

Franka and Antonio Mascherpa were among the guests. She was this distinguished machine tool manufacturer's much younger and second wife: he had gotten a divorce in Mexico and had married her in London. Most Italians refused to recognize that union and ostracized her. We soon became close friends. She clued me in to Italian customs, introduced me to out-of the-way shops in hidden courtyards. Without her, I never would have met the silversmith in a backstreet alley, the jeweler in a concealed hallway, or the dressmaker who in her dingy living room worked for a fancy Via Montenapoleone *couturière*. After their daughter was born, the Mascherpas built a villa in Arona, above Lago Maggiore. We spent

many a Sunday sailing and picnicking with them; and a number of ski
vacations in St. Moritz, Sils-Maria, and Courmayeur.

* * *

After freezing all winter long in the Baronessa's apartment, we moved
to the nineteenth floor of the Torre Velasca (a modern adaptation of
Florence's bell tower). This was the first rental structure in Milan featuring built-in closets, kitchens, and bathrooms. With Franca I roamed the
outskirts of the city, to acquire the necessary furniture from tiny start-up
firms for a total of $1000—beds, tables, chairs and so on, including the
Venini vase and ashtray I continue to treasure.

The American Consul General lived and entertained in our penthouse, a
New York manufacturer of bathroom fixtures, Harry Kleiman and his wife
Ethel, were below us on the eighteenth floor, and the elderly Urdahls—he
was a Washington consultant—a few floors above. The two couples ate
and shopped together, and when they took a joint trip to Jerusalem over
Christmas, the Kleimans were visiting Israel, and the Urdahls were retrac-
ing Jesus's path in the Holy Land. Apparently, they all had a wonderful
time. We took that sort of multiculturalism for granted. But after Harry
found that he was unable to convince Italian workers that in America
every pipefitting had to fit, and could not be "filed down" while being
installed, he gave up and returned to New York.

Over the years, such misunderstandings diminished. Many of them
arose from the profusion of the country's nationwide laws that often
contradicted those by local or regional authorities. For instance, when I
applied for a resident permit for our Chevrolet at the Italian Automobile
Association, I was advised that the import tax was close to the cost of
the car. Upon noting my upset, the man behind the counter motioned me
into the hallway. There, while furtively looking over his shoulder, he said:
"Why don't you do what everyone else does. Just take the car across to
Switzerland every three months, and import it anew."

That is what we proceeded to do. (When, in 1964, the authorities
clamped down, we traded our new Oldsmobile for an Opel.) During these
years, we spent many a Saturday in Lugano, lunching on Châteaubriand,
which was as yet unobtainable in Milan, "smuggling" coffee into Italy,
and giving our business to Franz Carl Weber's toy emporium, and to the
excellent English bookstore.

By then, Vivien had spent a year at the Lycée Français. When the following year the International School of Milan was founded, we enrolled
both children. It turned out to be a rip-off: teachers, for the most part,

were drawn from the pool of idle wives whose husbands were working for American and British firms. They were underpaid and kept coming and going. Ronnie, who never was enamored of school goofed off, and after much discussion and soul searching, we sent him to the American School of Leysin, and the following year to the Windsor Mountain School in Lennox, Massachusetts.

In 1961, after Artemis (Artie) Joukowsky arrived with his wife, Martha, to establish an Italian base for American Underwriters, Martha suggested we start a not-for-profit school for English-speaking children. I was caught by her enthusiasm and got involved in setting up the American Community School of Milan (ACSM). We made up for our lack of experience by zeal: we hired teachers from the U.S. before we knew that we would have enough students to pay their salaries; found more or less appropriate space; gave receptions to meet the parents of prospective students; and personally transported books from the U. S. in order to avoid customs. By the time Allen was two-and-a-half years old, I dropped him off at the nursery school and went to our tiny office. Every day brought on crises—when the nuns from whom we rented our premises objected to our girls' shorts at gym in the courtyard; whenever a substitute had to be found for a sick teacher; when a parent complained about a late bus or a lost lunchbox; after our new principal had invited our oldest boy on a ski trip, and we had to, quietly, keep that boy from accepting.

*   *   *

I was the only woman on our Board of Trustees, and its treasurer, and the only one who had no clue about corporate America. Robert told me that in addition to putting together balance sheets and budgets, I had to present these with the proper flourish. Dino Parenti, who was buying properties for Amoco gas stations, advised me, while walking me up and down via Manzoni at 2:00 A.M., that I had best present an issue I really cared about near the close of a meeting, when everybody wanted to get home. Robert agreed, and, once again, pointed to the comical aspects of these goings-on. After three years, Linda Beccio said at one of our receptions, "You all really put that school on the map. I wouldn't have given you two cents for it." Linda, a stunning, lanky blonde of Irish origins, was married to an Italian-American accountant, and the mother of an infant son. Her best friend, Cathy Zoccolillo, a somewhat shorter blonde with even longer hair, and whose husband worked for Rohm & Haas, also had a baby. She nodded in agreement. In another year or two, I calculated, they'll support our nursery school.

Our perseverance was vindicated. We soon organized fundraisers. Alas, our first concert was scheduled for the evening of November 22, 1963. While driving to the school, I heard on my car radio that President Kennedy had been shot. Thinking I had misheard, I remained in the car, and as people kept arriving they congregated around me. Crying in disbelief and sorrow, we canceled the concert. During the following week, countless Italians extended the sort of condolences that usually are reserved for the death of a close family member. When Helen and Bruno Menin—Roberts' old friend and the local head of Mergenthaler Linotype, had dinner with us two nights later, we saw Jack Ruby shoot Harvey Lee Oswald to death on our TV. What was happening to our country?

Both school activities and children's friendships were responsible for the close ties we forged with the architect, Tom Spiers, and his wife, Nancy, and with the Joukowskys. The youngest of the three Spiers boys, and Nina and Tiemie Joukowsky were around Allen's age. When, after my botched appendectomy, the American and Swiss consuls' wives made arrangements to have Robert bring me to Zurich on the double, Martha kept an eye on our household and had Allen for sleepovers. And when, on an evening while our husbands were out of town, Martha and I discussed curricular and other needs for the school, she unexpectedly went into labor. I checked her into the hospital at 4:00 A.M., where her pains continued, as did our deliberations. Upon his return the following morning, Artie took over, declaring to the staff:

"Either you induce labor, or I'm taking her home." A few hours later, a nurse walked the newly born Mischa through the hall. In horror, I observed her washing his tiny body under running water over the sink. Soon thereafter, Martha relaxed in her elegant room, where visitors were coming and going, a few of whom were smoking heavily. Clearly, we all had loosened up and had become somewhat Italianized.

*   *   *

There seemed to be no end to adventures. For instance, when we drove from Milan to southern Italy with Vivien, Ronnie, and Ashley Banks—the English, thirteen-year-old who had fallen in love with Vivien during our Christmas vacation in Gstaad—in the backseat, we showed them around Florence and Rome and ended up on the Amalfi coast. After basking in the sun and admiring the sunset over the Gulf of Salerno from Ravello, that magnificent old hill town, we turned back. I don't recall where we stayed that night, but will never forget our trip across the Abruzzi Mountains in order to reach Pescara on the Adriatic coast the following noon.

Along the way, we asked for directions, which inevitably were: "*Sempre diritto*." Not that there was a straight road. When we came to a fork, and there were many, we instinctively took the right one. After a while, and as the road narrowed and ascended, we no longer met anyone. Nor did we come upon any habitations. Soon, it began to snow. Robert and I were not only cold, but apprehensive after hearing the howl of wolves. We kept our fears from the children. As the snow fell ever heavier, and it was getting colder and colder, I worried that we might have to sleep in the car. Could the wolves bite their way through the canvas roof of our convertible? While grasping for Robert's hand, we suddenly came upon a large, lit up, building that turned out to be an elegant hotel. We not only had stumbled on a ski resort, but on one with heated rooms to let. The desk clerk was surprised only that we had not been warned to watch out for wild wolves and hungry bears. The following day, Robert's colleagues in Pescara told gruesome stories about travelers who had forever been lost.

*   *   *

Throughout these years, we spent numerous weekends in London, Paris, and Rome, in Florence, Venice and Zurich. We often took lazy drives along the Côte d'Azur with stops in Montecarlo, Cap d'Antibes and St. Tropez, while staying in Nice or Cannes. And winter vacations in the villages of the Val d'Aosta, in St. Moritz, Zermatt and Courmayeur, and most frequently in Villars-sur-Ollon—that Allen called his "home in Switzerland." With the Joukowskys and all of our children we vacationed in Gstaad. We frolicked in the snow with two dozen ACSM children and their parents in Madesimo. We even managed ten days in Greece, an unforgettable experience. And, like Italians, rented houses at the ocean side, usually in Forte dei Marmi for the month of July, and went to somewhere in the Alps, for the month of August—allegedly for the children's health. Just once, we sped to Genoa for lunch in Bruno and Helen Menin's convertible Porsche. More often, we attended opera performances in Parma and concerts on the Isola Bella. Our half-time subscription to La Scala (eighteen performances per season) gave us insights to the pomp and priorities of the old-time Milanese aristocracy, at least to the family that—reluctantly—was sharing its orchestra seats with us. (Most of that time Robert held two "full-time" jobs.) Intermittently, we dealt with the troubles our ex-spouses were causing, and were as loving as on our honeymoon when, on lazy Sunday mornings, we danced to "As Time Goes By," just like Bogey and Bergman had in Paris.

Altogether, we lived on the rollercoaster that then was Italy—before it was built-up and crowded with tourists in sloppy clothes, while the dollar was overvalued, and Americans were the kings of every mountain—whether they climbed it or not.

Inevitably, I also got more of a glimpse into America's diverse customs than I could have in New York—into southern hospitality and Methodist fundamentalism, the habits of Boston Brahmins and the convictions of Philadelphia Quakers. Lasting friendships developed across ethnic and religious lines. We had no elite I was aware of. Some of the Italians soon were eager to demonstrate that they were up to executive snuff by wearing crew cuts and giving cocktail parties. But even so, these individuals did not shed the political stances and beliefs they brought with them—be it from family backgrounds or Luddite traditions. Among these northern-ers the differences tended to be handled lightly, and with panache. Still, *nouveau-riche* entrepreneurs, who until recently had belonged to the working class, were torn by their workers' wild-cat strikes—which increasingly were mandated by the unions. In 1963, for instance, when parliamentary elections tilted to the Communist Party, Robert was not surprised. But our consuls were stunned: they had met only with Anglo-philes, with the friendly elites.

*   *   *

In close to eight years, Robert and I lived on this rollercoaster, enjoyed each other and the children—as we grew closer and closer. We built on the love that had drawn us together, while growing in lock step with the evolving "miracle." At the same time, our absence from America, as the cliché has it, made our hearts grow fonder of New York. Vivien was especially nostalgic for American teenage culture, mostly for Rock and Roll. After I watched Ronnie graduate from Windsor Mountain School, in June 1965, the children and I spent a week in New York, before visit-ing the Scotts who had retired to Sippewisset, on Cape Cod. And we looked at a few colleges around Boston, where to Vivien's delight we happened to stay at the same motel as the Beach Boys. She made sure to make their acquaintance.

At the end of July we met Robert in Copenhagen. For years, Allen recalled that he had lost a shoe while on the rollercoaster with his daddy, and Vivien recently said that the silver tea service we bought there has a special meaning for her. That August, we were in Forte dei Marmi for the customary *dolce far niente*. For the first time, Vivien was invited to join the Italian youngsters who spent their evenings at *La Capanina*, the hopping beach club-cum-restaurant. Although she was more of a mascot than a participant in the fun, she now was ready to spend the rest of her life in Italy.

But it was not to be. At the beginning of October, Robert flew to the machine tool convention in Chicago and expected to be back for the good-bye party we were giving for the Joukowskys. As usual, he stopped in New York for a medical checkup with Eric Nash. Before his expected return, he called and said, rather casually,

"Eric wants to have a look at my prostate, so I might not be back in time for the big bash. But there is nothing to worry about. I want you to go ahead with the party, as if I were there. And I may well make it."

The Joukowskys' departure was a personal loss and signaled a change in the dynamics of the American Community School. During the height of the adieus, Eric called, and, in his most relaxed bedside manner, told me that Robert's test had gone well, but that he would need another one, just to make sure. He ended by saying, "If you feel like it, come over and keep him company."

Within twenty-four hours, I had my plane ticket, and had arranged for one of our teachers to move in to take charge of the household. I arrived in New York long before the Joukowskys' ship, after an unusual flight. The hostess recognized the agitated shrimp in the seat next to me as the winner of the previous year's *Prix de Paris*: he was squeezing his rosary and praying, not too sotto voce, for the Madonna's protection. Because the plane's pilot wanted to meet him, he invited the two of us to the executive lounge: to cure the heroic champion's fear of flying, he held forth about the rigorous pilots' training on flight simulators, the safety of the automatic pilot, and so on. Although the trotting winner intermittently continued to mumble into his rosary, my more silent fear of flying evaporated. It never returned.

*   *   *

At the hospital, both Robert and Eric made light of the illness. Eric focused on whether or not to transfer Robert to New York Hospital for this delicate "procedure." He did not say that he suspected cancer, and that Robert might be severely ill. (All doctors then avoided that word.) About a week later, Eric assisted during Robert's "exploratory operation," but did not come and talk to me afterwards as he had promised. I had been worried only that Robert might not wake up due to the possible effects of his anesthesia. (Many years later, the unflappable Eric confessed that he had been too shaken to see me just then.) When Robert came to, I was overjoyed. Visibly moved, and happy that the surgery was over, he squeezed and kissed my hands, and made detailed plans for the following summer: we would rent a mobile home in order to travel throughout the U.S. with our five children. And we would visit Israel without them that winter. "We have a lot of living ahead of us," Robert kept repeating.

Now that physicians are expected to disclose the worst-case scenario, and often do so in the most brutal fashion, people cannot fathom that once upon a time death was a taboo subject. Neither Elisabeth Kübler-Ross's book on the stages of death and dying—denial and isolation, anger, bargaining, depression, and acceptance—nor the plethora of theses on the subject that were to follow it, had as yet been written; nor were there any therapists who specialized in helping survivors to mourn. Freud's legacy was restricted to uncovering unconscious mental functions. Most American psychoanalysts, who liked to think of themselves as scientists, were steeped in ego psychology; and tended to dismiss his writing on the death instinct as the work of a sick, old man. Only after I questioned Eric why Robert's recovery seemed exceedingly slow, did he suggest that I come to talk to him.

"How much shall I tell you," be began to say on that Saturday afternoon.

"Everything, the whole truth," I responded. That was when he informed me, slowly and haltingly, that the operation had been a failure; that the cancer had metastasized and had been inoperable. And he went on to say that I had to keep Robert in the dark at all cost, so that he would be able to live fully for at least another five to ten years—without turning into a hypochondriac. In sum, I had to live with this unbearable knowledge, while appearing cheerful and becoming super-efficient. Evidently, not only doctors in Vienna were living by the axiom "*lass ihn teppert sterben*" (let him die in ignorance). But how would I be able to keep secrets from the man I loved, and from whom I had learned never to withhold even my most intimate feelings and thoughts? I ended up veering between shaking with anxiety and trying to deaden my volatile fears.

At Eric's urging, we returned to Milan just before Thanksgiving—to resume our "normal" life. My close friend, Miriam, the wife of Martin Stahl, the director of the American Trade Center, picked us up at Malpensa Airport. After Robert was settled in bed, she turned to me saying, "I know that Robert had a hard time, but why do you look so awful? What is going on?" I broke down, swore her to silence, and told her. For a few weeks I focused on caring for Robert, on being cheery with the children, continuing my household and school routines—while trying not to spill my horrible secret. But I soon noticed that Robert was swallowing more and more painkillers, and seemed extremely tired—while pushing himself by making the rounds of his offices and even attending a few receptions. Against all odds, and despite my vague apprehensions, I counted on his eventual recovery. But I felt safer with New York doctors. Therefore, I talked our Italian physician into convincing Robert that he ought to take six months of rest in New York, where doctors could speed up his rehabilitation. On the sly, with the help of Martin and Miriam, I made arrangements to dispose of some of our furniture, to break our lease, and to sell my spanking new, red convertible. And I turned over ACSM responsibilities. As I jumped oodles of bureaucratic hurdles, I metamorphosed into my own version of Madame de la Marquise.

We got to New York on January 4, 1966. I had the children stay with Fred and Hannah Kurzweil in Queens, and expected to use my parents' extra room until the apartment we had rented in the newly erected Lincoln Towers would be habitable. However, my father, who always had been afraid to come in contact with illness, had decided to put us up in a studio apartment next door to them, in the Hotel Esplanade. The smell of cooking and genteel poverty was depressing, so we moved to our unfinished apartment after four days. One day later, Robert had a heart attack.

Just as Fred delivered Vivien and Allen, two ambulance drivers were carrying Robert out on a stretcher. Vivien distracted her little brother by telling him to look for his new bed. For nearly three months, our furniture consisted of four beds, a bridge table with four chairs, a television set and a vacuum cleaner. John Lindsay had just become New York's mayor, and the transportation workers had gone on strike. I left with Robert on the ambulance and sent the children out to eat.

While Robert's life hung on a thread, I zig-zagged between fear for him, for our future, and for Allen's psychic well-being. Yet all of that seemed to be happening as if in a movie, as if I were a spectator to my own life—while I went through endless hospital formalities, consulted with a slew of doctors, did the laundry, or kissed the children good-night.

*   *   *

My parents said all the right things. But during our long absence, I had forgotten their limitations, and that their lives were dedicated to "the business." Thus I had counted on more sympathy and family time than they were willing or able to give. My friends, Harold and Muriel Strauss, whose apartment was a few flights above ours, were aghast that my mother did not send over any furniture, and soon supplied us with an easy chair, a floor lamp, and a bouquet of flowers. I don't think I will ever be able to forget the hollow sound of a blaring television set in an unfurnished place, or my sleepless nights—after long and agonizing days in the hospital. Robert was suffering and wilting away, while I kept myself going by savoring his lucid moments, talking about the feats of our children and about returning to Italy. At times, his eyes would light up and he would reach out to me, planning the layout of the furniture in our apartment, and deciding whom to contact about work now that we were again in the U.S. During these fleeting moments, I was sure he would survive—and expected miracles I knew could not happen.

*   *   *

In the short run, I had to find schools for Allen and Vivien (Ronnie already was a freshman at Long Island University), but had to wait for the end of the Christmas break. My friends were certain that in the middle of an academic year none of the schools I considered would even be willing to grant us interviews. Almost on a dare, in the middle of January, I walked into the offices of the Ethical Culture School with Allen and Vivien in tow. With much hesitation, and after consulting the guidance counselor, the admissions director agreed to test Allen then and there. Since I had to leave for the hospital, Vivien stayed with him. When Allen came out beaming, and she was told that he had done well, she jumped for joy. This reaction by a teenager who did not yet know what would happen to her own schooling, so impressed the staff that they called Spencer Brown, the head of the Fieldston School, and, over his strenuous objections convinced him to interview her. In our nearly television-free Italian environment Vivien had read and lived in every book Brown mentioned. She had definite opinions about plots and protagonists, so that he was thoroughly impressed and accepted her into the junior class. (Robert glowed with pride when I told him.)

While recuperating from his heart attack, Robert was in ever more pain. For a few days he thrashed about and imagined that the patient across the room had it in for him. I worried that he was losing his mind. But after the cardiologist changed his prescriptions, the hallucinations stopped. The oncologist, however, thought it would be most human, and desirable, to let him die of his heart condition in order to spare him the extremely painful death this aggressive cancer was bound to cause.

"As long as there is life, we must do what we can," said the cardiologist, "who knows what cure for his cancer they might invent even within the next few months?"

I supported him wholeheartedly. But after six weeks, I was told to take Robert home, because New York Hospital could not keep terminal patients. Eric Nash declared that Allen ought to remember his father as the lively and extraordinary man he had been, rather than in this deteriorating state, and with tubes in his body. He had me accompany Robert in an ambulance to Parkway Hospital in Forest Hills, where he could care for him. On the way, Robert, while reaching for me, said that he was so glad to be brought to a place where he would be able to recuperate. At that moment, I again imagined us floating on a dance floor aboard a cruiser, and was sure that life would go on as before. While telling him about Allen's most recent bon mots, and the other children's doings, I wafted in and out of my trance: I didn't recognize until long after Robert had died, that his optimism and euphoria were caused by his addiction to morphine.

By then, I routinely dropped Allen off at school at 8:30 A.M. and went directly to the hospital. At 3:00 P.M., the mother of a classmate took him to her house, along with her daughter, and Vivien picked him up after she got back from Riverdale about an hour later. Allen seemed to like his kindergarten setting, but then he had been a social being from the day he was born. The only time I broke this routine was for the delivery of our belongings. That day, Vivien and I unpacked and placed the furniture. We were done by 2:00 A.M., and even had hung the pictures.

Allen spent many weekends with the Joukowskys, who now lived in Larchmont: Artie, who along with a few others at ACSM had looked to Robert as the wise elder, cried when he beheld him in his reduced state. For Allen, being with his playmates from Milan provided continuity. He knew that his daddy was sick. And he told me that he and his friends were praying for him to get better soon. (A few months later, he asked me to "please marry Mr. Joukowsky, because I need a daddy.") Vivien too lived under the cloud of Robert's illness, and did all she could to distract and protect her little brother. His half-brothers, Peter and Lenny, frequently visited.

When Robert died, on April 19, 1965, I collapsed. (On the following day, at the *Fiera di Milano*, he was awarded the first prize for his design of a modern kitchen "everyone" could afford.) Eric had to push me into giving permission for an autopsy, saying that the more we knew about that cancer, the better it would be, since, after all, we had to do this for his three sons. I don't recall, or want to recall, the stupor that overcame me even while I made plans at the Riverside funeral parlor; or sat, alone with his coffin, while waiting for Hannah and her sister to pay their respects. My father had bought a plot at the Westchester Hills cemetery in Hastings, my mother and brother met me to pick out the casket. The funeral parlor was full of people—Robert's former acquaintances, my pals from the Young Austrians, and our families, including his angry ex-wife, Ruth. Robert's best friend from Vienna, Frank Lustig, flew in from Chicago. After the burial, Marietta came from Boston and Marta from New Jersey. What are you going to do now, everyone was asking. I had no answer. When I showed my visitors Robert's extraordinary photographs, some suggested I get them published and exhibited. You need to work, and to earn money, said my family. I wholeheartedly agreed, but wondered to myself what Robert would advise me to do.

16

With Sorrow to a Profession

Robert's death left me crippled and drained. Whom could I rely on from now on, whose shoulders might I be able to cry on? After eight years abroad, I felt at sea in my own country. How would I support myself and the children? Most of my former friends continued to venerate suburbia and all that entailed, whereas my own horizon had expanded exponentially. I was unprepared for the everyday hassles lone widows encounter: reverse discrimination at the Social Security Office on 125th Street; having my personal property floater cancelled because widows were deemed to be greater risks than expatriates in Italy; getting Charlie, who worried that I now would sue him for having skipped child-support, to send his check. My parents kept berating me for putting Allen and Vivien in private schools. (The assistant principal at Hunter High had whispered, confidentially, that if I could possibly afford private schooling, the children would benefit. I believed her.) Moreover, I couldn't sleep, was dog-tired and weary, and in need of emotional support. New York turned out to be a rougher place than I remembered.

The day after the funeral, Vivien had a wracking crying spell. While in a tight embrace, and trying to console her, I said that after all she had Charlie, her own father. "Robert was my real daddy," she responded, "he understood me and took me places." Ronnie looked on, and when I collapsed on my bed, saying that I was utterly spent, picked up the yellow pages—wanting to find a psychiatrist for me.

*   *   *

For the sake of Allen, I had to be cheery and upbeat. He knew that his daddy had died, but given his age could not understand what that meant, except that he wouldn't see him again. Nevertheless, I was stumped when, on a glorious, cloudless morning, while driving him to school along Central Park, he asked: "When there are no clouds, Mommy, could we see Daddy?" (In his "interdenominational" prayers with the Joukowskys they had called upon God to take Robert to heaven.) A few days later he angrily accused me: "It's your fault that Daddy died. Why didn't you call up another doctor?" The guidance counselor at his school told me not to worry, and that he was doing well. But I had my doubts, as I answered condolences, cooked meals, and dragged myself through household chores. Another time, near tears, he burst out, "Remember, Mommy, when I told Daddy that his watch had fallen out of the window? Well, it didn't really fall, I threw it out, because I wanted to see time fly." (He had overheard a joke about that the previous day.)

Before long, I got into mothering *al'americana*: I sat on benches in Central Park and socialized with the mothers of Allen's classmates. They all were forthcoming and sympathetic—and went home to their husbands every evening.

To alleviate my financial worries, I contacted the director of the International School Services, who had sent teachers to ACSM. A few days after our cordial meeting, he telephoned, saying that he had the perfect job for me: Jim Huntley, a former Ford Foundation officer, was looking for an executive to replace him at the New York office: he was about to move to England, to start the first of a chain of Atlantic Colleges. I jumped at the opportunity, even though "this non-profit venture for now was unable to pay me what I was worth." Within a week, I realized that, at least for the moment, I had to type the letters my boss was dictating into a tape recorder; that my research would be limited to locating possible donors at the Foundation Center near Columbus Circle; and that he expected to add my Italian contacts to his rolodex.

With much trepidation, I called Jack Keller, Robert's boss from his Marshall Plan days, with whom we had had dinner whenever he blew through Milan, and who had sat at my bedside after my botched appendectomy. As the president of Eltra, the holding company that had bought Mergenthaler Linotype, he had 70,000 employees under him. He wanted to be helpful. Nevertheless, he ended up saying that I had excellent qualifications, but that his staff would not willingly take directions from a woman.

"Why don't you teach somewhere," he concluded while walking me to the elevator. At that point, I recalled Robert's frequent regrets that I had had to stop my studies when I came with him to Italy. So, after Allen sat at the foot of my bed one morning, with tears in his eyes, and said that he "didn't want that fat lady" to pick him up from school, I calculated that after paying for bus fare, lunch and her salary I was at most fifteen dollars ahead. And I figured out that I could afford to stay home for the time being—while acquiring a profession, in clinical psychology or in education. I didn't know just what I would do, but was as determined not to be anybody's secretary, as I was to pick Allen up from school. That summer, I enrolled at Queens College—in experimental psychology, two required courses for psychology majors.

The families of Robert's friends from Vienna, the Wessons and the Nashes, had been renting a cabana at Silverpoint Beach for some years. They invited me to share it. I found this overcrowded imitation of Forte dei Marmi depressing, but would have been depressed anywhere. I talked about everyday trivia with Liliane and Maggie, laughed at Eric's and Bernie's banter, and watched the children cavort in the water and in the sand. I was unable to concentrate on my school assignments. Liliane thought that if I were to become a travel agent (she now was scared that Eric too might die, and soon built up a most successful agency), I could earn "a lot of money." But like a mule on his track, I felt that I had to get that degree before embarking on any career, even as I doubted that I would be able to pass my courses.

Queens College's graduation requirements had been drastically lowered during the years of my absence, so I needed just another fifteen credits for my B.A. To fill an 11:00 o'clock slot during the fall of 1966, I registered for sociology of the family. When the professor, Cynthia Fuchs Epstein, returned our midterm exams, while explaining that she had arranged our blue books in grade order, she called my name first. I stumbled on my way to the front of the room, certain that I had gotten the lowest mark. However, I had come in at the top of the class. Now, she invited me to lunch in the faculty lounge. I spoke to her about Italy and the children, and about my disenchantment with the psychology department's shift from clinical to experimental psychology. Cynthia told me that my experiences were excellent preparations for sociology, and encouraged me to go to graduate school. Driven by my insecurity, I did not dare apply to New York and Columbia Universities—where Graduate Record Exams including statistics were required—and registered for the spring semester at the Graduate Faculty of the New School for Social Research.

Over the Christmas vacations, the children and I went skiing with the Wessons, the Nashes and a few of their friends. One of these was a divorcé, George Rowan. Born in Vienna, he told me of his army service and of some of the doings at the United Nations where he worked as a photographer. With much trepidation, I began to date him. He had had two heart attacks and advised me not to get attached to him. Two months later, after returning from an assignment in Haiti, he had another attack and died. I was more and more convinced that I was bad luck for any good man.

When not undertaking some activity with the children, I again buried myself in books. Only after Allen was in bed, did I allow myself to cry. During these sleepless nights, I again free-associated on yellow pads, as if Robert still were around to read my thoughts.

In the summer of 1967, I took the job my father had offered me. I invented a new bookkeeping system for the family's Austrian enterprise, Steinwerk Tribuswinkel—while Vivien and Allen played and cavorted in Vienna's parks. Soon, my father invited me to move to Vienna and run that company: under my oversight, we could expand it, while also putting an end to the manager's petty thefts. I accepted. However, when he stalled on his pledge of a 25 percent share of the business before my departure from New York, and quibbled about paying me a living wage, I was less inclined to go. On top of that, shortly after Thanksgiving, Allen came to my bed and sobbed, "I don't want to go to Austria. I like my school here. And if you get me a new daddy, I won't even understand him."

By then, the four-year-old black Cadillac my brother had inherited from my father already had been shipped to Vienna. That car, it gradually struck me, stood for what some of my fellow students thought of as a symbol of capitalism. I abhorred its useless fins and its size. Fast convertibles remained my preference. And I was frightened of being stuck overseas, and of being financially squeezed, balked at having to pay my moving expenses, and, foresaw Big Brother's control. Moreover, I was more and more worried about how Allen would adjust to yet another major change. Suddenly, it crossed my mind that when I had been a child, after having promised me time and again that he would take me to the Prater's amusement park, my father had quipped, "Yes, I've promised, and that's good enough. That is why I don't really have to take you." Of course, my father had good reason to be angry at me. My brother, though trying to hide the fact that he didn't want me as a partner, was pleased. To avoid trouble, or was it to allay my guilt, I continued to spend many a boring Sunday afternoon at my brother's home in Tenafly. They all talked about marble and balance sheets, while I sat by myself and watched the children. They didn't grasp that I preferred seeing the friends we had made in Pietrasanta, where American sculptors, among them Neil Estern, Jacques Lipchitz, and Stanley Bleifeld, had worked at a foundry. My parents were sure that they were bad influences, and did not realize that reading and writing term papers had become my work. Many a morning, my mother would phone and say, "Did I wake you up? You have an easy life, father and I have been at the office since nine o'clock." No matter how often, and in whatever way, I tried to explain what I was trying to accomplish, my family never could, or wanted to, understand. "Intellectuals" were the bane of their existence. Later on, the question would be "How much money do they pay you," or "you're teaching nine (or twelve) hours a week, what do you do with the rest of your time?" This anti-intellectualism didn't endear them to me, although I was not able to squarely face its disdainful undertone until after my father died many years later (see chapter 21).

* * *

In 1968, on the day Allen greeted me by saying that "this nice man in the elevator invited me to his apartment and wants to give me special chocolates," I decided that we had better move to a building with elevator men. I didn't want Allen to grow up as a mama's boy who had to hang on to my apron strings, but had to protect him. Soon, we moved to 1050 Park Avenue. Now, after Allen came home from school, we munched on our favorite Greenberg cookies, while he divulged as much as he thought appropriate about his day.

By then, he was in 5th grade, and after he began to come home later and later, I worried, especially when he let on that he had to escape from Joseph, one of the children who were being bussed in, and who was twice his size. But he refused to let me pick him up from P.S. 6. We both sighed with relief on the day he arrived home, dirty and bedraggled, and with a black eye—while bubbling over with joy and recounting just how he had managed to "sit on top of Joseph in the middle of Park Avenue."

* * *

While living in Italy, I had not followed American politics beyond what appeared in the *Herald Tribune* and *Time Magazine*. Although the number two official at the United States Information Service, had mentioned that he might leave the agency if they were to post him to Vietnam, I didn't pay it much heed. Subsequently, I was too taken up with Robert's illness to look beyond my own bailiwick. However, at The New School, I became aware of rumblings among classmates, mostly while discussing the Marxist theories I was eager to master. My fellow students in introduction to sociology seemed to know so much more than I. When I told that to the professor, Norman Birnbaum, he replied that much of what they were saying was nonsense, and that they were just showing off. He was impressed with my knowledge of languages and my European *savoir-faire*. (Actually, my lifelong habit of escaping into books came in handy, insofar as I drew, however vaguely, on some of the tales of Balzac and Dickens in relation to Marx's Communist Manifesto, and on what I had learned about Bloomsbury from an erudite English professor.) Soon, Norman asked me to be his assistant in a comparative study of West European universities, for which he had a Ford Foundation grant. I signed on, and began to summarize French and German books. That same semester, I registered for the first course ever offered on the sociology of women. All of the then available research on my paper, "Women in Management," proved that women could not make it as executives—either because men wouldn't take orders from them, or because they were emotionally unfit for such positions.

While discussing my research and sociological lacunae with Norman, he advised me on what to read and on what not waste my time on. On the one hand, he bolstered my ego, because I had a certain amount of sophistication you don't learn in academe. On the other hand, he berated me when he was in one of his bad moods. I did not understand that he was driven by instincts he was unable to control. Inevitably, we entered into a troublesome relationship.

At the end of May 1968, I brought Allen to Mrs. Houk's camp in Vevey, where Vivien was taken on as an (unpaid) counselor. I then joined Norman in Paris. Lo and behold, the "events of 1968" had just taken off. We stayed at the *Hotel du pas de Calais*, across the street from the Faculty of Medicine, a major meeting ground for protesters. All of Paris seemed to be in the streets. I found some of the students' flamboyant posters to be superior to those sold in the nearby galleries. They were denouncing the French state and its bureaucrats, and were demanding to be liberated from their authoritarianism. And they accused their professors of preparing them for a career they had no chance to pursue. In fact, the gates of the French university had been opened to masses of students, but no thought had been given to either "a theory or a practice" of mass education. Consequently, hordes of students were being exposed to "a system that was failing them." Unlike American students whose revolts were against consumer society, their French counterparts wanted the freedom to choose among courses that might prepare them for practical endeavors rather than for philosophies which might be of use only to the elite of the elite—to those who were aspiring to the highest governmental and university positions.

In this charged atmosphere, while trucks full of armed gendarmes were stationed around the corner on Boulevard St. Germain, and ambulance and police sirens were shrieking day and night, I was force-fed French politics and sociological theories. With success, the students kept raising their demands. Cheering left-wing professors, many of them Norman's friends, were getting ready for the revolution. We interviewed them. It was a heady time, even after May 30, when President de Gaulle's speech put an end to their dreams.

I was totally exhausted, if only because I prepared myself for every interview. For instance, before going to lunch with Alain Touraine, whose trim bearings and looks seemed to prove that he had learned how to present himself from his fellows at Harvard, I immersed myself in his *Workers' Attitudes to Technical Change*, (1965) and *La conscience ouvrière* (1966). These books however were of no help, because Touraine now was studying social movements. I was silent during the entire meal, but recall that Touraine was less certain of the students' success than Norman—who believed that because the Renault workers also were striking, another 1789 might well be around the corner. Hadn't Marx predicted that when workers and students united the revolution would begin?

Most Parisian sociologists cheered the students on the barricades—although those whose children were manning them seemed a bit less enthusiastic. (They all scorned colleagues, especially Raymond Aron, who remained on the sidelines.) We frequently visited Henri Lefebvre, the voluble Marxist "humanist," who officially had left the Communist Party in 1956, but not its principles. White-haired and erect in the black velvet suit he never seemed to take off, Henri took credit for the uprising, because he had been the student leaders' professor. His common-law wife, Nicole, soon became my friend. Lucien Goldmann, a rotund Roumanian Frenchman who spent hours at the café *Les Deux Maggots*, watching the "girls" who walked by, taught at the faculty of political science. He used to call us to hurry up and get to a specific *évènement*. But we never arrived at a single demonstration in time to witness it: only empty rooms and the odor of teargas proved that something had gone on.

So far, I have been recalling the world of left-wing academe and intellect I was determined to join. But, gradually, I became dubious of what contradicted some of my previous observations. This was nowhere more obvious than during our visits at the home of Denise and Serge Jonas. Whenever we got there, before dinner, the news would be blaring on television. For whatever rebellion or trouble, in whatever country around the globe, and whatever car accident or other mishap in France or the rest of Europe was being reported, Serge declared it to have been the work of the American CIA. Since I inadvertently had known some of its representatives in Milan, who had been too inept even to keep secret their identities, I occasionally dared point to one or another irreconcilable fact in Serge's scenario. He would dismiss me with a shrug or a grimace as unable to grasp the hold that my capitalist background had on my thinking. His co-editor of the journal *L'homme et la société*, and of *Anthropos*, a tall, swarthy man, was even more of a practicing Stalinist. I then already had heard of Party discipline, but was as yet unable to distinguish between run-of-the-mill leftists and liberals, and dyed-in-the-wool communists and idealistic socialists. Even Denise, who was unhappy because Serge never had divorced his first wife so that their two children were "illegitimate," and who confided to me that she was too scared to tell him of a lump in her breast, never referred to Serge's political doctrines. (She died of breast cancer two years later.)

On our tour of universities, I admired articulate women students, especially at the University of Grenoble, who drew crowds while arguing that the revolution must go on. On our visit to Bochum University, the assistant professor showing us around complained about the shoddy construction and box-like shape of the classrooms—as we were strolling on a wrap-around terrace. His deep anger, however, was directed at the centralized German university system that overpaid arrogant senior professors and underpaid overburdened assistants like him. We heard similar (justified) objections in Munich and Berlin.

On our excursion to East Berlin, the young man in front of us was stopped at Checkpoint Charlie by a hefty woman inspector. She angrily grabbed his identification card and his package—small blue bathing trunks wrapped in newspaper. After more than twenty minutes she came out, threw the bathing suit at him and said that this time she wouldn't arrest him, but told him never again to try smuggling unwanted information across the border. I was ready to turn back, but Norman insisted we go on. As we walked up the *Kurfürstendamm*, I was struck by the overall shabbiness of people's clothing, and by the dirt and broken windows in the art deco building we entered—to visit a sociologist Norman knew, but who wasn't at home. Norman pointed out, correctly, that books cost much less than they did in the West. I noted, however, upon opening a tome on women, that its content didn't correspond to what we were observing.

That summer ended with a conference in Cérisy, near Geneva. Its ecumenical institute had invited student leaders and professors from the countries that had had demonstrations, to find out about connections reaching across national borders, and about plans for future collaboration. Simultaneous translations were provided in German, French, and English. To my amusement, the students of each country were speaking in their own professors' voices. So, when at one point I didn't understand what was causing such boisterous laughter (I didn't use earphones), I was told that the interpreter from German had said to "wait a moment, the verb is still to come." In any event, it was found that all these students had acted spontaneously against specific local conditions, although they had watched one another's spectacles on their television screens.

*   *   *

Overseas student riots and opposition to the Vietnam War conspired to increase, and heat up, the discontent that was brewing in American universities. As did the activities of the women's liberation movement. That fall I returned to The New School, and Norman—who had been denied tenure—started to teach at Amherst College. Resistance to draft registration was in full swing. Protest marches to Washington were successfully organized. Altogether, these activities convinced President Lyndon Johnson not to stand for reelection. The New School faculty had agreed with the radical student leaders to turn over the first ten minutes of each class to them. So, before every lecture someone would come in and ask: "Is there any value-free sociology?" Invariably, the conclusion would be that Max Weber had been wrong; that capitalism had to be brought down; or that it already was on its last legs. I had trouble believing that America was as bad as they decreed, but was pleased that they trusted me even though I was over thirty. Still, I kept wondering how dropping out and moving to rural communes, or stealing books from the 8th Street bookstore, was going to stop capitalist production.

Despite my unease about the war in Vietnam, I continued to concentrate on my academic work. From Peter Berger I learned about the theories of Max Weber and about myths; from Benjamin Nelson I heard of Jacob Burckhardt, Max Weber and their antecedents. Arthur Vidich expanded on the makings and underpinnings of communities; Trent Schroyer looked at Marx and other radical thinkers, while Emil Oesterreicher taught about Gyorgy Lukacs, Georg Simmel, and Ferdinand Toennies. Hannah Arendt and the Frankfurt School luminaries became household words, as did Joseph Schumpeter, Alfred Schütz, and Edmund Husserl. Visiting scholars brought yet other perspectives. And these differing ap-proaches and areas of expertise reinforced my own tendency to question taken-for-granted assumptions, and to act as the devil's advocate. As I increasingly grasped what sociology was about, and turned in "well-written" and "well-argued" term papers, fellow students as well as professors and their families became personal friends. Already before I received my M.A. in 1969, I no longer doubted what I was cut out for. When appointed teaching assistant (T.A.) to Digby Baltzell who visited from the University of Pennsylvania, to John O'Neill who came from Toronto, and then as senior faculty assistant, I nearly felt like Croesus. Before Christmas of 1970, my thesis proposal on Italian Entrepreneurs was approved by the entire faculty of sociology. And I had been offered a fellowship at the Agnelli Foundation in Torino. Consequently, Allen was to spend the school year at Aiglon, a boarding school in Villars-sur-Ollon. Charles Fisher, a friend and psychoanalyst suggested that on my way to Italy, I might want to attend the meetings of the International Psychoanalytic Association (IPA) that, for the first time after Freud's departure were to take place in Vienna. Anna Freud was to attend.

That week's visit to the city of my birth put my mind on fire. To me, the theoretical arguments—among ego psychologists, Lacanians, inter-relational and other factionalists—though extremely heated, did not set me as much on edge as did the interactions, or lack of them, among the psychoanalysts and the Viennese. The visitors, in tourist-type fashion, liked the food and fancy receptions. The handful of local psychoanalysts, who didn't get along with one another, pretended to be wearing Freud's mantle. The population looked askance at the foreigners with gray conference folders, when not openly voicing their hostility. Altogether, the Viennese carried their provinciality and anti-intellectualism on their sleeves—which most of the psychoanalysts ignored. One evening, when I expected to hear light classical music in the courtyard of the *Rathaus* (city hall), the orchestra played romanticized rock and roll. To relieve my revulsion at the superficiality and pretense of it all, I began to free-associate on my yellow pad, while the music played: I juxtaposed contradictory clinical presentations; differences between conference participants and natives; and marveled at the adulation of Freud's daughter.

After polishing and expanding my notes, I hesitantly sent the essay to Norman Podhoretz, the editor of *Commentary*. He was surprised that I was "a writer," and offered me $350. After "The Freudians Meet in Vienna" was printed in November 1971, I received many friendly letters, and a few attacks, and was invited to psychoanalysts' meetings and parties. Inadvertently, I had achieved recognition. My father let me know that he was glad I no longer used my maiden name, because that might have been harmful to his Austrian enterprise. For the first time, it crossed my mind that he might be envious of my success as a "journalist," the profession that had been his dream while he had served in the Austrian army, but had renounced to join his father's business.

* * *

By the time I was on the plane from Vienna to Rome, I put that week of Viennese schmaltz and hypocrisy behind me. Instead, I savored the familiar mayhem greeting me at Fiumicino, Rome's airport. Why did I feel so comfortable in this clatter and commotion, so relieved to exchange Austrian duplicity for Italian cunning? Yes, Italians too fleece their foreigners, but their Machiavellianism can be hilarious. Of course, I am biased; like Ignazio Silone, I clue into their "feigned exaggerated gaiety, [their] awkwardness [and] passion for women, for food, for their country, and, above all, for fine-sounding words."[12] I found Austria's "wine, women and songs" more scripted than Italy's "*dolce vita*," its *machismo* more genuine than Austria's—whose shopkeepers tended to imitate the Habsburgs' courtly manners; and its women's pushy coyness, à la Arthur Schnitzler, many with a heavy touch of anti-Semitism. In any event, my upcoming Italian year promised to be enlightening in a country that never lacks in surprises.

Still, that August, family matters predominated. After a leisurely jaunt along the Amalfi drive with Norman, we picked Allen up at Rome's airport: he had spent the month of July at a camp in New Hampshire. A few days later, Norman's two daughters arrived. Anna, prettier than her younger sister Antonia, who was Allen's age, was a handful. In the hills above Forte dei Marmi, the children played and fought, both verbally and physically. Only after Anna had coaxed Allen to retrieve a handkerchief she had dropped out of her window, and he had fallen into a wasp's nest, did they get along a bit better.

Vivien had been on a trip through Northern Africa, where she had escaped more dangers than even I had foreseen. Only gradually did she tell about some of her close calls—of the romantic setting in a Spanish cemetery, where three guys had driven away with her and her two friends' possessions—including their shoes; about the Frenchman who nearly had raped her in Tangiers; and about the seductive Egyptian who almost had stolen her return ticket to Italy. Still, how could I not value her new ability to apply mascara in the artful manner of the women in Morocco's harems?

In September, Norman and I settled down in Turin, in a comfortable studio apartment, the *Casalbergo*, not far from the Agnelli Foundation. I was assigned to a spanking new and perfectly equipped office, with bookcases all around, and a view of the lawn in front of my wall-size window. As a fellow, I was entitled to secretarial and library services, and was the designated American "expert."

Under these circumstances, my 120 requests for interviews with family owned, medium-size entrepreneurs in the provinces of Lombardy, Piedmont, and Veneto had been mailed without delay. Among them, sixty turned out to be suitable. Before then, I had designed my questionnaire, and had gotten in touch with Flavia Derossi, a highly intelligent industrial sociologist. She was a friend of Mara Mosca, my former Italian teacher. Flavia praised my questionnaire, but said that in Italy, you cannot ask people whom they voted for: "This is a very personal question, it is even against the law to ask it, and you might well be thrown out of some offices for posing it." When I told her that this item was crucial for my study, that I expected to focus, among other things, on political changes due to the major workers' strikes in the "hot autumn" of 1969, she suggested: "If you have to ask, tone down this question, and keep it for the end, just in case." I followed her advice. As it turned out, none of my respondents threw me out, but I did get many cagy responses. I published the book some years later.[13] But in that scholarly study I could not convey that my spirits rose when drifting through an abundance of colorful foliage and blooms on winding paths, when slowing down in alleys of cypress trees, or when traversing a secluded orchard while in search of a forlorn village. Invariably, in such hamlets, my respondents would tell me, proudly, of their ancestors' exploits that had started in a barn, a lean-to or a kitchen; and when and how they had expanded production, built the mansion they now inhabited—next to a textile plant, a shoe factory, or a foundry.

Many of these off-the-beaten-paths boasted of no known tourist attractions: they were quiet havens with splendid sunsets and secluded grottos. Despite the countrywide workers' strikes in 1969, rural entrepreneurs expected to preserve their relaxed way of life. Some asked me how they might be able to reinstitute industrial peace, now that labor relations had broken down; profits had shrunk; and Italian unemployment had jumped through the ceiling, while its compensation (nine months full pay) had contributed to the inflationary spiral they had to cope with. The majority of respondents also decried the demise of paternalistic relations—which massive unionization, and new laws, had destroyed. They felt deeply hurt by their workers' actions. How would they manage to *arrangiarsi*—that is, to muddle through, legally or illegally.

No two of my respondents were alike. Most of them had traveled extensively, many owned *pied-a-terres* in Milan. Even the manufacturer of machine tools who bragged that he had stopped school after fourth grade, spoke French and was knowledgeable, however superficially, of European history. Many said they belonged to the Liberal party (its tenets are close to those of our Republicans), and nearly as many were Social-Democrats; an impeccably dressed "anarchist" drove up to our meeting in a souped-up Ferrari; and neither of the two members of the Communist Party saw any conflict between their self-interest and their ideology. Luigi Barzini might have argued that they probably were expressing loyalty to strong (Mafia?) friends, whom every successful Italian needs to survive.

*   *   *

During my life with Robert I had learned to keep house Italian style; and to diplomatically refuse propositions—this time by my respondents. The researchers at the Fondazione Agnelli who were conducting their Valetta project—which was to help entrepreneurs and managers to become more sensitive to social needs— invited me when world renown economists and political figures came to give talks, which put me into the right place, at the right time. (Only some professors at The New School had trouble understanding that my entrepreneurs were Catholic rather than Protestant, and worked hard while adhering to the pope's dicta.) When I wanted to interrupt my routine, I spent a weekend with Maria Assunta Graziano in Tortona, or with Franka in Arona or in Crans-sur-Sierre.

Norman was an esteemed member of the Left. Thus, he (and I) met with its luminaries, such as the philosopher, Norberto Bobbio, the sociologists Franco Ferrarotti, Paolo Farneti and Allessandro Pizzorno. When he received an invitation to the (closely guarded) fiftieth anniversary celebration of the founding of the Italian Communist Party (PCI), in Rome, I was allowed to come along. Norman was pleased to recognize the leaders and theorists of the various factions—from Enrico Berlinguer to Gian Enrico Rusconi, from Palmiro Togliatti to Luigi Longo—who were among the approximately 100 participants. After I remarked that the morning's speaker had read a long paper, to which the afternoon speaker had responded with yet another prepared paper, and that the atmosphere among the panelists was strained, Norman told me that such trivia was unimportant. But when Franco Ferrarotti, who for a time had been a deputy of the Socialist Party in the Italian government showed up and made a similar comment, he only nodded. This experience reminded me of my brushes with communists in Milan, and I began to read yet more about the ins and outs of, and the strong disagreements within, the Partito Communista Italiano (PCI).

Vivien came over during her Christmas break, and we once again visited Rome and Sicily, on a whirlwind tour of archeological sites. All went fairly well, until, at Norman's insistence, I took the right rather than the left fork on our way from Siracusa to Agrigento, and we got lost. Even worse, after daring to take a shortcut down a shallow staircase, its bottom exit was blocked by stone pillars. I had to back up on these steps: after ordering the children off the backseat and unloading our luggage, I drove while Norman applied and released the emergency brakes in sync with my use of the gas pedal. The entire street's population emerged on their stoops to loudly cheer me on. I was afraid only that I might run over a child that came too close—and to end up being lynched. By then tempers were short, and got even shorter after we found out that our hotel was out of rooms and out of food. Just before midnight, we finally were settled in two tiny maids' rooms. Once again, I wondered why I still was so fond of Italy, and of Norman. That morning, I had my answer: the Valley of the Temples and the archeological museum, in that green landscape next to the sea, were as irresistible and memorable as had been our visits to Palermo, Taormina, and Catania. Although we looked for signs of the Mafia, we didn't find any.

*　*　*

Throughout that fall, I drove to see Allen across the treacherous St. Bernard Pass, or via its tunnel. (Only many years later did he let on that he had been unhappy: and that his roommates were giving him a hard time because he was Jewish.) One Saturday morning in November, my car was the only one braving the snow while descending into Switzerland. All went well, until I missed seeing a patch of ice in the Rhône valley, and my car spun around and around on its axis. Luckily I was not hurt. However, a few months later, I slipped while walking to a pre-ski lunch with Allen and his friend, Jeffrey Stefani, and broke my left arm in five places. (After his mother, Elinor, nursed me for a week, I returned to Turin. But the arm needed to be re-broken, and reset at the hospital in Aigle.) Was I accident prone, or just unlucky? Norman left for Paris. Flavia lent me her loden cape and invited me to dinner and the movies. Every day, I dragged myself to my office to work on my thesis.

Fortunately, I already had interviewed all of my entrepreneurs. By 1972, the workers had won many concessions, and Italy's industrial miracle appeared to be over. And yet, when I revisited my respondents in 1977, their versatility, combined with persistence and pride, had kept them going: they had employed managers and enlarged their production and foreign markets; had fired their workers and hired them as (unregistered) subcontractors; put sons in charge; and were cheating even more on taxes than they had earlier on. However, my shoe manufacturers, unable to compete with Korean and Czech labor, had gone bankrupt. They all told of having drastically curtailed their lifestyle in response to the threat of "kneecapping by communists and/or crooks." But somehow they managed to stop that sort of terrorism. Still, Italy's inflation has not gone away any more than have the volatile spirits of Italians.

When my cast was about to be removed, my Swiss surgeon suggested that I get therapy in New York. I did during Allen's Easter vacation, at the Rusk clinic for rehabilitation. Indeed, this was a good move, since Allen now could be interviewed and tested at the Dalton School—where he entered seventh grade the following September.

*   *   *

At New York dinner parties, especially at Charles (Chuck) and Betty Fischer's, I met psychoanalysts who had read my *Commentary* article. (Then, most people shied away from mingling with "shrinks"—afraid that they might be "analyzed" while at table with them.) To reciprocate, Norman suggested we invite the Fishers to dinner, together with Edna and William Phillips, the editor of *Partisan Review*. "After you get to know William and the circle of writers around him," Norman informed me, "you'll never want to have any other friends. They are more intelligent than run-of-the-mill academics, even than psychoanalysts."

On the following Saturday evening, upon answering the doorbell to my spacious but somewhat threadbare Park Avenue apartment, a medium-size woman with dark hair hesitantly lingered in the doorway, while making elaborate excuses for being late. Her husband, in a dark shirt, knit woolen tie and tweed jacket stood two steps behind her. He loosely swung his walking stick, while peering over his wife's shoulder. Soon he interrupted: "Why don't you go in, you're a roadblock," which I thought of as rude from this white-haired, self-possessed man. Given my nomadic education, I didn't know that William Phillips had co-founded *Partisan Review*—the magazine he edited—and that every serious young American writer wanted to be published by him. Nor did I fully find out for years, the extent of his incisive judgment of situations and people the moment he laid eyes on them—which he was hiding beneath his sharp wit and ability to entertain. Or that among his intimates in England had been (and were) George Orwell, Stephen Spender, and Doris Lessing. Or that he and his co-editor, Philip Rahv, had been the ones to first publish Delmore Schwartz, Saul Bellow, Ralph Ellison and Czesław Milosz, as well as Sartre, Camus, and Raymond Aron in the United States. Of course, I had read essays that had appeared in *Partisan Review* in conjunction with my sociological studies, but had not known that William Phillips had had to vet or solicit them.

As soon as the Phillips's entered, Norman introduced everyone, and it was clear that our guests knew of each other. Since William had edited a collection on *Art and Psychoanalysis* (1957), the table talk should have been easy and cordial. But when Chuck was about to tell William about his most recent dream research, William indicated, somewhat impatiently, that he already had read all about it. Norman's various stabs at political chitchat also fell on deaf ears, if only because in an editorial, William had deplored the low level of such table talk. But Norman kept on trying to find topics that might engage both honored guests. Clearly, Chuck had not read *Partisan Review* in some years, and William refused to report on what could be read in his magazine. So, they fell back on praising my *blanquette de veau*, which was about the only topic agreeable to everyone. I vaguely realized that that was why William, on my left, spent much of the evening worrying about my injured arm, told me about the thumb he had broken a few years before then, and made a point that either he or Norman had better volunteer for kitchen duty. (As yet, I had no clue to the fact that both of Chuck's and William's wives were rather quiet, not only because that is what the wives of prominent men were supposed to be, but because they were angry that their husbands had serious girlfriends.) All in all, this was only the first time that I spent an entire evening with people of distinction whose small talk was no different than that of less exalted ones.

*   *   *

By the time we returned to Europe, my arm was fairly usable; I had been asked to review Nathan Hale's *Freud and the Americans*,[14] to write an essay about Italian sociology for the Sociological Review, and one on Italian universities for Change: The Magazine for Higher Learning. And after a talk I gave at the Agnelli Foundation on *il sistema imprenditoriale italiano*, they wanted it for their bi-monthly publication. Even though my thesis would not be accepted for another year, I already was treated as the professional I aspired to become.

After two more uneventful months in Turin, Allen, Vivien, and I left for Santa Margherita. There we frolicked with old friends: Pietro and Pinuccia Pecora and their children; the Grazianos, the Stahls. Ing. Fedelini, who had been Robert's boss on two of his projects, also came to see us. This tall northern Italian, in natty clothes and with a crew cut *al'americana*, had tears come to his eyes while we looked out on the peaceful Mediterranean. He complained that ever since Robert's death, his own career had gone downhill. Did he not realize that I had been hit even harder than he? Or, that while Robert was alive, he primarily had been concerned to get credit for Robert's achievements? I marveled at his narcissism and kept silent.

At the end of July, we returned to the U.S. and rented a cottage at the Stefanis' Colony of Wellfleet. I took Allen, Jeffrey Stefani and Ken Lifton for sailing lessons, and went swimming every afternoon, often at Lewis and Rose Coser's pond. I particularly admired Lew: he could compete with the best sociologists when it came to theory and to its jargon, yet his writing was totally accessible to laymen. I then did not know that he had started out as a journalist, and that in the 1940s already had written for *Partisan Review*, under the pseudonym Louis Clair.

On mornings I worked and stewed about my dissertation. Norman and Bob Lifton were planning a meeting about psychohistory. Erik Erikson was to be the honored guest, and it seemed that whom to leave out was as important as it was to decide whom to include, and to seat Erik at the head of the conference table, and Bob opposite him. But Erik soon upset these plans by moving next to me onto one of the couches—that were set up for wives and other onlookers. This was only the beginning of unforeseen snafus.

In retrospect, I believe, that the eventual splits among the so-called New York intellectuals were foreshadowed that day. Of course, I did not yet grasp anyone's underlying motives and ideologies. But I do recall a disagreement between the foremost German psychoanalyst, Alexander Mitscherlich, and the sociologist, Richard Sennett, about the consequences of architectural design on the inhabitants of cities. And that the Yale literary critic, Peter Brooks, commented in terms that clearly were derived from French structuralism. William Phillips dismissed it as French rhetoric and as "bullshit"—before getting into explaining why. Bob, as moderator, kept deferring to Erik, who didn't want to commit himself, and, once in a while, threw in something on one or another of the stages of life. Now that he was physically de-centered, he was fairly relaxed. Not so the persons around the table, who had their backs to him: they had to swivel back and forth, crowd onto a couch or pull up chairs. The basic problem, however, was that almost none of the participants had a prepared talk.

The political was mixed into the personal, at least for me, when, while wading in Great Pond, the psychoanalyst Margaret Brenman told me that there were troubles in every marriage—an indication that Norman had told her that I was about to leave him—without saying why I was unable to stay. Apparently he also had informed the Mitscherlichs while in Frankfurt, the Eriksons while passing through Stockbridge, and the Liftons. That Caroline was living with Richard Sennett and about to break up her long-time relationship with William was not yet an open secret—when Norman and I met William and Edna for dinner.

Although I still was extremely shy at talking up from the floor, I could not contain myself when, during the Liftons huge party, that was more like a political rally, Noam Chomsky said that one had to encourage students to protest—even to the point of laying down on a railway track while awaiting an oncoming train. I said that a young Italian demonstrator had been killed that way. He dismissed this as okay, or worthwhile, if it had furthered the cause.

On the following morning I left for the American Sociological Association meetings in New Orleans. There, I made up with Norman, presented a paper, and looked for a job. I was offered an adjunct teaching position in Hunter College's department of sociology. The pay was minimal, but having a foot on the lowest rung of the academic ladder made me feel high. Except when I thought of the hurdles to my Ph.D.

Bad Gastein, 1958
with parents

Ernst Weisz

Edith and Hans

Mimi Weisz

With Robert in Rome, 1959

Robert

Brussels World Fair, 1958
with our four children

William in the late 1960s

William with Czeslaw Milosz

Conference at the 92nd St Y, 1980s
(Roger Shattuck on right)

William in Wellfest, 1980s

Edith, 1990

Part III

17

How I Became a Professor and an Editor

While strolling to Hunter College, I walked on air. I over-prepared for my courses in Introductory and Industrial Sociology, and was worried that my students might not like me. They did. But why did the lanky, blue-eyed Debbie fall asleep by 9:30 A.M.? What could I do to keep her interest? When I hesitatingly asked her, she said that she "falls asleep for all her teachers," because her roommates, a bunch of nursing students, start talking when they get in at two in the morning. Somewhat relieved, I suggested that she ask for another room. A week later, she idled up to me, and wondered whether I had noticed that she now remained awake.

But more serious troubles arose, due to the newly instituted open admissions. For instance, after a sweet little girl from somewhere in the South ate her pencil during the midterm exam, and produced just a one half-page run-on sentence, I asked the chairman, Nelson Foote, to get her extra help. He was sympathetic, but advised me that there was no money for such instruction.

We all came to know soon enough the disastrous consequences of this well-meant policy—for students who floundered and gave up, for professors who lowered their expectations, and for universities that kept dropping admission standards. At the time, however, my liberal and well-meant enthusiasm blinded me.

That fall, Norman and I occasionally had dinner with Edna and William Phillips. I liked them, but was embarrassed when Norman made provocative statements that William contradicted, especially when it concerned the early days of *Partisan Review*. As yet, names such as Delmore Schwartz, Isaac Rosenfeld and Lionel Abel did not mean much to me. I listened more closely when they mentioned Daniel Bell, Daniel Patrick Moynihan or Michael Harrington—some of whose books I had studied. One evening, during a visit to the Phillips's comfortable apartment in a run-of-the-mill brownstone on West 11th Street, while Edna brought out cheese and hors d'ouevres, Norman once more began to talk about the CIA's funding of Encounter. When he heckled by intimating that *Partisan Review* also might have received such secret funding, William got angry.

"Why were we always so poor, while Mel Lasky was rolling in money? He had a grand apartment in Paris, and flew to London for lunch whenever he felt like it. And he could afford to pay writers much more than we could. Governments have no business meddling in literary matters. Still, how can you go on believing that America doesn't need a secret service," he continued, "since the Russians were (and still are) winning the propaganda war, especially among intellectuals? Just look at yourself."

This was only the first time I would hear William explain that he was against the CIA's secret funding of cultural magazines. But when reflecting on the issue, he would say that he didn't know of any way that a democratic society could counteract the clandestine influence wielded by its totalitarian enemies.

That November, William and Edna invited us to a reception for Doris Lessing. Upon entering the fairly dark hallway of the building, we walked upstairs to a party in full swing: the Phillips's two large rooms were stuffed with writers, journalists and politicians whose names often appeared in the press, whose books I had come across, but few of whom I had met. I recognized Lillian Hellman and Hannah Arendt, and saw eager hands stretched out towards Doris Lessing. She was standing with her back against the fireplace. I was too shy to enter into a conversation with persons I didn't know, or to approach any of the celebrities. I felt out of place. Since Norman was in his element, I decided to leave by myself. But William stopped me in the doorway.

"I read the article you had in *Commentary*, about the psychoanalysts' meetings in Vienna. That must have been quite a show," he said while looking at me somewhat quizzically.

"But tell me, did all these psychoanalysts really suck up to Anna Freud as much as you indicate?"

"Yes, they did," I said. "But I was more annoyed at the Viennese. Since I was born there, I couldn't help but understand its citizens' two-faced remarks. Also, when I had dinner with my former nanny, she talked about the Austrians' ingrained, knee-jerk anti-Semitism, and its distrust of intellectuals and especially of psychoanalysts."

"You must tell me more about that, but at some other time," William said while gesturing at the mob in back of us. Still, where do you think psychoanalysis is going from here?"

I had just come across a book about encounter groups, which then were the most recent therapists' fad. Hesitantly, I told him that, for the most part, these pseudo-therapies might be harmless, and did serve as a way for singles to meet potential mates, but that they might be dangerous for disturbed persons who truly needed professional help. I also mentioned that there had been a number of suicides that might well have been "helped along" by such encounters.

"Why don't you write about this trend for *PR*," he suggested. I was flattered and agreed.

Between Thanksgiving and Christmas, Norman and I split up for the last time. Arthur Vidich, the chairman of my thesis committee, was putting me through the wringer—mostly by changing his mind about the focus of my introduction—from Italian history to types of organizations, to economic history, to entrepreneurship and to industrialization. (He believed that no more than two students per year ought to be granted their Ph.D.—to uphold the discipline's reputation.) After a frustrating year, I sent him a long letter summarizing this harassment, and ended up by stating that I would follow his latest suggestion, but that that was it. And I sent a copy to the dean, Joseph Greenbaum. He intervened. Eventually, we agreed to get outside readers, and after more back and forth settled on the sociologist Lewis Coser and the political scientist Juan Linz. (I was forbidden to get in touch with them.) After they sent in favorable reports, and I had a few more contretemps with my chairman, my thesis was accepted—one week before the deadline. Now, I hired a copyeditor.

Under the circumstances, I couldn't think about encounter groups, and was convinced that having left Norman, William wouldn't want me to write for him anyway. Reluctantly, I called him to check.

"Of course I want this piece, just go ahead with it," he told me rather gruffly. On that Saturday, while my copyeditor and I were pouring over my dissertation, and Allen was watching television, William phoned: "How is that piece coming along," he asked.

"I don't know how to start it," I said, "and I can't really concentrate on it before I have handed in my thesis. I'm busy copyediting it."

"If it's all right with you, I'll come over to discuss this piece with you," he replied. Since I had had a few colleagues for beef stroganoff the night before, and had leftovers, I invited him to join us.

William arrived about an hour later. I don't recall what we talked about during this awkward dinner. We didn't linger, if only because William said he was not hungry, my helper wanted to get on with her work, Allen was eager to get back to his television program, and I was nervous about obtaining the Ph.D., on which my prospects for a regular teaching job, and my financial security, depended.

After William and I went back to the living room, he somewhat perfunctorily asked about the state of my dissertation, and soon moved our conversation to the article he wanted. I showed him *Encounter Groups: First Facts.*

"Why don't you review this book," he said after leafing through it, "and bring in what you think of the phenomenon, just as you told me about it the last time we met. Keep it simple and use the book to make your points."

He made it sound easy. Now that this problem, at least for William, was solved, he switched gears.

"When you left my madhouse of a party," he started, "you said that you would tell me what it was like to grow up in Vienna. But I don't see how you can remember any of it, you must have been a baby."

Though flattered, and not wanting to give away my age, I let on that I recalled not only traumatic events after the Nazis marched in, but many incidents of my earliest childhood—that had seeped into consciousness during my analysis.

"You cannot possibly recognize in me the child and adolescent I was before the Anschluss," I went on. "Maybe that is why I occasionally sound defensive of Freud, especially when his thoughts are being attacked by people who haven't read anything by him."

Now, I let on that I had immersed myself in Freud's works at the age of seventeen.

"Who was your analyst," he interjected. I said that he was an M.D., but not a strict Freudian, was analyzed by Erich Fromm and belonged to the William Alanson White Institute.

"Hm. I went to a European woman, a senior member of the New York Psychoanalytic Society. They're the best," he stated, while shaking his head somewhat astonished. He hinted that Norman had come to see him, and had told him that he was unhappy about our breakup. I briefly said something about finding the sort of yo-yo relationship Norman needed too hurtful. As one thing led to another, he implied that he too felt upset, because the woman he had been close to for nearly ten years had left him. (I had heard vague rumors of that.) After a long pause, William asked me how I had come to this country.

I didn't know where to start, and felt tongue-tied about telling this relative stranger at the other end of my L-shaped couch about the troubled relations with my family, which I was unable to separate from that story.

Nor did I want to paint the fake picture of a happy family my mother routinely presented to the world. So I recounted fragments of my escape, mostly of the nearly missed connections in France and Spain.

In 1973, there was little public interest in Holocaust survivors. I still tried to be as American as the proverbial apple pie. Thus I had relegated these experiences to the Ditta of my childhood. I also assumed that only those who had gotten away from the death camps could be called "survivors." In fact, William had touched a subject I still tried to ignore. I don't recall exactly what I told him on that cold spring evening. But I remember that I felt attracted to him, and anxious. He was married and I liked his wife. So, I was determined not to get involved. Still, as soon as he was gone, I looked forward to seeing him again.

*   *   *

William called me the following day and wondered whether we might be able to meet for lunch, and that he wanted to hear more about my hair-raising escape. We met at the Right Bank, a small, informal place two blocks up from my office on Madison Avenue. There was something mysterious in his straightforward manner. He was an enigma. We arrived almost simultaneously, and William seemed preoccupied. He told me that his stomach was out of sorts, and that I shouldn't pay attention if he were to fiddle with his walking stick. He took a long time over ordering his tuna sandwich. (I did not yet know just how fussy an eater he could be.) After that was taken care of, he asked me to tell him more about my escape from Europe. Not wanting to keep talking about myself, I countered by asking him about where he and his pals had stood while the French were deporting their Jews, and the Germans were bombing London and strutting around Paris.

"It was complicated," he said, "we didn't have reliable information about the ins and outs of the war, and although we all were strongly anti-fascist, we couldn't agree on what position to take. The magazine primarily was literary, and we were modernists as well as Marxists. And anti-Stalinists. Both the Allies and the Axis basically were capitalist states. Personally, I would have wanted to vote for getting into the war against Hitler, but I knew that I would not be drafted because I have a bum leg, a leftover from the polio I had as a child. (He now pointed with his stick to the double-sole on his left shoe.) So, I didn't think it was fair of me to send others to fight. But this is not the whole answer, and I may be making excuses for myself. In fact, our editors took a variety of

positions. You can read about some of them in the editorials and ex-
changes we published at the time.

Still, I want you to know that I couldn't sleep last night, thinking of
how irresponsible we were—while kids like you were running for your
lives. By 1942, if I recall correctly, Dwight (Macdonald) and Clem
(Greenberg), who were on our editorial board, argued that America had
to remain neutral rather than support England. Philip Rahv and I, gradually, agreed that we had to fight Hitler. We split up over this issue, and
Dwight started his own magazine. Before then, we had printed a statement
to the effect that Partisan Review had 'no editorial line on the war, only
individual positions.' Sure, I heard rumors about the Holocaust, and at
the time Edna and I got a few people to send affidavits (we were too poor
to give them ourselves),[15] but we didn't experience any of the hardships.
We did solicit reports from England, by Stephen Spender, George Orwell
and some other Europeans. Of course, we did not have any direct lines
to our government. In any event, I would never have been able to cope
as you did," William concluded categorically.

"When you have the devil at your back, you just know you have to
run. Fortunately, I ran fast enough and was lucky a thousand times over,"
I said. "Somehow, I always trusted trustworthy people—people whose
vibes go out to youngsters" I added, and went on to ask about his relations with the communists, which I had not always clued into, in some
of the arguments he had had with Norman.

"Yes, we had a terrible time with them, not only when we split off
and restarted the magazine in 1937, but during the McCarthy period.
Both Rahv and I were called before the House of Un-American Activities Committee (HUAC). They had all the names, and we knew them as
well. But neither of us cooperated by giving them to the interrogators:
we were against these tactics as much as against the communists. Still,
in this country you never had to worry about your life, unless you were
Leon Trotsky, only about getting or keeping a job, or going hungry," said
William. (I took note that I had better read more about the depression
era, and about who was who among American leftists.)

After a long pause, we switched the conversation to my need for a job,
and to my review for Partisan Review. That review[16] became the reason
(or excuse) for us to get together rather frequently. We went walking in
Central Park, or met for coffee and cake in one of the German pastry
shops on East 86th Street, such as Bremen House or Café Geiger. When
I finally hunkered down to writing the review, I consulted William when
I thought I might be too critical, or too simplistic. He kept egging me

on to give it my all. I was fascinated by his mercurial mind, and by his facility of blurting out what came into his head, in his idiosyncratic way. (Mary McCarthy's son, Reuel, recently told me that when he was a little boy, and William had visited them for a day in Wellfleet, William had been the center of attraction.)

At the end of one of our lunches, while ambling up on Madison Avenue towards home, to 87th Street, I saw a typical Chagall—all primary colors—in the window of the Seidenberg gallery as we were about to cross 79th Street.

"That's a wonderful painting," I exclaimed.

"What do you know about painting," William countered in a rather aggressive tone. I was taken aback, and began by telling him that I had wanted to be a painter; that I had attended Saturday classes at the Art Students League for a year or two, in figure drawing and oil painting; and that sporadically, here and there, had taken lessons at Queens College, and with a teacher. I went on to add that I had visited many a museum in Italy, and that Robert had been an admirer of de Kooning, and had introduced me to Rothko's color fields at an exhibition somewhere on 57th Street before we were married. (Only years later did I realize that William knew the ins and outs of the Western history of art, that he had been writing, critically and in the vanguard, about artistic traditions as far back as 1935, and that my practical familiarity might well have meant nothing to him.) William mellowed. I did not yet know that this was not his customary reaction to amateurs.

"You don't have to get so defensive," he said, "I was just asking a question."

He went on to inquire about what else I had done in Italy, and was impressed— overly so, I believed—with my command of languages.

"That's no big deal," I explained, "after all, German was my native tongue. I had to learn French while in a Belgian pensionnat in order to get along, and English to make my way in America. When I planned my trip to Europe, in the summer of 1956, I decided to return to Queens College to get a smattering of Italian. (Not only to learn that language, but to work towards the B.A. I had dropped when getting married.) How else was I to get a sense of what people were talking about?"

Our meetings brought us closer. William seemed to appreciate that I was a neophyte in his world, and that I had a certain amount of savvy about things European. I found him fascinating, unpredictable and appreciated his quick and whimsical take on serious questions. After one of our walks in Central Park, I received a phone call from Barbara Probst Solomon.

We had met through Norman, and as two widows with young children, we got together—often for Sunday lunch at the Russian Tearoom, and for occasional dinners. We commiserated about problems widows with children faced, and she told me about her active sex life.

"You have been seen holding hands with William Phillips in Central Park," she began angrily, "and you ought to know that he is married, and always has two women, sometimes three." Barbara went on giving me the lowdown on him, and berating me at length. (He had already alluded to having had [mostly meaningless] relationships, that two or three of these had been serious, and that he remained loyal to Edna—even though there had been problems and ambivalences in the marriage almost since the beginning.)

I was upset by Barbara's attack, and mentioned it to William. He joked about it and calmed me down. But a few weeks later he was less laid back, while pulling an invitation to Barbara's home from his pocket. It was for the book party she had been consulting me about—in honor of the sports writer Roger Kahn, with whom she then was going out.

"I never go to most of these book parties," William began in his most disgruntled tone, "and I won't go to this one." He feigned surprise when I said that I had not been invited.

"Maybe the letter was lost," he speculated with a touch of irony. I did not want to ask Barbara about it, but William went on to say:

"I will stop respecting you if you don't at least find out from her why she is cutting you out." So I called Barbara. She claimed that the publishers, who allegedly were cosponsoring the event, did not want to have too many people. (I still was in the dark about the politics of book parties, and of literary "friends," but felt hurt.)

I soon forgot about Barbara, if only because William and I had become close; I had been offered a few teaching jobs; and had presented a paper at the Eastern Sociological Association before flying to Italy for a talk. And I was about to accept a professorship at Montclair State College.

Alexander Mitscherlich, who with his wife had reintroduced psychoanalysis to Germany after 1945, had asked me to write about the International Psychoanalytic Congress in Paris for Imago, and I planned to leave for Paris at the beginning of July. However, just two days before my scheduled departure, I fell down a flight of subway stairs, broke five bones of my left leg, and was forced to spend July and August in a heavy non-walking cast that extended from my crotch to my toes.

Fortunately, I had offered my apartment to Angela Zanotti, my Italian friend and fellow student from the New School, who now lived and taught in Rome. She made my breakfast and kept me company when she came home from her summer job at Queensborough Community College. William was sorry for me, and visited on many an afternoon. Angela, who was a staunch member of the Italian Communist Party (PCI), soon tried to—unsuccessfully—convince William that Italian communism did not follow Moscow's line. Then, Angela was certain that Enrico Berlinguer's communism was an exception, and was totally independent of Moscow. William, who in the 1930s, had been the secretary of the communist affiliated John Reed club (the equivalent of chairman) had known Stalin's representatives in the American Communist Party, and that they were receiving instructions from Moscow. He argued that there was no such thing as an independent PC. Still, neither William nor Angela wanted to upset me, their friend who was suffering from an itching cast, and from enforced bed rest. I tended to agree with William. But I stayed out of the fray by praising the Italian Socialists, especially Bettino Craxi.

Actually, they were enjoying their heated arguments. After William left, Angela commented on his distinguished looks and on his original ways of argumentation, and egged me on to pursue an intimate relationship with him.

"Why should you care that he is married," she stated, "since you said you never want to get married again? But, what is he afraid of," she nevertheless kept wondering, "didn't you notice that when I first walked in he scuttled to the corner of the room behind the door, trying to hide like a scared rabbit?"

*   *   *

By the beginning of September, Angela had flown back to Italy, William and Edna had returned from their vacation on Martha's Vineyard. I stopped feeling abandoned and no longer waited for the phone to ring. My cast had come off, and I began teaching in Upper Montclair. Still, when William complained that he did not have enough people to weed out manuscripts, I volunteered to drive down to the *Partisan Review* offices in New Brunswick on Wednesday afternoons. Selma Rudnick, who presided over the office and the work-study students, handed me a stack of fiction and essays. William's instructions were brief:

"Pass on whatever you think might be publishable."

After a few weeks, he went over my selections, discarded most of them as unusable, while judging one to be old news, and another one as repetitious and badly written. He then handed me an essay by a well-known sociologist, and asked me to take out the jargon and to put it into plain English. I labored over it, before daring to hand it to William.

"It reads well now," he said to my relief. "But does it say anything we don't already know," he went on. I had to admit that it did not. William rejected the essay, which had been solicited by Norman. This was my first lesson on how an editor makes enemies without trying. Soon, I found the loose atmosphere, the stimulation of reading manuscripts and learning to make literary judgments more challenging than most of what I had done up to then. Even sociology.

On Thursday afternoons, William conducted his poetry seminar. About a dozen students were sitting on chairs and at his feet in his office. When I occasionally came to listen in, I too was handed a pack of poems, all of whose authors' names had been removed. The students were asked to read these published and unpublished verses—some masterpieces, others of dubious quality. William, in his sonorous voice began to read each poem aloud. His listeners were spellbound, and soon associated to what they had heard, commenting about meaning, successful execution, rhythm, aim, and I don't recall what else. (I was silent, thinking of the poetry course I had taken during the scorching summer of 1944, when I had been asked to identify allegories and meter, alliteration and versification, pentameter and hexameter, and all sorts of other abstract concepts in medieval and romantic poems—without ever having properly heard them read. That experience had turned me off poetry.) Before the end of the session, William asked the class to rank each poem and to comment on their rankings. The ensuing discussions often lasted long after the end of class. I admired William's Socratic and relaxed way of reaching out, and of engaging every participant.

I was less impressed by the way he ran the office. In fact, I was struck by its havoc and inefficiency. Students and teaching assistants were walking in and out. William kidded around, and seemed to focus on where his lunch—of the best and least fatty, roasted or grilled, chicken— would be coming from, and which one of the teaching assistants was going to fetch it.

"If the four of us who are able to discard unusable manuscripts quickly were to spend one morning going through these five shelves of submissions," I timidly suggested one day, Selma would not have to spend so many hours answering calls by impatient writers." Halfheartedly, William agreed. We soon reduced the pile by three quarters. I found an accountant at one third of what was being paid for the yearly tax return. Of course, William spent most of his time on the phone, soliciting pieces for the magazine, or editing some he had on hand. He also took his afternoon nap, and a short walk when he woke up. (He did not yet speak to me of his money worries.) He relied on his managing editor to take care of office routines, and to set up public meetings.

By the time I arrived, managing editors were coming and going. William enlisted me to help select them. I recall the pleasant but depressed one, who quit in order to return to the husband she had left; the one who needed a dictionary on her lap when writing the letters William had dictated; the one who preferred sitting on the floor rather than at her desk; and yet another whom we didn't hire, and who then brought a formal complaint because William had asked her whether or not she was married. He was upset after having hired Rosalie. She not only "mixed everything up" but while taking dictation kept piercing overly ripe pimples on her face. William kept complaining about this to him disgusting habit, but neither had it in him to ask her to stop or to ignore it. Finally, on the afternoon she got off the phone with Philip Roth, and declared that after having talked to her idol she had to stop working for the rest of that day, he used the occasion as a pretext to ask her to leave.

"You're not firing me, I'm quitting, because the two of us don't get along," she announced haughtily. He sighed with relief. Finally, we hired Linda Healey, who became a close friend, and who, in 1978, however briefly, would move with us to Boston University.

18

Intellectuals' Friendships and Deceptions

I had slaved over my Ph. D.—my passport to academe. Sociology was thriving then, and sociologists didn't yet know that their successful splits into criminology, family studies, women's studies, organization theory, and endless other sections, would cause the breakdown of the discipline as a whole. As to myself, I still was keen, as my mother had been saying, to "dance at every wedding,"—because I assumed that I had to make up for all the years I had lost.

I was invited to Brussels to speak about Italian entrepreneurs. At the Fernand Braudel Center in Binghampton I met the luminaries of the *Annales* school, who first made me ruminate about the differences of discourse in Paris and New York. I befriended colleagues in Bled, Vienna and Uppsala, in Little Rock, Chicago and Oslo, and in Geneseo, Geneva and in Alpine resorts. The meetings of Historians of Psychoanalysis in Trieste, and the ones at the University of Southern California's (USC) Annenberg Center of Communications were memorable for their elegance. As was the reception after a heated conference of editors, again at USC, under the auspices of the *Nation*—at the home of a movie mogul, where white-gloved attendants parked guests' cars, served mountains of lobster, caviar and other delicacies to Greenwich Village characters who reviled capitalism and filled their bellies while carelessly leaning on Calder and Moore sculptures.

I came to reflect on the human condition under Communism while attending a feminists' conference in Dubrovnik, in June 1974—after an angry waitress refused to let me join a friend's table; a taxi driver declined to start his engine before receiving his tip; and where dirty tablecloths, cold coffee, and overbooked hotel registrations were the norm. Moreover, I had never met up with people who so aggressively pushed others to get onto a bus—as in that hauntingly beautiful city. (However briefly, the 1971 meetings of the International Sociological Association in Varna,

Bulgaria, crossed my mind—where all local women wore black kerchiefs, poverty was blatant, and heavy-set KBG agents who doubled as waiters kept Westerners and Eastern-bloc participants apart.)

* * *

From there, Rose Coser, Helena Lopata, Allen, and I departed for our first visit to Israel. While descending on Tel Aviv, tears unaccountably welled up in my eyes. Did the Jews really have a land that might save them from the next Holocaust? My brief brush with Zionism during Nazi times—unbidden—rushed through my mind.

In Jerusalem, the sociologist Rivka Bar-Yosef escorted us to religious and Arab quarters, introduced us to professors and high-ranking politicians, sent us off to Tel Aviv, to Masada, and to bathe in the Dead Sea—where Allen unearthed bones he thought were pre-historical. We ate in Arab restaurants, were driven by Arab cabbies, and upon leaving were thoroughly questioned (and searched) by El-Al's quick-witted interrogators. Clearly, nearly thirty years before 9/11/01, the country's security system already was in place.

Subsequent visits to Israel were more troubling, especially when, on the eve of the French-Israeli meeting of psychoanalysts, I asked the suave receptionist at the American Colony hotel for directions to the old city, down Nablus road.

"Don't go there," he said.

"Why not," I asked.

"Because there will be trouble," he responded. Shrugging my shoulders and thinking of the negotiations of 'land for peace,' I innocently asked: "When is that going to end?"

"Not until we win all of our country back," was this educated Palestinian's answer.

Ever since that day, I have been suspicious of "Oslo," "Camp David," and the other peace initiatives, although hoping against hope that my Israeli friends, most of whom belong to the Labor Party and have been willing to give up anything and everything for peace, know what is best for them.

In 1989, before participating at a conference in Tel Aviv, William and I spent a week at the Givat Ram campus of Hebrew University. During that stay, a member of the faculty was ambushed and killed. We were more shocked than our Israeli friends—who seemed to be used to living under threat. Our mood did not improve when during that conference Americans presented anti-American papers, and generalized from our left-right splits to those of Israeli society. William tried to intervene, but gave up after being dismissed as a fascist for contradicting this taken-for-granted bias. Since more than others, Israeli professors depend on travel to the West in order to keep informed, it may not even be calculation that makes them listen to our "politically correct" professors, who are nearly the only ones they meet.

* * *

Now, I routinely taught on weekdays, read manuscripts for *Partisan Review* and met William in New Brunswick and in town. I cooked less, and took in an *au pair* student. William shook his wise head, shrugged his shoulders, marveled at my energy, and got me to walk and swim. When I had gotten involved with him, I had not minded that he wasn't free. But as we were getting ever more intimate, and he spent half a week away from me and yet was jealous when he thought I might "meet a man" at a dinner party, or at a meeting, I was annoyed. But how could I stay angry when receiving a letter that begins:

> It is very difficult to write to someone whose existence is in doubt. This is my third letter [to Dubrovnik] and I haven't heard a word from you. I don't even know whether you've gotten my two letters. It's like sending a rocket into space though there at least one gets signals back. As you can see, I'm somewhat annoyed. It would seem to me you could spare a few minutes from the fascinating sessions to write at least a corroboration of your existence if not some news about what has been happening to you.

Before long, I actually liked seeing my friends when we weren't together, and my parents for Saturday dinners. I looked forward to my weekday "honeymoons" with William. He came with me to Wellfleet. I accompanied him to meetings of the Coordinating Council of Literary Magazines (CCLM), the organization he had set up at the behest of Roger Stevens, the first head of the National Endowment for the Arts (NEA).

In a letter to the representative of the government for NEA's literary program, Carolyn Kizer, William had written:

> Like you, I feel very strongly about the magazine project, and not because I'm connected with a magazine. As I've said many times, I'd support it strongly even if PR weren't involved. At the risk of sounding pompous, I'll say that it's just something the country should have done long ago.

Since I still was unaware of William's standing among the literary elite, and never had judged people by their reputations, I did not find it extraordinary that I regularly met writers and poets who were full of countercultural opinions. Among them were Kenneth Koch, Russell Banks, Mark Mirsky, Donald Barthelme, Elliot Anderson, Ronald Sukenik, Daniel Halpern, Charles Simic, and so on. The cheap dinners near Columbia University were expensive for William who—however annoyed—always ended up with the check. I was bothered only by sensing the rivalries among them, by their ambivalence to William, and mostly by my own ignorance.

The first time I accompanied William to the 1974 CCLM's meetings in San Francisco, already about one thousand little magazines had been founded. There, the government's representative, Leonard Randolph, whose poems had been rejected by *Partisan Review*, attacked William brutally from the dais, and not only in the name of regionalism. Had Randolph not been restrained he would have physically knocked him down. Others denigrated William as a member of the establishment. There were women who accused him of sexism, and newly minted editors who deemed him "elitist." One of them came to our room, trying to convince William that it was elitist to print and bind *PR* rather than mimeograph and staple it.

"What is the world coming to," was William's comment after he had more or less politely gotten rid of this upstart—who had created a magazine only after learning that government subsidies were in the offing. While staying in our room during official meetings, I answered countless phone calls asking me to put in a word with William, to appoint this caller to the about to be created panel that would take decisions out of the hands of the Board of Directors—the most "established" of the little magazines. The following year, in Winston-Salem, this panelists' board, led by Ishmael Reed, "kicked William upstairs," by elevating him to "honorary chairman." In another of his Dubrovnik letters to me, he states:

> Telling Jim Boatwright at lunch today about CCLM, about the possible destruction, made me sad, not only because it doesn't continue to exist like one's own writing or magazine. I guess this is why I think action is needed but not for me.

After CCLM had spent over half its budget on panelists' travel, the NEA decided to shut them down. Now, they pleaded with William to save the organization. Reluctantly, he went to Washington, came down with the flu, but won. And after he managed to get them a large Ford Foundation grant as well, *Partisan Review* was deemed too "established" for his erstwhile friends to receive any funding.

As could be expected, the increasing influence of friendships and ideology of the by now tenured activists of the late 1960s, soon invaded the NEA—via the choice of administrators and panelists. Still, we did not waver in our belief that Congress ought not to abolish our arts and humanities endowments, thereby upsetting, for instance, Hilton Kramer who, correctly, criticized the abominably low standards the grants by both endowments had reached. We argued that they needed to be fixed rather than abolished, if only because every civilized nation has to have, and is judged by, its advanced arts and intellectual activities.

So when a Yale University administrator asked William, confidentially, to evaluate the *Yale Review*, he gave it a better report than he thought it deserved, saying to me that "the more little magazines exist, the better this is for the literature of the country." This concern for literature, and his gut reactions to political issues, also led William to join, for instance, Penn Kemble at Freedom House to support the Contras; and to consider Ronald Radosh's and Robert Leiken's proposal for adding a political section to the magazine—which never managed to get financial support.

* * *

As sociologists became ever more engaged in women's liberation, and were supporting its most extreme advocates, the man-hating and bra-burning types, I thought they were going a bit far: my patriarchal father was so much more domineering than the husbands they were denouncing. In any event, when during a Sociologists for Women in Society (SWS) meeting it was suggested that we ought to know what the men were up to, I decided to focus on the classical and evolving theories that had appealed to me already in graduate school, when I had written well-received papers on Talcott Parsons and Claude Lévi-Strauss. Now, I kept wondering why French academics so easily could talk to colleagues in other than their own disciplines, and Americans could not. That led me to write a book on French intellectuals that would be original enough to get me tenure.[17]

Now, I frequently had to travel to Paris—not exactly an unpleasant experience. After combing that city's many bookstores, and much reading, I felt too antagonistic to Louis Althusser's "scientific Marxism" to want to interview him. I kept meeting Henri Lefebvre socially, and talked to Alain Touraine. Jacques Lacan already was too sick to receive me. I had spent time with Roland Barthes long before, at the Lefebvre's in Navarrenx and now interviewed him by phone. And I set up an appointment with Michel Foucault. Because William at that point was in Paris, I took him along, to the Collège de France. Foucault was mobbed by enthusiastic followers after his lecture, but soon escorted us to his spacious office.

(A handsome male student hovered in the back of the room and seemed to be smirking.) During this dialogue, William occasionally interrupted my theoretical questions by wondering about the political implications of Foucault's fairly careful answers.

When I began to present papers about Althusser's Marxism and about Foucault's approach to history, many leading colleagues came to listen: they wanted to learn about the radical political potential of French thought. Only years later did it occur to me that that was why I was invited to a number of job interviews, and eventually moved to Rutgers University.

*   *   *

While at the Rockefeller Foundation's Villa Serbelloni, in Bellagio, during the summer of 1977, I revived my Italian life—and came into daily contact with renowned American academics, such as the literary critic René Wellek, the political scientist Richard Rosecrance, the future Supreme Court justice Ruth Bader Ginsberg, and the former president of Cornell University, James Pearson. We all worked on long mornings and went swimming on hot afternoons. On many an evening, we presented our research. During our gourmet dinners, we often met high-ranking politicians and internationally syndicated journalists who held their meetings on cutting-edge and sensitive topics at the conference center on the property. (The oil crisis and international trade come to mind.) Towards the end of my stay, I visited the Grazianos in Tortona, and initiated the restudy of my entrepreneurs. (A few years later, that research resulted in a book.)[18]

My Bellagio companions frequently reminisced about the 1968 upheavals, so that I began to better understand what as a student I had only vaguely grasped. Unlike my fellow academics, I had not been inducted into the ways professors try to both undercut one another and cooperate, something that most resident students get via osmosis and absorb as part of their subject matter. Moreover, my habit of mulling over the many sides of each question had not lent itself to fully articulated politics: I tended to look for the flaws on all sides—which only added to my insecurity. Did this allow me to perceive what others missed? Or did I keep myself too open? Indeed, unlike most academics, I did not pursue just one or two specialties. I looked for larger trends. Like my young self, I still wanted to "know everything," but realized also that I never could fully catch up with the "area specialists." What's more, I aspired to write like the best of novelists, while mastering sociological language when publishing in professional journals. Increasingly, I tried to find a manuscript or two for consideration by *Partisan Review*, and possible participants for future conferences, wherever I found myself.

*   *   *

These peripatetic activities had kept me fairly ignorant of William's relations to the university. At *Partisan Review*'s Christmas parties I met his colleagues from the English department, who drowned whatever gripes they might have had in wine and the Christmas spirit. I chattered—as I did during receptions for visitors such as Frank Kermode, Christopher Lehman-Haupt and Stephen Spender. I knew that Richard Poirier chaired the English department and had brought the magazine to Rutgers in 1963, and that he had resigned from *PR*'s editorial board in 1971. William had a way of forgetting bygone quarrels and troubles. Every day brought new ones that required his attention. What else could an editor of an intellectual journal—that tried to get to the root of controversies—do? He spoke to writers who thought that their own pieces were more topical and important than everyone else's and ought to be published at once; he persuaded others that their articles would gain by cutting out repetitions; and inveigled yet others to write about to be hot topics.

At my first Advisory Board meeting, my first at Joanna Rose's apartment, I met the former president of the university, Mason Gross, and the soon to be deposed provost, Richard Schlatter. But they didn't say much when lunching with the wealthy people from whom we hoped to receive financial help, and who preferred to give advice rather than money. If they were aware that a few of William's colleagues were eager to take over the magazine before he was ready to retire, they did not let on. Thus William was stunned when Schlatter's successor, Kenneth Wheeler, invited him to his office to tell him that the university might not want to live up to the informal agreement he had had with the previous administration—to teach and put out *Partisan Review* for as long as he pleased and in exchange to leave the magazine and its archives to Rutgers University when he died. So, when William received a letter stating that he was expected to retire the following fall, in 1978, and that a younger generation would take over *Partisan Review* unless he were to find another sponsor, he blanched and disappeared into his office. He didn't speak of it to anyone for nearly a week.

My impulse, when facing a crisis, is to do something, anything at all. So I was unable to stand by while William appeared to be sleepwalking. After talking to him, Edna and Linda, I got in touch with the president of the New School, John Everett, to find out whether they would want to take on *Partisan Review*. He did, but without paying William a salary. Around then, Carolyn Rand Herron, the former managing editor, who now was at the *New York Times*, tried to take over the magazine. Together with her husband, Richard Sennett, a professor of sociology at New York University, she had gotten its president, John Sawhill, to back her. Now, William woke up. He called a few university presidents. They all wanted the magazine, but did not offer William a salaried teaching job. However, Bard College did not balk at his age.

We met and negotiated with its president, Leon Botstein, at least a dozen times, at New York's University Club and in Annandale-on-Hudson. After we had run the gauntlet of the English and sociology departments, the faculty offered us teaching positions. We settled on office space, salaries, and living quarters. When we met to finalize these arrangements with the Board of Trustees, they agreed to everything, but then insisted on owning the magazine. Since this meant that William could be fired at any time, we pulled out. By then, we had an offer from Boston University. They stipulated that the magazine be incorporated in Massachusetts, that two out of five directors of that entity be appointed by the university and that the *Partisan Review* papers—though not the personal ones—go to the Mugar Library. (It took three years to finalize details.)

* * *

When we were ready to move, the Rutgers librarian refused to release the magazine's files. In *A Partisan View: Five Decades in the Politics of Literature*, [19] William summarized the legal hassle that started on August 4, 1978, the day the movers came to pack up the unsold back issues. That morning, when William and I got to our office, we couldn't open the front door. He called the vice-president for real estate, who had been pushing us to vacate these premises. He arrived at once. He found an improperly closed window, crawled inside, and let us in. A few minutes later, the provost came running, while waving a letter by the president of the university. It informed William that all the files and whatever else he had on Rutgers property was being impounded. While they argued, I called our pro bono lawyer, Robert H. Montgomery. Bob was stunned, said that we were in America and not in Nazi Germany, and added that he wanted William to call him as soon as possible. William did. Within an hour, on a conference call with Bob, the provost and a Rutgers lawyer, they agreed that Rutgers would copy whatever items we needed to put out the next issue of *PR*.

"They can fire a professor," Bob maintained, "but in America they cannot close down a business."

William was devastated, looked ashen and ill. I talked him into taking a meprobromate, while Linda and I were dealing with the "authorities." The day seemed like a dance on a high wire: we didn't yet know that William had been betrayed by his (solicitous) friends. Linda and I tried to get out as much material as we might need to keep functioning. At one point, the graduate student, who had been brought in along with a huge copy machine, told William that he didn't want to be involved in this chicanery. But William convinced him to stay on, saying that he had better think of his own career, and that they just would find someone else to do that job. (In 1991, while serving on a search committee for the head of the Rutgers library system, a man on that committee sidled up to me to whisper that he had been that student.) All day long, Linda and I had to show the assistant provost, John Salapatas, every item that was to be copied. He had been put in charge to see that we would not steal what belonged to us. But he had no clue as to what PR was about, and why we needed whatever it was in order to go to press. In other words, we gave him a crash course in magazine publishing. For instance, when Linda playfully yelled across the room whether I wanted an unpublished manuscript of mine, he said that it belonged to the university—obviously a violation of copyright. When I had to go to my office, a policeman walked up the stairs ahead of me, which exposed the gun he had strapped to his leg. I began to shake.

Scenes from Nazi days flashed through my mind, and I wondered whether I would be getting the tenure I had been promised at Rutgers, Newark. This was my first semester: because I already was tenured at Montclair State College, I had been told that it would be a formality. But all tenure decisions had to be approved by the provost, by Kenneth Wheeler. We knew that William would have to sue the administration for his archives—as he did after we got to Boston University—which meant I would have to go on the stand as a material witness. Ultimately, I made it through that process, either on the strength of my curriculum vitae, or because Wheeler signed everything put in front of him. Still, I kept worrying that entire academic year.

Basically, the legal hassle revolved around the word "deposit." The rather casual 1963 letter of appointment to William for a one-year lecture-ship, with time off for editing the magazine, had stipulated that during that period he would deposit the files of *PR* in the library. Under these terms he had been reappointed year after year. The trial was held in New Brunswick about eight months later.

"Deposit does not mean give," was our lawyer's, Albert Bessie's, basic argument. On the second day, the judge, David Furman, told the Rutgers lawyers that they had no case, and asked them to settle in order to save the university embarrassment. After another day they capitulated. It was agreed that they were to ship everything they had impounded to Boston University, but could copy whatever files they wanted. In turn, William agreed not to speak to the press and to refrain from suing for personal damages. What a relief: I would not have to appear in court. As if by magic, the nausea and headaches that had been plaguing me for some weeks, disappeared. During our "victory lunch," William wondered how much worse businessmen would act. According to Bob Montgomery, they were "much more ethical than academics."

*   *   *

Before the end of the decade, I moved from my large Park Avenue apartment to a small one on the West Side. Instead of teaching in Upper Montclair I was teaching in Newark and New Brunswick—exchanging a suburban park for brick and cement, and for a more prestigious institution. I had delivered *The Age of Structuralism* [20] to my publisher. Allen was a student at Yale, and I had set up a Boston home with William. I worked on manuscripts, met with students, and was most contented when William came over. In my spare time, I read, trying to make up for lost time: guided by William, I developed literary judgment. Indeed, I now was integrating my sociological training and my practical and pre-academic background—not only for the benefit of PR, but for my own satisfaction. I had gotten used to William's "double life," especially after Edna and I came to recognize and accept that he needed each of us. (When he unexpectedly was hospitalized for a prostate operation, Edna called me; we sat together while he was in the operating room and then went out for dinner.)

After a month at Boston University, Linda went to live with her future husband, J. Anthony Lukas, in New York. Now, every Thursday, after I finished teaching in Newark, I caught the four o'clock plane to Boston from the nearby airport. As executive editor, I was responsible for the overall functioning of the office. William and I spent Thursdays to Saturdays in that beautiful, laid-back city. Whereas at Rutgers our office had been in charge of all details, including the disbursement of moneys, we now were on a university budget line. This added a great deal of paper work, since expenditures had to be requested on specific forms, and we were mandated to raise money for some of our routine expenses. Under the circumstances, I had to negotiate these terms, and to make sure that our two young assistants adhered to them.

To get a sense of Boston's intellectual life, we invited many of its leading figures for Friday afternoon discussions. Among the regulars, the philosopher Robert Nozick jogged over from Harvard, Daniel Bell was being driven over, Helen Vendler, Millicent Bell, Eugene Goodheart and Alasdair MacIntyre already were on campus, and Peter Berger was about to move there from Boston College. We went to the Harvard and St. Botolph clubs for dinner, attended concerts and plays, and dinner parties. But the English department remained inhospitable, with the exception of Eugene Goodheart, Millicent Bell, and two junior members. The others perceived us as "stooges of the administration," probably because we had arrived at a time when the faculty was particularly discontented, and was about to go on strike. William as yet was not teaching, and I was a one-day-a week staff person. We couldn't afford to close the office, even if we had wanted to, because we had to get the magazine to the printer. William didn't really mind these colleagues' neglect. He shrugged his shoulders, saying, "Who wants to bother with all that academic nonsense anyway?"

To welcome us, Vice President Gerald Gross invited us to lunch at the Hyatt Hotel in Cambridge, and John Silber asked us to a dinner party at his sumptuous home. I recall only that Keith Botsford and an award-winning actress were among the twelve guests. When the talk turned to our eventful departure from Rutgers, William, who was in one of his entertaining moods, recounted that the husband of one of my (Bellagio) friends, the Harvard historian, Barbara Miller Solomon, had said that in Massachusetts, the possession of a weapon without permission to carry it mandates a year's prison sentence. Was that true, and if so, how could he dispose of it? (In the confusion of our departure from Rutgers, it had been shipped to Boston University.)

"I'm thinking of dropping it into the Charles River," William mused, "but Edith says that it might be spotted, dredged up and identified."

"Where is that gun now," John Silber demanded in his most imperious voice.

"In the back of my closet in the office, behind some old clothes," William replied.

"Don't you know that keeping a gun on university property carries a mandatory sentence of one year," John Silber sternly replied.

After much back and forth, Keith thought he knew someone with a gun permit who might take it off our hands. William regretted giving away his cherished weapon. I, however, was worried that if a burglar were about to appear, William might accidentally shoot himself rather than the intruder. All ended well, when a week or so later, two university policemen came to pick up this worrisome object. They drove it, along with a frightened William, to the apartment of the man who did have a gun license.

Now, we could truly settle in. For a while we added Daniel Bell and Leon Wieseltier to our editorial board. During these meetings, Dan talked a mile a minute, Leon did his best to keep up with him, and William interrupted with clever verbal undercuts. We were unsuccessful in setting up a Boston Advisory Board. Why support a little New York magazine, our contacts implied, when they had obligations to Harvard and to its many institutes? Also, Gerald Gross, who originally had promised to help raise funds, became more and more involved with getting the Huntington Theater off the ground.

All in all, we liked the calm of this beautiful city, yet were a bit taken aback when some of its inhabitants kept asking: "How can you possibly keep living in New York?" William's pat answer was: "I don't. I live on the New York-Boston shuttle."

To watch him get on a plane was to believe him. Although he always stuffed his coat pockets with eyeglasses, tissues, nail file, toothpicks, Tylenol, Maalox, eye-drops and pocket knife, and with a manuscript or two, he would walk on unencumbered, carrying only one of the many walking sticks he kept collecting.

19

Domestic and European Ventures

From day one, *Partisan Review* had brought European thought to our country. Now, William, who was eager to keep on top of it, encouraged my research on Europe. It was a boon for the magazine. At my professional meetings and in French bistros, in English pubs and German restaurants that served neo-Italian food, or when consuming the fare of my Viennese childhood, I listened to what was on people's minds. In the 1970s, *Partisan Review* held evening discussions on relevant topics such as "The Political and Economic Crisis in America and Europe," "New York and the National Culture," "Euro-Communism," "The Art Scene Today," and "Psychoanalysis Today." After moving to Boston University we extended such events into two-day conferences, beginning with one on "The State of Criticism."

William kicked that meeting off by pointing to the widening gap between impressionistic and journalistic criticism and its more technical and theoretical practices—Marxism that traces the social origins and meanings of a story or poem, and structuralism that analyzes a poem à la Lacan's treatment of Poe's "The Purloined Letter." Participants disagreed but remained polite, as academics usually do even when undercutting one another. But the nasty assault on Clement Greenberg by a dedicated structuralist, and a memorable interchange between the art critic, Rosalind Krauss and William were foreshadowing larger troubles.

"When I was standing up there," Rosalind commented, "I heard William start rattling the change in his pocket because those terms [denotation and connotation] make him very nervous."

To much laughter by the audience, he shot back:

"I thought you were a structuralist, not a psychoanalyst."

For the moment the tension was diffused, but these differences never were resolved, as can be noted when comparing the contents of *Partisan Review* and *October*, the magazine Rosalind soon was to launch.

Around then, the National Endowments were beginning to fund conferences that would help raise the level of all-around knowledge. Now, I taught myself to write grant applications. I assumed that some Europeans' expertise might open the eyes of at least a few university professors, as well as bridge the gap between "old-fashioned" (modernist) and "new-fangled" (post-modern) critics.

As a product of American public education and a traditional liberal, I strongly believed in integrating immigrants and minorities via our public schools. But I could not help recalling that in the 1940s we all were expected to measure up, and to repeat, whatever subject—in my case the proper pronunciation of "th" in speech class—we were not able to master. Keeping these experiences in mind, I invited experts—among them the president of the teachers' union, Albert Shanker, historians Arthur Schlesinger, Jr., Eric Breindel, Gertrude Himmelfarb and John Patrick Diggins, sociologists Peter Berger, Brigitte Berger, Irving Louis Horowitz and Nathan Glazer, literary critics Robert Alter, Cleanth Brooks, Dennis Donoghue, and Stephen Marcus, the directors and theater critics Robert Brustein and Gitta Honegger, and a large number of poets and novelists—to conferences that would further these ends.

To reach a broader public, we published a special issue of a 1990 conference [21] in 1994, in an enlarged version. But our politicians neither paid attention to Vienna's school chancellor, nor to Frankfurt's university provost, or to Paris's and Hungary's leading psychoanalysts. Or to the top writers from Eastern and Central Europe, most of them as yet unknown to American readers. (Even Lynne Cheney's comparative NEH study of student achievement a few years later did not have much impact.)

Like Freud, who, while exploring unconscious phenomena believed that some day science would be able to ground these in neurology, William kept speculating about theories of human evolution. This was not a new interest, at least according to Mary McCarthy's novel, *The Oasis* where she maintained that the original *Partisan Review* group had assumed, however briefly, that they had the "right to think that [they] could resist history, environment, class structure and psychic conditioning."[22] Although William no longer believed in any sort of Utopia, he wondered what changes President Reagan's "Star Wars" (SDI) might wreak, if it were feasible. To find out, we convened a meeting at Joanna Rose's apartment in order to understand the nitty-gritty facts of a ("potentially impenetrable") defensive shield in the skies. We asked George Chapline, a physicist at Lawrence Livermore Laboratory, to debate John Pike, then the Associate Director of Space Policy for the Federation of American

Scientists, which opposed that program on principle. (In 2004, he is described as "a private satellite expert" advising U.S. senators.[23]) Inevitably, the deliberations grew increasingly heated. Pike's supporters came out against SDI, and maintained that even though no one could truly guess at Soviet intentions, they won't strike first since they had not done so up to the present. His opponents held that deterrence, so far, had worked, and that we therefore should build it up further. Although I didn't think that any of our guests had changed their minds, I was pleased that we would be able to print a full range of facts and opinions of the issues at stake. Was I naïve or moving to the political right?

* * *

Of course, just as in the 1930s, *Partisan Review*'s literary mission was being sidetracked by politics. But whereas then intellectuals had been free-floating and poor, most of them now were in the universities and financially secure. The 1960s generation had become the 1980s professors. Predictably, they were upset at the indifference to politics, and the cynicism, of a large segment of their students. I was more disturbed by their anti-intellectualism, their lack of curiosity, and their ignorance of history, even of current events. Our conferences were to be sort of antidotes, if only because sharp disagreements were interrupted by witticisms, so that even the most controversial topics couldn't become clichéd. The more ideological the arguments became, the more strongly William spoke up against the dangers of group-think, this time by the leftisants. Now, some among them started to call William reactionary, conservative, or a traitor to his past. And neoconservatives berated him for having printed some left-wing pieces. (See below.) Frontal attacks came from Norman Podhoretz, the most effective and visible of the neoconservatives; and nasty ones from Joseph Epstein and Hilton Kramer. Of course, we too thought the Soviet Union was as much of a danger as they did; but we were softer on domestic issues, if only because our tax code so obviously kept favoring business interests and the rich; and because we were pro-choice, at least for the first half of pregnancy.

When, during the first post-war congress of the International Psychoanalytic Association held on German soil, in 1985, in Hamburg, the London psychoanalyst Hannah Segal, and the Boston psychiatrist John Mack sponsored an anti-American peace rally, I was perturbed. At the time, the Soviets had placed ballistic missiles facing the West, and our Congress was debating whether to vote for deterrence by having our own missiles oppose them, or to turn the other cheek. The one psychoanalyst,

Otto Kernberg, who pointed to the negative consequences of unilateral withdrawal, was shouted down. How could he not be for peace? I didn't trust my ability to win an argument against the organizers' Trotskyist methods of crowd control. Instead, I pointed to this growing anti-Americanism in the pages of the magazine. William and I kept trying to get peaceniks and liberal fellow travelers to see the larger picture, and neoconservatives to recognize some of their domestic short-sightedness. We did get a few converts, but most of these didn't come out publicly—akin to the registered Democrats in New York City who vote for Republicans but make sure not to let their friends know.

*   *   *

After receiving NEH and Rockefeller grants for comparative psychoanalysis, and fellowships at Harvard's Center for European Studies, Paris's Maison des sciences de l'homme (MSH), Frankfurt's Sigmund Freud-Institut and Vienna's Freud Gesellschaft, I contacted scholars and psychoanalysts in these cities, and in London.

I had been in Vienna countless times before 1982, but had been steering clear of the most loaded memories—personal humiliations and the loss of relatives at the hands of Nazis. So, when I was assigned Freud's first consulting room, at Berggasse 19, and sat in the exact spot where he had written his "Introduction to Psychoanalysis" and his "Essays on the Theory of Sexuality," in front of the window that in his day had been a garden and now was displaying motorboats, I spent the morning daydreaming, not doing anything. Probably for the first time since Robert had died, I seemed to have shed *all* of my anxieties.

"What am I doing here," I kept asking myself as in a dream. I knew that research in my hometown would require a special effort to maintain the objectivity sociological inquiries call for. But the most upsetting incidents of my late childhood and early teens, of what Freud called the latency period, still remained unconscious. My Belgian memories, for example, had not yet fully surfaced. During previous visits, I still had shied away from some of the negative feelings my parents never had permitted themselves or me to express, not in Vienna nor in the U.S. Like most Jewish parents, they had believed that they were protecting their children when keeping from them what they thought of as unseemly, or shocking, such as talk about money, pregnancies, unhappy marriages, politics, servants' illegitimate children, divorces, marriage swindlers, infidelities, family feuds, and all other forms of behavior not fit for bourgeois ears.

"Not in front of the children," my mother would routinely declare, while shooting her right forefinger to closed lips, when anyone was about to touch on a forbidden topic. Only after my father's death, when she was in her nineties, did she open up, however cautiously. Until then, she had resented my growing spontaneity as much as my frequent withdrawals. Added to that was the Austrian dictum: *lass sie teppert sterben (let her die ignorant)*

* * *

On that first sunny afternoon in Freud's office I left early and seemed propelled along the Schottenring to the Donaukanal, towards Obere Donaustrasse 63, my maternal grandfather's carpentry shop. That formerly busy courtyard now served as a parking lot. Instead of the ugly U-shaped grey cement building that faced me, I imagined it as it had been, with its delivery boys and apprentices running about, with its sounds and intermittent shrieks of wood-saws and drills; with the occasional booming of my grandfather's voice; and with the nooks and crannies, one of them my grandmother's bookkeeping office, that had vanished. These visual memories gradually brought tears running down my cheeks.

When I re-crossed to the center of town, I was struck by the meticulous restoration of Vienna's previous grandeur. Unlike Frankfurt or Munich, for instance, where in the 1950s roads had been widened and buildings torn down to renovate and modernize, the city of Johann Strauss, Jr. had reconstructed the glories of the Austro-Hungarian Empire. As melodies in three-quarter time were wafting out of storefronts and open windows, I reflected on the ease with which the Viennese had reinstated the political triangulation of the Austrian republic—into Socialists, Christian Democrats and Nazi sympathizers. This was confirmed by Vienna's psychoanalysts, who, when realizing that I was a native of Vienna, often told me more than I had hoped for, or informed me of their love of Jews and alleged resistance to the Nazis. Viennese hypocrisy was alive and thriving.

Still, there were exceptions. At the psychoanalyst Harald Leupold–Löwenthal 's party of Vienna's hoi-polloi, I met Marta Halpert, a peppy journalist who has remained a close friend. (Marta's parents had been through the death camps, and she was born after the war.) Although I subsequently met others of her generation, I still sense the anti-Semitism in many persons of my age. And I am not fully cured of my own ambivalence and sensitivity—the push-me and pull-me of my childhood.

Like their counterparts in other cities, Vienna's few practicing psychoanalysts were badmouthing their colleagues. True, in each location animosities result from specific personal histories and individuals' psychoanalyses that have to do with the history of the discipline, starting with Freud and his disciples' utterances.[24] To put it crudely, Frankfurt's Freud is read à la Mitscherlich, as the proponent of civilization without discontents and prejudices. Paris's version ends up as a cross between Freud's ego psychology and Lacan's rereading of texts à la Saussurean linguistics and Hegelian philosophy; the Londoners' is an outgrowth of the 1944 controversies—and subsequent accommodations—between Anna Freud's and Melanie Klein's followers; and the Berliners' judgment depends on where the founders of the post-Nazi institutes (their analyst-fathers) had stood during Hitler's reign. Had they adapted? And since those who had practiced had to have had the regime's blessing, they must have done so. Had that prevented them from becoming "real" psychoanalysts? Had they, therefore, turned into charlatans, hypocritical careerists, or even imposters? Of course, this sort of navel gazing derives from the necessity of psychoanalysts' transferences and counter-transferences—without which unconscious material cannot be reached.

*   *   *

In Frankfurt's Sigmund Freud-Institut, I was treated as if I were the Queen of England. I was given a large office, secretarial and library help, and was invited to candidates' seminars. Was I being courted in order to let it sink in that anti-Semitism was of the past, at least among the members of that institute? Yet, for the psychoanalysts Margarete Mitscherlich and Mechthild Zeul and for the sociologist Karola Brede I was Simmel's "Stranger" to whom they poured out endless stories about former Nazis, and not just of far out skinheads, who still were holding on to their bigotries. Altogether, the majority of Germans remained guarded: they lived up to their stereotypes, except for the ones who made sure to inform me of their (real or invented?) Jewish grandmothers, and who allegedly had been hidden.

Still, what could I make of Hotel Mozart's dour desk clerk, who had looked askance when, in her lobby, I insisted on watching a Holocaust film on television. I wanted to know what Germans were being exposed to, and she did not: she rushed to turn off the set every time I was summoned to the phone. Yet, after a caller had asked for me as "Frau Professor Doktor Edith Kurzweil." she oozed with obsequiousness. Was she anti-Semitic or anti-American? This subject needs to be aired, I thought, and what publication would be more appropriate than *Partisan Review*? Of course, the good Germans now were on the political left, which led them to be somewhat soft on communism. Relations with the German Democratic Republic (DDR), and with family members across that divide, complicated their feelings as much as did anti-capitalism and environmental issues. I increasingly was reading newspapers from the far left to the far right.

During the 1984 summer semester (April through July), I taught at the social science faculty at Frankfurt's Johann Wolfgang Goethe University. This was a challenge, not only to my German vocabulary, but to my familiarity with philosophy: I never had had students who were thoroughly steeped in Hegel and Kant, and capable to debate the views of Horkheimer, Adorno and Habermas in depth. And who wanted to make presentations—which entailed preparing them (and myself) for their topics.

Some of these students ambled in late and left early, brought their dogs, and felt free to interrupt—which was contrary to stereotypical Germans. Most of them were serious, often debating issues long after the end of class. During the weekly seminars of the faculty of social sciences, the split said to be between right and left, revolved more around the bureaucratic management of the university rather than around the country's politics. And while they fiercely argued about how best to protect the German forests, I nearly choked on the smoke of their cigarettes.

At conferences around the country, I often gloried in being the lone woman among German men: their chauvinism still was in high gear—across the political spectrum—although women were beginning to make inroads. My visits to Herbert Strauss's Center for Research on anti-Semitism at Berlin's Technical University, and those to the German Psychoanalytic Verein (DPV) were especially helpful insofar as they often provided the grist for my "Comments" in *Partisan Review*.

Again and again, I was struck by the gap between linguistically oriented and fast-stepping French intellectuals, and the preoccupations of their German peers with anti-Semitism and their fascist past. In fact, one of my German students remarked how ludicrous it seemed to him that they had to bring me, an American, to instruct them about intellectual life across the Rhine.

*   *   *

Even before the fall of the wall, Berlin was incomparable to any other German city—as if the specters of Auden, Isherwood and Spender, and of "Sally Bowles," had returned. On a trip in the summer of 1989, from a window of the Gropius Haus, I looked at the close-by electrified wall—a wide strip of dirt-strewn, dusty emptiness guarded by armed soldiers on watchtowers. Ten months later, there no longer remained a trace of it. When shortly thereafter, William and I participated at a conference of editors of literary magazines, we got a look at the flimsy construction of communist housing: its depressed inhabitants; its overall grisly grunginess. By the summer of 2004, I was convinced that present-day Berlin might be counted as the eighth world wonder. In contrast, I found Frankfurt sleepy and depressive.

*   *   *

By the early 1980s Parisian psychoanalysis already had turned into a hot public topic. Feminists, among them Julia Kristeva, Hélène Cixous, Luce Irigaray, and Cathérine Clément, who soon would rise to fame among postmodern American feminists, were watering down their attacks on men and were becoming psychoanalysts and writers.[25] By then, Jacques Lacan's Freud was flooding the city's cultural scene. In cafés, would-be intellectuals no longer read Herbert Marcuse's *One Dimensional Man* (1964), but were working their way through Lacan's *Écrits* (1966) and *The Four Fundamentals of Psychoanalysis* (1977). Public performances and conferences on psychoanalytic controversies— from what Freud had said and "really" meant, to clinical terminologies and arguments about translations and practices—no longer were restricted to professional therapists. I had access to every bit of this Freudian free-for-all. What was propelling French Freudians into the limelight, and turning them into fashionable icons, just as their American brethren's (public) fate was so rapidly sliding? Before long, I was asked to speak during some of these "confrontations," if I recall correctly about the errors of Freud's American followers.

*   *   *

Whereas I winged it in continental Europe, William's priorities differed from mine. When we first were planning to take a trip to Paris, he grilled my travel agent about the state of the heating system of every hotel she suggested. In 1983, when thanks to a friend I had a luxurious, well-heated duplex on the Quai des Bourbons, he soon joined me. The chill he had suffered in his hotel room on his visit in 1949 had shaken him up.

Saul Bellow recalled it when I was there for dinner, shortly before William died:

"Did William ever tell you that I saved him from freezing to death when he and Edna first came to Paris?"

"He did, but not in any detail," I answered.

Well, I received his phone call at the crack of dawn on a Sunday morning. William demanded that I come over immediately. He had called the proprietor of the hotel to turn on the radiator, and she apparently couldn't do it. He sounded desperate. So I rushed over there, and after looking at the radiator asked that woman for a wrench. She didn't know what I was talking about. Eventually I procured one and showed that helpless lady how to use it. Now, William was able to thaw out.

With his customary irony, Saul went on to talk a bit more about their Parisian adventures. Among other things, he wanted to know whether William had spoken about their visit to the Follies Bergères. He had not. Saul recalled:

William one day asked me, cautiously, what these girlie shows were all about, and let on that he wanted to go to one of them, but neither with Edna, nor alone. So we went together. The strip-teasers did their usual thing. And, after having stripped down to their g-strings, one of them danced around our table and ended up sitting on William's lap, while making a play for him. He knew that he was expected to slip a dollar into her belt, but was too shy to do so. He squirmed and couldn't bring himself to touch her skin. After much hesitation, and while she kept on flirting with him, and teasing him, William convinced me to take his dollar and give it to her.

When I repeated this anecdote to William, he said that he didn't remember it. Instead, he recalled that he and his friends—Bellow, Raymond Aron, Manes Sperber, Albert Camus, H. J. Kaplan (Kappy), René Liebowitz, and Hannah Arendt—had fallen out with Sartre and the rest of the communists, existentialists, and fellow travelers. They had had the courage to publicly go against these taken-for-granted beliefs. He recalled a meeting with one of them (Merleau-Ponty?) at the Brasserie, who said that opposition to Sartre was no problem—while putting his hand over his mouth and looking around to see who might be overhearing him.

By the time William was with me in Paris, he had become accustomed to red carpet treatment, mostly on his "good will" trip around the world. Then, he had been able to indulge his fussy eating habits, whereas now, since we often ate in cheap bistros, it was more difficult to get perfect service. Not all waiters were patient enough to reassure him that his chicken was soft yet not full of butter, his soup not too salty, and that his vegetables would be cooked into mushy softness. Occasionally I would be embarrassed. But this was a small price to pay for having him around. His off-hand comments and cutting or hilarious remarks made up for having to translate everything for him, even the French he understood. He managed to make me laugh at the many ways he invented in order to make a fuss. I loosened up.

After William had joined me, I still went to my office at MSH on weekday mornings, but either met him for lunch or stopped working at teatime. We explored bookshops and clothing stores, looked for walking sticks in antiquarian establishments, strolled through the Louvre or the Jardin de Luxembourg, and almost bought a pied-à-terre in the Marais. Whenever William felt the least bit tired, he insisted that we rest up in the nearest café. We also found the "flea bag" where he had "frozen to death;" and the exact spot where Hannah Arendt had told him that: "It is so much easier to walk in Paris than anywhere else in the world, because the cobblestones are so much softer."

After we had found out where the Soviet writer, Andrei Sinyavski, (alias Abram Tertz) lived, we ventured beyond the last stop of his *métro*, walked another mile or so, to a house that was almost hidden behind high weeds. His take-charge wife opened the door, and after we cooled our feet for a while, said that he was ready for us in his upstairs study. Books were stashed on every step of the staircase, on radiators and other surfaces, so that reaching him presented a number of hurdles. But once we sat across from this courageous dissident, his modesty and pleasure to see us were overwhelming. He answered all of our questions, and promised to send us a chapter of his forthcoming book. We were less successful in reaching Milan Kundera, who, after finally giving us a four o'clock appointment, didn't open the door when we got there.

*   *   *

My landlord's stand-in was Annie Cohen-Solal—whom President Mitterrand later would appoint as Cultural Attaché to New York. She was writing her book on Sartre, and after I told her that William had known him, I got them together. They hit it off. William elaborated on Sartre's hold on Parisian intellectual life after World War II. This is not to say that Annie had been unaware of it, but only that she had been as uncritical of it as were most French intellectuals. Then, Gaullism, anti-Americanism and pro-Communism had gone together. William was partial to Camus, who, he said, combined independent politics and courage with good looks and perfect demeanor. He recalled that:

> When he came to New York soon after the end of the war, he called me up, and I gave a party for about forty people. All the women went for him. That Saturday evening, he asked me to introduce him to American intellectuals. He was stunned when I told him that nearly all of them were in the room.

William was negative about Simone de Beauvoir, whom he had welcomed to New York in 1947. He said:

> She was ignorant and arrogant. And she never let go of her fixed ideas. For instance, she insisted that John Steinbeck was the best American writer and was dismissive of most of the ones she now met. She requested that someone accompany her to Canarsie. I couldn't imagine why. "That's where the workers quarters are," she replied. Also, she was certain that "imperialist America was in its death throws." I was relieved when she left for Chicago.

William wasn't traveling anywhere in order to look at nature. "Nature is for tourists," he declared. This was not entirely true, because I never met anyone more concerned for the life and health of trees, or aware of the blight in his environment than William. Actually, he meant that he was visiting foreign countries to learn about their people, to meet persons who could inform him of "what *really* was going on." And to find material for *Partisan Review*. Nature could be absorbed by osmosis.

After William rekindled his friendship with Manes Sperber, Munyo, as he was called, we often dined at his home on rue Notre Dame des Champs. Jenka, her husband's muse, was a cook who managed to combine the best of Viennese and French cuisine. She became one of my close friends, and after Munyo's death made sure that his many autobiographical novels remained in print. However, only after the first of these dinners did William tell me that they had been on the outs for a long time, because "Munyo's anticommunism had moved him too far to the right." Now, they both criticized communist influences and the knee-jerk left, as well as the establishment. (Solzhenitsyn's *Gulag Archipelago* had made a splash in Paris only after 1975.)

One day, Henri Lefebvre invited us to a typically French Sunday lunch, which lasted from 1:00 P.M. to 9:00 P.M. The two prima-donnas were seated at opposite ends of the long table. In between were Henri's hangers-on. Henri had said his official good-byes to the communists, in his two volumes, *La somme et le reste*,[26] but still defended Russia's politics, allegedly because he was outraged at having to curtail his travels within the U.S.—after having told an immigration officer that, "yes, I have been a member of the Communist Party." Was he upset by that intrusion, or by the fact that his interlocutor did not know of his importance?

Nicole's elaborate feast eased the tensions of what I perceived as a civilized cockfight. Of course, everybody spoke French, which handicapped William—who kept turning to me as his "mouth piece." In fact, there was no way, at least for me, to properly render William's barbs and ironies while, also, remaining alert to Henri's equally acerbic utterances. Moreover, Henri had invited Catherine, a nineteen-year-old student, who seemed to be a cocotte rather than a budding thinker, with her scarlet mouth, painted eyes and brows, and her seductive baby-voice. Some time before then, Nicole had taken seriously Henri's dictum that 'intellectuals ought to bond with the working classes, and had befriended the handsome Spaniard who was painting the house they were building in Spain, and whom she soon would marry. Catherine was Henri's answer to her infidelity, though far from the first one. (Clara Malraux, an inveterate gossip, confided to me that according to rumors Catherine had been planted by the Communist Party to seduce Henri back into the fold. She soon would succeed, whatever her motivation might have been.) That afternoon, however, her presence and her inappropriate questions provided the diversion that kept Henri and William from going at each other.

William's and my meetings with Pierre Bourdieu, Clemens Heller and Pierre Rosenvallon, the leading figures at MSH, were suffused with mutual admiration and competition. We resolved to cooperate in a variety of projects, but none of these came to fruition. When we met Raymond Aron at his office, the two men spoke of the olden days, of their lonesome stand against the anti-American left in the early 1950s, and, of course, of the political future at this moment of tension: the Russians' positioning of ballistic missiles facing Western Germany. (I had admired Aron's sociological works and now was listening quietly.) Alas, it was the only time I would encounter him. He died that fall. Soon thereafter, his brilliant daughter, Dominique Schnapper—who was spending a year at Princeton with her husband, Antoine, a distinguished seventeenth-century art historian—became my friend.

*　*　*

When William joined me while I was teaching in Frankfurt, in 1984, he was self-conscious of his American accent, and of a possible touch of Yiddish in his less-than-perfect German. Nevertheless, he explored everyday life; checked on the prices of chicken and pasta; observed the dedicated services by the women at supermarkets; and compared the costs of oversized portions of food in restaurants. He was pleasantly surprised that the mail was delivered at 9:00 A.M. on the dot, and that every bus ran on time. (My colleagues deplored punctuality as "a disgusting and typically German defect.") During drives along the Rhine into Frankfurt's surroundings, and at dinner parties with colleagues, William probed, not always in the most polite manner, into his hosts' and their guests' stances on specific political issues. His inquisitiveness was never-ending, especially when it came to relations with East Germany (DDR), and to the presence of—possibly hidden— fascist tendencies. (Margarete Mitscherlich still recalled his provocative queries when I met her in 2004.)

In Vienna, I introduced William to my childhood haunts. Now, his inquiries, if anything, were even more thorough. Just once, we took the Badner Elektrische (the tram that connects Baden to Vienna) and met my parents for lunch. There, William got a whiff of Austria's wine country and of my father's nimble cynicism. Somehow, that was where we came to talk about religion at great length. Neither one of us was observant. But I did wish I were able to give up my secularism for some sort of religion. I was Jewish and a supporter of Israel, but didn't know any Hebrew. I perceived Yiddish as a poor aberration of German. I didn't wait for the arrival of the Messiah, and didn't even know the ritual Friday night prayers, much less any of those for specific holidays. Neither did William. But, at least, he understood Yiddish.

* * *

In 1988, after a conference in Frankfurt and talks in Heidelberg, we flew to Toulouse. For some time, William had wanted me to show him my escape route from Europe. We tarried in Toulouse: its City Hall was still where it had been, but nearly unrecognizable in its cleaned up splendor. The pinkish hue of that red and white stone structure was plunged into total, almost eerie, quiet. It did not much distinguish itself from the seats of France's other ninety-eight provinces. (In 2005, it was overflowing with tourists.) Its foreign consulates had moved to the even sleepier outskirts. My memories not only were of another time, but of another place.

Before entering Spain, we stopped for a few days in romantic Collioure—staying in the hotel room from which André Derain had painted the fishermen's dense, overlapping patterns of sails, and where Henri Matisse had spent years. Then, on to Port Bou, across the Pyrennées from Cerbère. Alas, the frontier's control hut and its inspectors were gone, modern trains were swallowed up by the tunnel, while we drove unimpeded on a paved, deserted road. No trace of my bloodcurdling escape any longer existed.

Until then, William had relied on *my* languages, and I had done all the driving. I was tired and expected to relax, counting on his knowledge of Spanish. However, when I found myself on a sixteen-lane highway outside Barcelona, and asked William to read our roadmap and/or to ask for directions from one of the speed demons on an adjoining lane, he asserted that he never reads maps, that his Spanish was rusty, and that my Italian might well get us by. I lost my cool after spotting our hotel on the other side of that route, about ten lanes away. Before we got there, about an hour later—we had the worst fight in all the years we were together. But on the following day, we were at one while admiring the most unforgettable Miro show that ever was assembled.

Now, we took the train to Madrid and settled in with Mechthild Zeul, who by then had married her Spaniard, José Antonio Gimbernat. We ate well, and whiled away much time at the Prado. Mechthild took us into the luscious countryside—to buy ceramics, visit ruins, and Toledo.

*   *   *

Whereas William tended mostly to rely on me and my friends on the Continent, when returning to New York via London, we primarily met *his* friends. Early on, John and Miriam Gross gave him a party, which *tout-Londre* attended. I knew nearly no one, and if I had they all had bigger fish to converse with. I recall sitting on a bench next to James Trilling while making small talk. At Noel Annan's public discussion with William at London University, I fared a bit better. We saw Doris Lessing nearly every time. Just once, William invited Juliet Mitchell to the very British Garrick Club. The high point of amusement was reached when Juliet and I on our way to the bathroom were stopped, because we had put our feet on the staircase that led to the (male only) bedrooms—right after Juliet had been deploring British machismo. That evening, we accompanied her to a lively party in a woman psychoanalysts' home. I remember only a huge living room in a suburban house, and excellent food.

Then, I was unaware just how highly British intellectuals and playwrights valued William. I found them all exceedingly sharp, maybe because in these London circles wittiness counts for more than friendship. (Still, years later, at Jonathan Miller's fancy reception, I was astonished at the host's warm greeting—because I was William's wife.) But then, William, too, was a master at snide humor and quick, situational come-backs. Thus he recalled with pleasure the occasion when together with Cyril Connolly he was crossing Venice's Piazza San Marco, and they ran into a disgruntled writer who buttonholed Connolly, demanding why he had not yet printed a story he had accepted some time before.

"It was good enough to accept, but not good enough to print," said the editor of *Horizon*.

While shrugging his shoulders and smiling, William would quote that line when having second thoughts about a piece we had accepted, but never without attributing it to Connolly: to use another's *bon mot*, or *mauvais mot* without attribution was worse than plagiarism. William deemed every bright saying clichéd the second time around. To compress what one had to say, often kept him from writing more than he did. He was a perfectionist whose every word had to count. No padding. No frills. He once showed me a tiny notebook where he had jotted down epigrams. I have as yet not been able to find it.

Only when two years after his death I looked into William's personal papers, did I come upon a clipping from the *Guardian* announcing his forthcoming arrival in London. Recently, both Doris Lessing and Natasha Spender recalled that his presence always produced a flurry, although they could not reproduce the upbeat atmosphere of these earlier days. Doris recalled William's frantic search for the "real London Left" he apparently had heard about, one that was not just ideological, or posturing. That was in the early sixties, she thought, and remembered, also, that she then had not believed that such a Left existed, but had assumed that she just might have been too shy or critical to tell him. Were they referring to the New Left that was led by Perry Anderson and Raymond Williams?

20

Editing *Partisan Review*

"I am the Resurrection and the Life
I am the things that stay, and those that flow.
I am the husband and the wife
And the victim and the sacrificial knife
I am the fire and the butter also."
—T. S. Eliot [27]

About a year after William's death, I opened the posthumous volume of T. S. Eliot's *The Waste Land* his widow had edited. It included an unpublished poem marked with a piece of paper. One of our around-the-clock attendants had left him that crumpled purple square with her phone number—after he had told her not to come back. I will never know whether he then inserted this bookmark to identify himself, or to describe me. Or whether he was thinking generically of "the editor," the one who is stricter on him- or herself than on the manuscripts he or she receives—and whose judgment had better be faultless. Like Eliot's?

After William had invited me to meetings of his editorial board, around 1974, three years before he put me on the masthead, I listened with awe to the deliberations about manuscripts by the members of that group. They were debating the merits and weaknesses of each submission, and blaming William for delays and errors by the staff. Although we all were aware of the cultural shifts, William was most keen on digging into their causes, expecting to fully anticipate every rumbling, and then to call attention to it in the magazine. Intuitively, he had a nose for trends that were in the air, while they still were incubating. But his innate caution, his care not to jump to precipitous conclusions, also, led him to hold back. Late in life, he told me that in the late 1960s he had been full of enthusiasm for the emerging liberation movements, yet had been skeptical. At the time, he neither had given up on most of his left-leaning hopes, nor on his strong belief in the viability of the democratic process.

By then, there was much tension between William and his co-editor, Philip Rahv. When they first had broken with the communists, they had stood together against the world. They both had been accused as traitors to the cause, as running dogs of imperialism, Trotskyists, enemies of the working class, informers, and literary snakes. Former friends had stopped talking to them. But gradually, as the magazine became the beacon of American intellectual life, the friction between the editors came to the fore. By nature, Philip was assertive, William reclusive. (In a letter to his wife, Edna—from Yaddo, the writers' colony—around 1936, William informed her that she would have been proud of him had she heard him speak up to Malcolm Cowley, then the editor of the *New Republic* and a prominent fellow traveler.) According to all accounts, Rahv was not only highly intelligent but domineering. Increasingly, his ruthlessness and disloyalty took over. He made sure to arrive at their office early in the morning and to answer letters to known figures and promising writers, even when they had been addressed to William. At first William didn't care: he was busy attending to practical matters. Later on, he fought back. Actually, all the so-called New York intellectuals were honing their mercurial minds and ironic insights at each other's expense.

In 1957, after Rahv went to Brandeis University, the relationship between the founding editors further deteriorated. Now, Phillip sent aggressive letters about manuscripts he allegedly had not received or that had been delayed. To begin with, William's responses were substantive, but increasingly, his annoyance crept in. He alone dealt with the nitty-gritty problems inherent in legal and tax questions, hired office help, saw to the printing and layout of each issue, and spent his days trying to raise money—while Philip insisted on his equal rights, objected to William's entitlement to a salary, and complained about having been left out of some (last-minute) decision-making. He had been bad-mouthing William as well as other associates behind their backs for years. Recently, Dorothea Straus recalled that "Phillip would ask her husband, Roger, about money raising opportunities, but then would not follow up," because, ultimately, he "wanted no connections to 'capitalism.'" Eventually, people would be William's friends, or Rahv's, but found it impossible to socialize with them both. William, (somewhat enviously?) would refer to Philip's talent to find wealthy wives. By then, Dwight Macdonald quipped that the relation between Philip and William "was the only marriage held together by a magazine." When the situation was close to breaking, Rahv who had insisted on an office of his own that he never used, met with

William, Marcus, and Poirier every few months in New York. After they designated William as editor-in-chief, Philip sued them in court. Soon, he started another magazine, *Modern Occasions*—and they finally split. By the fall of 1969, Rahv's name no longer appears on the masthead of *Partisan Review*.

At that point, William decided to form a larger board. By 1971, Peter Brooks, Morris Dickstein, and Richard Gilman were listed as contributing editors, along with Steven Marcus and Richard Poirier as assistant editors. Before long, William appointed Norman Birnbaum, Frank Kermode, Christopher Lasch, and Stephen Spender as consultants, and added Susan Sontag a year later.

Their expertise varied. Marcus, Lionel Trilling's star student, had written on the Victorians, on Dickens and on Marx. Brooks, the blond son of an American father and a French mother, was as at home in Paris as at Yale, where he taught comparative literature. His colleague, Gilman's, specialty was theater. Dickstein, whose dissertation Marcus had supervised at Columbia, concentrated on American twentieth-century intellectual history and increasingly on the movies. Their differing talents seemed comparable to those who originally had helped *PR*'s impetus and its renown.

In any event, William had not expected that Brooks's allegiance soon would change from T. S. Eliot to Jacques Lacan, or Dickstein's to the New Left, or that the upheavals within the universities might turn into liabilities, not only in some of their thinking, but in their characters. William's mistake, I believe, was not only the assumption that, as in the 1930s, he would be able to create a circle strong enough to keep cultural extremism at bay, but to expect that, together with these collaborators he would manage to buck the right as well as mass and popular culture, or at least stem its tide. He thought that by keeping a firm grip on traditions while keeping an ear to the ground, that is, by listening to the rumblings and grumblings around him, he would get a proper grip on the volatile present.

It took me some time to catch on that in wily and underhanded ways some of the younger associates were trying to take charge of the content and direction of the magazine, and that my being "nice" and reasonable would not dissuade them. William defended himself against their maneuvers, and could become quite angry while deftly navigating around their manipulations, even plots. He too had watched the success of the free speech movement of 1964, and later on the shooting at Kent State by police, and the occupation by Columbia University's students of

Hamilton Hall. While scrutinizing what was printed in *PR* during that period, I found that William had been more sympathetic to these "revolutionaries" than he later recalled—if only by publishing Susan Sontag's "The Pornographic Imagination,"[28] and Steven Donadio's[29] interviews with seven Columbia professors. The letter he wrote to Richard Poirier on 3 May 1968, clearly describes his thinking:

Dear Dick,

Though things have been churning, I find it hard to write about them, I guess because when being caught up in them is a way of life, or more accurately a kind of routine, nothing seems to stand out, and I tend to confuse the events themselves with my own sense of involvement or rather of being bogged down by them.

The after effects of the King assassination seem to involve more black militancy and anti-white solidarity, but maybe this was in the cards anyway. I had some dealing with blacks recently, and as on other political questions I was divided: my youthful, irresponsible radical self was with them; my tired, sober, wise self said I was partly with them, but that they went too far.

The same thing with the Columbia rumpus; half of me is with the kids, half is for sanity, one-half of which is on the side of the students, which makes me three-quarters for them. As you probably know, the issue has focused around the question of amnesty, which I am for, perhaps a little irresponsibly, because as has been pointed out to me over and over, the kids are insatiable, they want the fight, and they will start one up again at the first opportunity. Almost the entire faculty is in effect against them though it is trying to work out compromises that the kids so far won't go for. The revolution is here, and I have no time to either join it or oppose it.

The election stuff you know about. Most writers, etc., are for [Eugene] McCarthy, the core being made up of the Kunitz types, full of virtue, sanctimony, heroism, honesty, loyalty, last-ditchism, and café idealism, though there is a lot of straightforward decent feeling for McCarthy. Many for McCarthy say they feel they ought to stick awhile and though they may shift soon, it is still too early. Out of a limited type of conviction and a Poirier type of perversity—I am more like you than I am willing to admit—I've accepted a co-chairmanship of the arts committee. On the practical side, I have the feeling it will be Kennedy vs. Humphrey, whose credibility gap is in his mouth when he opens it. A certain number of people have come out for [Bobby] Kennedy, the most notable—predictable or unpredictable?—being Mailer. I assume you will sign up and I assume I'm to put your name down, as you told Goodwin you would be available to help. Of course, I have reservations, but not so much about Kennedy personally—who knows about the others personally?—as about the politics of moderation in general. I wish I knew which half of me to listen to.

The magazine shlepps along, after me and Steven, with Rahv barking at our heels. Nothing exciting or spectacular has happened . . . .

At the time, the situation at Yale was especially tense, since it was the home of the Black Panthers, and Bobby Seale was on trial in New Haven. Peter Brooks's overly long essay explained the Panther's phrases as "metaphor[s] of argot, a secret language designed to identify members of [their] group."[30] He claimed having avoided the turmoil until he realized that his students were using that same language to disrupt his classroom.[31] At that point, he went on, he thought that the faculty should intervene, although he did not know just how. But soon he too was calling for "a fair trial for Bobby Seale"— which apparently was perceived as a verdict on the Panthers, and by extension on all Blacks. Brooks allegedly was swayed by a Panther who argued for a "new and more difficult level of consciousness. . . in those who had tried to understand." (Did he ignore that his career depended on supporting that side?)

William commented that Brooks (and Leo Bersani) had substituted literary criticism for politics, and had overvalued literature and undervalued politics; that he had "maneuver[ed] himself to the side of good (meaning new) politics . . . . [by means of] fancy footwork about language, literature and politics. . . . [that contained] a hodgepodge of old socialist ideas, pacifist feelings, liberation and national movements, Keynesian panaceas, vague notions of central planning, environmental and antinuclear concern." [32]

* * *

While exposing the underlying motives and agendas of the Left, William did not spare the Right. But instead of creating the dialogue he expected *Partisan Review* to print, he was assailed in the neoconservatives' publications. (Mary McCarthy commented favorably on his position in a personal letter, but not in the magazine.) Brooks responded, angrily, in *PR*, that reality is better understood via literary interpretation than by "politics as usual." The lines were drawn, and William's efforts to make our editorial board "see reason" remained elusive. As we know, the polemics continued, the polarization between the right and the left accelerated, and by 1980 the neoconservatives helped elect Ronald Reagan.

I cannot possibly record all the back and forth, nor do I want to. I tended to agree with William but was upset by the aggressive tone of these discussions, mostly because I am not an experienced debater. Our views, I believe, were expressed in an undated letter from that time to a number of Norman Birnbaum's long communications:

Dear Norman,

I am answering you in haste, as we are up to our necks in getting the issue out and various other chores connected with the magazine—and don't have too much time at the moment for controversies that lead nowhere.

I also see no use in answering you point by point, since that simply leads one to lose sight of the main issues, which are, themselves, fairly clear.

I'm glad to hear that you are honoring me by saying we are becoming indistinguishable from *Commentary*. Norman Podhoretz would surely appreciate this. May

I say in reply that I would like to honor you by saying that your views are becoming indistinguishable from those of *The Nation*.

Your letters have two main arguments. One is the ad hominem argument that what we are doing is moving to the right, thus making us indistinguishable from *Commentary*. This is obviously a phony charge, since even a child can see the difference between us and *Commentary*. Also, Norman Podhoretz, who is a better witness than you are on this question, has broken with us. But more important is the fact that you are echoing the typical slander of the left when it doesn't like certain views: it disposes of them simply by calling them conservative or right-wing or Reaganite—or like *Commentary*. This has been the classic tactic of the vulgar and simplistic left ever since I can remember. I have thought of you as an independent thinker, but reading your letters and the piece you sent me gives the impression that they could have been signed by any of *The Nation*'s ideologists.

If you are serious and want to discuss the issues, the way to do it is not by personal letters and by innuendos, but by writing something that can be printed and to which I can reply. This would make for open and serious controversy.

I should say that I feel what's involved here is more than simple differences of opinion. You are acting like an ideologist for a given side. And this, Norman, aside from the merits of the arguments, I do not like to see. I don't like to see you being sucked into predigested positions. I would prefer to see you in the role of independent thinking.

I repeat, it would be much more serious and responsible to conduct the polemic in public. Of course, both agreements and differences depend on the extent to which people have common assumptions. It seems to me this is what we have to explore.

Best, [Wm]

The boiling point, in 1982-3, was our editors' response to an editorial William had written. He had begun by questioning "the meaning of *left, right, conservative, liberal,* and whether these characterize specific and consistent bodies of opinion." He described the confusion by the right as amorphous and reacting to liberal trends, which included, also, America's conservative populist strain, as well as reactionary, racist, and moralizing currents, and from which the neoconservatives were eager to distance themselves. He found the position of the left more complicated, due to the relation of the Soviet Union to radical and liberal thinking.[33]   In other words, he tried to clarify that muddle. He also maintained that the radical mind was a parody of itself, in its belief that disarmament would magically lead the Soviets to follow suit, and that demonstrations in the West alone would bring about peace. William did not mention Brooks and Dickstein, although he pretty much used a number of points they had made at some of our meetings. In any event, they asserted that as contributing editors they had the right to present their positions in print. After much to-do, William agreed—provided that the other members of the editorial board would follow suit.

Now, Brooks dismissed William's editorial as a caricature of the American liberal left. Dickstein dubbed him a neoconservative and accused him of being obsessed with "the specter of communism" and the ghost of Stalin; and charged him of helping to turn the cold war into a hot one by refusing to support the peace movement. William responded that Brooks and Dickstein were "offering a brief refresher course in attitudinizing," and, ultimately, "were celebrating the sixties, and forgetting that, though full of enthusiasm, [these had come] to nothing because they [had] substituted slogans for programs, and because they [had] ended up in terrorism." I accused both Brooks and Dickstein of reducing complexities to the lowest common denominator, and pointed out that even French socialists were continuing the Gaullist policy by building up their *force de frappe*, and maintaining that they did so because America had not kept pace with the Soviet Union. Marcus thought it was unfortunate for literary critics to write about politics, and that "one of the luxuries of living in a political democracy is that one can indeed behave like a political infant." Leon Wieseltier answered Dickstein's "anthology of assumptions" point by point, and concluded that intellectuals were mandated to remain "thorns in the sides of both the left and the right," but that, instead, Morris "want[ed] a rose." Dennis Wrong proved that they "often confuse the two separate dualisms of left-right and domestic-foreign," and found that "the ghost of Stalin is simply irrelevant to strategic issues today." [34] (When I wanted to reprint some of these pieces in a reader on *Political Writings from Partisan Review*,[35] Dickstein refused permission.) By that time, the shilly-shallying Richard Gilman no longer attended meetings, and Daniel Bell kept himself out of the fray. After Brooks resigned, William hoped that Dickstein would do so as well. He did not. (A board member told us, that he was claiming to be *PR*'s fiction editor to get himself onto the influential Book Critic Circle's Awards Committee.)

Clearly, our editorial meetings had become too loaded to be of much use. Tension had built up, tempers had risen. Brooks stopped writing for us, and Dickstein kept needling. In arguments about specific manuscripts the line-up was predictable. (For overlapping, mostly short, periods, Ed Lehman, Lionel Abel, Daphne Merkin, Kay Agena, Rachel Hadas, Mark Lilla, Barbara Rosecrance, Rosanna Warren, and Dennis Wrong were on this board.) William increasingly told me that he dreaded the silly arguments that were taking the place of serious discussions. An Advisory Board member asked for permission to attend this "circus." I believed that it was hopeless to expect reconciliations, as did Steven Marcus. However, William alone paid for our board's antics: the right never forgave him for having printed these polemics.

The tempests in our editorial teapot replayed earlier ones: different issues, same political divisions and power plays. After a major blowup about the Iran-Contra scandal, William and I had to come to terms with the fact that this board had become useless. By then, Brooks was the head of the Whitney Humanities Center at Yale, and Dickstein soon started a similar center at the Graduate Faculty of the City University, with funding from, mostly, the *PR* Advisory Board, and with (at least some) ideas picked up at our meetings.

*   *   *

I slipped into editing *Partisan Review* in 1987, while William was hospitalized for nearly three months, and then broke a hip while recuperating. As soon as he was on the mend, he gradually took over, but never completely. By 1994, we decided to designate me as the official editor, and to elevate William to editor-in-chief. Near the end of his life, when I came to him with an idea or tried to push him for an opinion, he would smile lovingly and shake his head in amazement, saying: "Who ever would have thought you would turn into an editor?"

As executive editor I had not fully felt the editor's burden. It is the editor of any little magazine who carries *all* responsibilities. Now, I grasped why William had been so leery of publishers' parties. For people began to buttonhole me in order to criticize the content of a piece they didn't agree with, to point to a typo, a printer's poor inking, the wording of an advertisement, a postal error, or an assistant's mistake. Publishers and writers approached me to protest that their books had not been reviewed. (When going over the stacks of volumes to decide which ones to consider for attention in *PR*, we judged quality, content and topics, rather than literary politics.) I gradually learned not to take such reproaches personally, but did not have William's experience, or his clever comebacks. I easily got defensive.

It did not occur to me until recently that, possibly, when William had first called me, nearly thirty years before, he had been searching for a muse as well as for someone to write on European and psychological topics. (Diana Trilling remembered that the "*PR* boys of the 1940s," though valuing the smarts of the women around them, also had appraised their sexual potential.) Be that as it may, William never could willingly spend an hour with anyone, male or female, who was not straight forward and on the ball. In fact, he forever pushed me into writing about topics that relied on my understanding of European issues.

By the end of the 1990s, we met with Dickstein and Marcus alone. They often had not read the manuscripts before a meeting, and their verdicts, even on purely literary pieces, rarely seemed to agree with each other. By then, Morris tended, in a casual way, to walk in while commenting on a current political topic that would inflame William. Sooner or later William would explode, and Morris would dismiss him as irrational, or as an angry old man. Steven tended to remain silent. True, as William was losing strength he became increasingly impatient with what he found to be provocations, and a waste of his (diminishing) energy. To me, all of that was draining. I had to get the magazine to the printer. By the time William was very ill, and I was yet more pressured for time, I would meet with one at a time, or get their opinions of pieces over the phone. Occasionally, I called on the reliable Eugene Goodheart to check on my own literary judgments.

I then did not realize how these internal battles were seen by the world that still looked to William as some sort of guiding spirit—while neoconservatism was rising to its heights and personal friendships were being trampled on for the sake of ambitions. Still, I should add that William and Steven also were friends. They had long telephone talks, not only about literary modernism and political topics, but about a shared past. This is not to say that they always agreed on anything except football: they were rooting for the Giants, and on Mondays, after one of these games their conversations were endless.

21

From Political Issues to Personal Ones

In November 1989, the Berlin Wall had come down; the communists no longer dominated the Czech parliament; and on that Christmas day the Romanian dictator, Nicolae Ceausescu, had been executed. "We've been vindicated," was the general gist of our conversation, while wondering what the political future of a suddenly free Eastern block would bring. More assassinations, exiles, or purges? A resurgence of democracy? Would a soon to be reunited Germany present a new danger? William and I guessed at myriads of scenarios, interrupting only to decide on what to pack for our routine exodus on New Year's Day—to the tedium of the Sunshine State, to Palm Beach. William was convinced that two weeks relief from ice and snow would save us from sniffles and the flu. In our comfortable hotel room we continued speculating about the future of the West, as our eyes moved from glorious sunsets over the ocean to CNN, and to the pages of the *New York Times*. The *Partisan Review* office was a phone call away.

We hunted for seashells or looked at condominiums we never bought, and decided where to stroll or eat. William regretted that his hero, Sakharov, had not lived to see this happy turn of events. With a scornful wave of his right hand, which he accompanied by clearing his throat, he wondered what some of our American leftists, who for years had ridiculed him for his anti-Communism, would concoct to land on their feet. (Later on, he could not grasp, or grasped only too well, how so many among them adapted without ever admitting their ideological flip-flops, and soon morphed into one or another civil rights movement—for women, gays, pro-choice, and so on.) More immediately, we read whatever fiction and political thinking came out of that "former East," and tried to get the best of it into the magazine.

In 1982, we already had gotten a whiff of the psychological impact of communism at our first "Conference of Soviet and Eastern European

Dissidents." I had been surprised that, when greeting them in our office, they ogled me suspiciously. Uneasily, I asked our translator to find out why. Apparently, they could not understand the reason for this gathering, except to suspect that the KGB was behind it. Yet, as soon as I explained that we had admired their courage, and might want to translate some of their essays, poems or fiction, they loosened up, a number of them to the point of clinging to my arm for comfort. A few preferred vodka. Still, when after two exciting days—with an overflow audience—we were taking them to the New School in New York, two men refused to get on the Boston-New York shuttle. They suspected it might be bombed. Neither did most of the participants sleep in the hotel rooms we had reserved for them, feeling safer with Russian immigrants in Queens or the Bronx. Only then, did we catch on to the emotional damage they had suffered.

"I could not have survived in such conditions," William maintained. Were our visitors' outstanding contributions and deliberations an indirect result of having had to dissemble, of having had to invent ever newer and newer metaphors for what they dared not say openly? Clearly, we were learning more about life under communism than we had bargained for.

Ten years later, in 1992, we set out to capture these authors' responses to the demise of the USSR, and to their take on life in the West. So, we brought them together with the best of American writers, at a conference of "Intellectuals and Social Change in Eastern and Central Europe." Since as a faculty member at Rutgers, Newark, the university's stepchild, I had been asked to "do something for us," the administration was delighted with my idea for such a conference—as long as I would do the work and raise the money. I received a grant from the National Endowment for the Humanities (NEH), which a few private foundations supplemented. When representatives of the press asked me how I had managed to assemble such a star-studded cast, I summarized, somewhat tongue-in-cheek: "They came because we told them who else was going to be here."

Actually, we knew that Saul Bellow and Ralph Ellison had been close friends, and that they had been out of touch. When Saul let on that he wouldn't mind getting together with Ralph, William invited him for lunch at the Century Club. The impeccably dressed and affable Ralph seemed favorably disposed to participate after hearing that Saul would be there. The rest was relative child's play, since the other figures I then got in touch with were more or less eager to join.

In the course of that lunch, nearly every "Centurion" who entered the dining room approached our table and warmly greeted Ralph. William wasn't used to such neglect, so he wondered why they pretty much ignored him. Ralph explained a bit pompously: "They all know me, because I integrated this joint."

For me, this was my first (and accidental) stab at seriously bridging the gap between my literary and academic pursuits. In the opening session, Lynne Cheney, then the chairman of NEH, praised writers as those who "speak the unspeakable," who understand the underlying truth of their condition rather than follow what their contemporaries consider the correct stance, and who keep digging for that truth however uncomfortable their conclusions might be. William moderated the first panel— all of them Nobel Prize winners. Saul started off by outlining the different values upon which American and European democracies were based—the former on reason and dedicated to the conquest of nature that would eradicate poverty and create conditions for peace, justice and order, and the latter, following Aristotle's *summum bonum*, on establishing principles that would do away with civil wars, tyranny and internal chaos. He reminded us that our founders had promised relief from hunger, disease and fear, which to a large extent we have achieved, and that has become associated with capitalism; and that most Western intellectuals had hailed the Russian Revolution of 1917—against all evidence—by upholding Marx's stages of development that would achieve an ideal communist society. Alas, people in the East discovered that the state did not wither away as Marx had predicted, although the individual did—while struggling for material goods as well as for freedom. Ultimately, Bellow concluded that speaking the truth in the East sent you to the gulag, whereas in the West you could say anything you wanted, but no one listened.

The atmosphere was intense. Still, when Bellow was interrupted by a fire alarm, he smilingly paraphrased Marx: "No matter what you do, it always turns into a farce." Ellison picked up on this note, explaining that writers portray reality by means of comedy, satire, tragedy or the blues—to point to the absurdities around them. He called himself an outsider-insider, a descendant of slavery, who had been left out of the American equation. He suggested that the break-up of the Soviet empire might be better understood by focusing on chaos—as had the (white) Southern writers who explored the improvisations after the chaos of the civil war, and those who had dealt with the clash of ideals, or with the reality of the Depression in the 1930s. He ended saying that writers have to take the punishment that goes with telling the truth. As to the Invisible Man, he patiently explained to a student, he not only had been invisible to those around him, but to himself.

Czeslaw Milosz, who in 1950 had defected from his job at the Polish Embassy in Paris, told how he then had been of no interest to either the right or the left, in an intellectual milieu dominated by Sartre. *The Captive Mind*, his book about politics behind the Iron Curtain, he went on, actually was disdained by his peers, the poets, who now thought of him (negatively) as a political scientist.[36] And he speculated, just as we had, on how intellectuals would deal with the unknown, now that they had no "ideal society" to look to.

The panelists' seemingly off-the-cuff contributions were relatively brief. But the audience was electrified by the profundity and immediacy of the speakers. When the apologetic Joseph Brodsky belatedly arrived at the podium, he predicted that since the fall of the Soviet Empire, which he soon referred to as the Ruble Zone, writers' and intellectuals' roles would be substantially diminished; would be more and more atomized; would be controlled by self-interest and marginalized—in a "lumpen context," and in a breeding ground for fascist and other organized groups.

Bellow then distinguished between intellectuals who like Marx, Rousseau, and Lenin continue to dominate our lives and our minds, and writers who react to their surroundings with their feelings, and indirectly are involved with the intellectual project—which the masses of mankind are incapable of handling. Ellison added that the novelist "is stuck with what he can make of social reality by reducing it to manageable proportions through forms and techniques of fiction." Milosz, referring to academic writing, saw a "direct connection between intellectuals' and writers' aspirations." William kept the ball rolling, when, to everyone's amusement, he asked Milosz whether he was sure that academics ipso facto are intellectuals. Brodsky then defined them as systematic persons who look for order or social models, unlike writers who tell a story which unfolds as it develops. Students went on asking questions, not about, for instance, the recent Gulf War, but about their hopes for a world without wars. Smilingly, the panelists agreed that such a utopia was unlikely to come about, and averred that they would not relinquish their relationship to literature and art, despite its diminishing returns.

Susan Sontag had not wanted to prepare a talk, I assumed because she had grown ambivalent in her relation to William. Line by line, he had edited her "Notes on Camp,"[37] which had catapulted her into the limelight. Personally, they continued to like one another, but less so when Susan morphed more and more into an idol of the far left. When in 1982, she spoke of "Communism with a Human Face," Diana Trilling was outraged and stopped talking to her, saying: "where has she been when we were fighting the communists?" William had been equally annoyed. But that did not keep him from calling up his wealthy friends to help pay her bills after she had breast cancer and had no health insurance. While she was recuperating in Paris, we had a most enjoyable lunch with her. William understood her need to shine and to attract a large public, and he valued her ability to sense emerging trends.

At our event, Susan moderated the session that dealt with the legacy of communism—which the Hungarian writer, George Konrad introduced historically, and the Bulgarian and Russian authors Blaga Dimitrova and Tatyana Tolstoya, enlarged on, as did the Roumanian, Norman Manea. Doris Lessing discussed the "unexamined mental attitudes left behind by communism," and gave telling examples of the way liberal and conservative writers, almost inadvertently and without awareness, were continuing to use the communists' empty language. Adam Zagajewski, Walter Laqueur, Valery Golofast, Ivan Klima, Eda Kriseová, Slavenka Drakulic, Dubravka Ugresic and Hans Magnus Enzensberger were just a few of the illustrious panelists, all of whom approached the issues with a view to their own experiences. During leisurely meals, that included dancing in one of Newark's Portuguese restaurants, and a formal dinner in New York, old friendships were renewed and new ones formed. (The Viennese journalist, Marta Halpert, recently told me that this conference was of lasting benefit to writers who until then probably had read one another but had not met.) Even now, I still run into people telling me that this conference was the most memorable and eye-opening gathering they ever attended.[38]

*   *   *

About a month after that conference, on a glorious May day, William received an honorary doctorate from Adelphi University. By then, I no longer was happy at Rutgers, mostly because the newly appointed (female) associate dean kept making inappropriate demands from all department chairs, but especially from me, the only woman. She even had gotten the writers' organization, PEN, to invite the participants of my conference to dinner—on the very evening we had our gala event.

By contrast, Adelphi seemed to be a more appealing campus, and not only because of its manicured gardens. The university president's wife, a lively young blonde who presided at our table, complained of her misery in a comparative literature course, saying that she did not know anything about French structuralism and postmodernism. I promised to send her my book. Her husband, Peter Diamandopoulos, an energetic, volatile Greek philosopher, who was hell-bent on improving educational standards, read *The Age of Structuralism*. He was impressed by its interdisciplinary range. I was taken by his determination to turn Adelphi into "the Harvard of Long Island." When subsequently, at one of his receptions, I expressed my respect for what he was doing, he invited me to participate in a seminar about the formation of a core curriculum. Now, it became clear to me that a few among the participants were dubious about this enterprise. But I was impressed by their serious and candid disagreements, and didn't pay that any heed.

Soon thereafter, I happily accepted a visiting professorship. After two months, Dr. Diamandopoulos asked me to lunch at the Faculty Club. As soon as we sat down, he said: "Edith, you know what I am trying to do here, and you're the perfect person to help me upgrade this university. I need you. What will it take to have you join us?"

By then I was Professor II at Rutgers, received a relatively high salary, and was on nearly every important committee in New Brunswick, often as the only Newark representative. But I wanted to get out from under that associate dean's control. So I decided to take the leap, and to move to Adelphi as University Professor of Humanities and Social Thought. I cannot know to what extent my innate (though then unconscious) fondness for challenges led me to that decision. Or whether I primarily left Rutgers because I was dissatisfied with the leveling of admission standards at my campus, and with the rumblings of political correctness that were roaring ever more strongly.

At Adelphi, I threw myself into developing courses in the core curriculum, and into teaching at the Honors College. I had close contact with the best of our students. After starting a Humanities Institute for faculty members, I invited *Partisan Review* authors and other luminaries to present their books and research, and encouraged colleagues to participate. Even more than at Rutgers, I was encouraged to organize conferences, which of course came more easily now that participating in a *Partisan Review* event had become a feather in most academics' caps. Still, a conference on "The Politics of Political Correctness" took place at Boston University, as did "The New World of the Gothic Fox," and "Education and Integration: Europe and America." "Knowledge and Information Technology," with Ray Kurzweil, Edward Rothstein, Gunther Stent, and Guy Burgess was held in New York City. Adelphi University hosted, among others, "Psychoanalysis and Psychotherapies," and "Breaking Traditions: *Fin-de-siecle*: 1896 and 1996" that was celebrating the university's centennial and Austria's millennium. When I arranged major talks by, among others, the writers Doris Lessing, Gitta Honegger, and Saul Bellow, the social scientists, Ronald Radosh, Rita Simon, and Robert Wistrich, the philosophers John Gray, Susan Haack, and John Searle, and the psychoanalysts Janine Chasseguet-Smirgel, Julia Kristeva, Helen Meyers, and a bunch of lively Hungarians, many faculty members came to hear them. The professors who had been selected to receive a small stipend and a course reduction presented their research. But after a few people used these occasions to derail our discussions in order to criticize the university president's initiatives, attendance dropped. Much of that might have been predictable. Some was absurd: for instance, a philosopher accused Rita Simon, the loving grandmother of a biracial child, of racism; another one, almost routinely, turned every topic into a Marxist free-for-all. At first I wasn't too concerned, and didn't pay much attention to the mumbles and grumbles by colleagues who were out to get rid of "Dr. D." (He was berating them for their lack of productivity.)

Eventually their tactics bore fruit. Soon, more and more members of the faculty stayed away from the events I arranged. When, for instance, the professors from the English department were not invited to the small dinner with Saul Bellow, they boycotted his talk. Administrators who had to teach a course were angry because they were not on tenure lines. And as his opponents were gaining strength—with the help of the originally secret committee of about eight people—Dr. D. turned into an increasingly harder taskmaster, into a micro-manager. And after his assailants managed to break into the university computer and found that he was receiving one of the highest salaries among American university presidents, that became the only issue. The faculty's low productivity, its discontent about salaries and opposition to curricular innovations, and changes in student requirements no longer were on the table. The university's Board of Trustees backed the president, allegedly because they did not want to lose him. Basically, the faculty and its union wanted control.

One time, as the controversy was heating up, and I ran into him while crossing the campus, a large athlete interrupted our conversation, complaining that there was no money for a campus paper for black students.

"How much do you need," said Diamandopoulos.

" Fifteen hundred dollars."

"Go to my secretary and get it. Tell her I'll sign," he answered.

This good deed did not go unpunished, because he had not consulted with the designated faculty committee. On another such occasion he said, "Look at me, Edith, I'm a little guy, the president of a little university, and up to now they have written fifty-five articles against me, most of these in the *New York Times*."

I had heard through the grapevine that at least one of the insurgents had a close (family?) connection to that paper's inner circle. I openly took the president's side after, at the beginning of an early morning class, a student asked me whether or not he ought to transfer to New York University. It was what one of his professors had advised him to do—while announcing that Adelphi was about to close down. I was stunned, but answered that we weren't going to spend class time speculating on that subject, that we could discuss it after the bell rang. That was when the students informed me that "all the professors are talking about this during class time."

Of course, I was shocked at the lack of professionalism, and in the back of my mind wondered how to handle the situation. (I had suggested, while sharing an umbrella with a Board member, Hilton Kramer, during graduation ceremonies, that if the president were to announce that he would take half his salary, the opposition's entire case would collapse. He responded: "Absolutely not.")

During a *Partisan Review* evening, I asked a friend who was on the New York Times Op-Ed decision-making board, whether he would print a piece by me about the Adelphi situation. After saying, "of course," he changed his mind when I told him where I stood. He suggested that I write a "Letter to the Editor" instead. I told him that I already had done that and that it had been ignored. After one of the university's lawyers came to see me, I agreed to testify in what to the best of my (informed) knowledge would be a kangaroo court. They did not call me. Nor did the press indicate that what came to be called the Adelphi case was to be the test case for the success of faculty unions in private universities in New York State. (I had been a loyal union member all along, to the point of going on strike at Montclair State College in 1974.)

Ultimately, Peter Diamandopoulos was fired by a state appointed board. The insurgents got their spoils: they became provosts, deans, and vice presidents. They abolished the core curriculum, lowered admission requirements, furthered personal interests, and gloried in their success. This is an insider's summary of a shameful episode during the height of political correctness.

*   *   *

I now expended more of my energies editing *Partisan Review*. It has been observed that no matter how attuned a junior editor is to the ideas of his or her mentor, a slight change in the emphasis of articles in the magazine occurs. William and I were not conscious of such an adjustment, if only because, all along, my interests had converged with his. He always had egged me on to write comparative pieces for the magazine, to investigate and follow up on my hunches, and to trust my instincts. These tended to concentrate more and more on the slipping of educational standards, and on students' lack of knowledge and interest in history—that were reinforced by recalling my past, which, also, was triggered by the books on universities and the Holocaust that were being published in ever larger numbers. I reviewed many such tomes, and assigned others.

Because both William and I were put off by the post-modernism that now was sweeping the humanities and the social sciences, we furthered writers and critics who, too, were questioning that trend. We were leery of what soon became an avalanche of relativist and convoluted criticism. Still, we were cognizant that we did not have a voice in government, and that Washington policy makers were beyond our reach. Basically, we featured avant-garde literature, and tried to encourage readers to think outside of their boxes.

*   *   *

While working on *The Freudians: A Comparative Perspective*, I had stumbled on the fact that the first book on French feminism published in the U.S.—a mass of short excerpts—came out in 1980, in the same year that these celebrated French feminists were refuting many of Jacques Lacan's theories—which had been their original inspiration. In sum, I wrote *Freudians and Feminists* [39] primarily to point to this error. (Except for a mixed review by Juliet Mitchell in the Times Literary Supplement the book was ignored.) My essays during that decade also tended to doubt the unified worldview espoused by well-meaning American liberals—who, fortunately, never had been exposed to the vagaries of war on home soil. For I recalled the praises Chamberlain had received in 1938 after successfully appeasing Hitler—which in effect had served as the green light for the invasion of Poland. William, on the other hand, pointed out that if the German communists had not refused to join the socialists in 1932, Hitler would have been kept from power.

Many academics now talk of American "exceptionalism"—which explains our differences theoretically but leaves out what Milosz summarized at the 1986 PEN congress:

> Innumerable millions of human beings were killed in this century in the name of utopia—either progressive or reactionary, and always there were writers who provided convincing justifications for massacre.... Recently I read, in a French translation, an article by a West German literary critic glorifying Sartre for his assault on Camus, but not mentioning what was really at stake. Camus's offense was mentioning the existence of gulags. Sartre was concerned with injustice in his world and unwilling to pity millions of victims sacrificed in the name of a presumed historical necessity. [40]

Both William and I kept groping for ways to get our readers to understand the perils that lie in denying hidden realities. (Yet, why was I unwilling, or unable, to uncover my family's concealed secrets?) Was it because, as William used to say, most individuals cannot keep two conflicting ideas in their minds at the same time? Or, what may be called the paradox of open-mindedness? We continued to look for pieces on subjects that foresaw and explored coming "hot issues," rather than one-sided arguments. When we couldn't find anyone to do so, we wrote editorial comments, or reviewed a relevant book. To that end, I occasionally covered the New York Film Festival, or commented on an overly praised movie or play. In 1996, for example, William cited his experiences during the early years of *Partisan Review* to refute some of the revisionist histories that set out to prove irrelevant or ideologically driven points. In 1998, I suggested that to combat terrorism we follow the lead of other countries and recruit the best and the brightest, and whose ethics pass muster, to our intelligence services; and William detailed why the provenance of today's Left was not rooted in Marx's or in Lenin's revolutionary socialism but in a belief in its own moral, intellectual and political authority. In 2000, after Ralph Ellison's death, he recalled some of his encounters with him; and I reminded our readers that it was about time for some of our historians to stop speculating how the U.S could be held responsible for the start of World War II, and to recall, instead, that the Japanese had sneakily attacked the U.S. at Pearl Harbor.

While on a panel at the Czeslaw Milosz festival in California, in 1998, I again met like-minded people, such as Adam Michnik, Adam Zagajewski, and Richard Lourie, and the best of our contemporary poets, among them W. S. Merwin, Seamus Heaney, Edward Hirsch and Robert Hass. The private dinner with Milosz, whose smile and laughter remain unforgettable, was an extra treat, as was the ease with which everyone took scholarship for granted and moved beyond it, including the lively, Polish journalists who had arrived from Warsaw and Krakow. We printed a good part of these proceedings.

22

Family Relations and Marriage

I could not help but know that I had disappointed my father by pursuing my academic interests. He disdained "intellectuals" as goof-offs, as non-productive members of society, almost as akin to parasites. He tolerated lawyers because they were needed. Doctors were necessary, but one had to remain on guard with them, since they were apt to exaggerate the seriousness of debilitating conditions in order to overcharge. Academics, psychologists and psychoanalysts were beyond the pale. After all, what tangibles did they produce? So, for him, I was a fictitious doctor. I don't even think that he meant to put me down when, the only time he ever referred to my title, he introduced me to the surgeon who had operated on his ulcer: "This is my daughter, she is a doctor too, but not a real one."

It is useless to speculate whether my father's scorn for intellectuals went back to childhood problems with his mother who was a bookworm and wrote poetry, or to his strong identification with his less educated father. When he mailed me editorials critical of professors or universities, I didn't take them as affronts, because I shared some of his criticisms.

The more I fell in my father's esteem, the more I looked for his approval. We skirted most topics of conversation. Before William had come to live with me "uptown," in 1985, our Saturday dinner talks had been restricted to the price of fish and marble, and to the suffering of businessmen. After William moved in, we saw my parents on Saturday afternoons at one of the inexpensive diners on Broadway. My father lived as if he still were a poverty-stricken refugee, alternately preparing himself for run-away inflation or deep depression. But to show to the world that his business was thriving, he traveled only in first class, stayed at the best hotels, wore expensive clothes and drove costly cars—not classy Porsches or Mazzeratis, but luxurious Cadillacs—even in Europe. My mother went along, at times flaunting, other times glorying in fancy vacations.

Whenever we met, I was told of my brother's lavish spending habits, his wife's laziness and their *nouveau riche* life style, which usually ended with my father's fear that "the business" would come to naught after his own death. (It didn't.) Allegedly to stave off such an ending, my parents kept going to the office. Behind their backs, my brother dubbed his place of work the "old age home of the marble industry." But when it came to running down professors, they were at one.

Inevitably, we evaded more subjects than we addressed, and thus were restricted to the sort of small talk William abhorred. My father was as adamant about picking up the (minuscule) check, as he was at insinuating that we only saw him because we were freeloaders. William would wrinkle his forehead, shrug his shoulders, fiddle with his walking stick, and tell me that he disliked these outings. I preferred having him along, because his presence put the brakes on more direct charges and disparagements.

By then, my mother's fear of conflicts—which she occasionally alluded to during the rare occasions we were alone, and which apparently were rife between my father and my brother—dominated her existence. When my father accused Johnny of selling too cheaply, or of wasting time and money on tennis courts or golf courses, she backed her husband. But she adored her son. And yet, in a conspiratorial voice, she once confided to me that they had seen a lawyer because they suspected that their business lawyer was in cahoots with John. As my mother's anxiety mounted, so did her anger at the husband who didn't seem to know even how to get himself a glass of water from the tap, or to insert his own hearing aid. (During her only hospitalization for minor surgery, he met me for breakfast and dinner that entire week.) Increasingly, he refused to listen to her prattle—that became more and more annoying the more put-upon she felt, and the more helpless. Yet my mother seemed unwilling, or unable, to change these dynamics. Only after she took a fall on West End Avenue, incapable of pulling her shopping cart up onto the curb, could I convince my parents to hire a caretaker. In sum, I suspected that something was amiss, ascribed it to their strained relationship, and did not really want to be drawn into their tangled psyches—my father's ever growing despotism, my mother's angry passivity, and what I perceived as my brother's evolution into a caricature of his father.

Sometime in the mid-1980s, as my father was nearly euphoric while telling me that the business was thriving, my mother suddenly jumped in, accusing me of "having seen Franzi," the sister-in-law they both hated. (I had made a condolence call in 1973, after my uncle Felix had died—which my parents interpreted as treason. I had not seen her since.) This was strange behavior. So was my mother's furious outburst on a Saturday afternoon, when William, who no longer wanted to listen to my father's jokes, or to his predictions of impending chaos, commented about my feat of having saved myself and my brother in 1940.

"She did not, it was our money that got the children to this country," my mother responded angrily.

"Why is she denying that you were an extraordinary youngster, and what is going on here," William kept questioning afterwards. I wrote it off to her poor memory. Because I did not want to confront her, I pushed this incident to the back of my mind, along with others that were belittling me. Intermittently, I was overcome by a deep longing for my mother's affection, and speculated what I could do to regain her love.

I often guessed that my father wanted to tell me something urgent, which my mother didn't want me to know. Particularly during the last six months of his life, when he no longer went to "the business." He did articulate more than once, usually with a sly smile, that after his death my brother and I would fight. My mother always intervened by changing the subject, and never left the room during my visits. Yet, ever so often, unbidden, and in moments of relative closeness, she cautioned me not to ask him about his will, which, in any case, I would have considered an unseemly thing to do. When she told me that I would receive less than my brother, I thought that was only fair since he was dedicating his life to the marble business. And because she also repeated that the first item in his will was the repayment of his debt to me of long ago, and with interest, I didn't worry—if only because that alone now came to a considerable sum.

On the eves of Jewish holidays and Thanksgiving—the mandated events at my brother's house in Tenafly—family conversations had become ritualistic. As if on cue, before repairing to the dining room, my brother would launch an attack on "teachers" who don't work: "How many hours per week are you teaching, is it nine or twelve? And what do you do the rest of the time," he would begin. Soon, there would be an *encore*, about the fact that it was their New Jersey taxes that paid for William's and my salaries at Rutgers University. At that point my father would smile mockingly, and I would choose to keep quiet. Only once, did I interrupt the tirade to launch into one of my own—about businessmen who are said to have nothing on their minds but money. Straight out of Karl Marx. They were stunned but did not hear what I said. And I was unaware that my family's disdain for academics (or was it unconscious envy?) seemed to increase with every one of my promotions, and with my visibility. At these gatherings, my sister-in-law, Sonya, kept assisting her efficient Irish housekeeper in the kitchen, and when she finally did emerge, did not seem to be there at all. These holiday meals were an ordeal for William and the children, who dutifully, if reluctantly, accompanied me.

*   *   *

On Friday, November 20, 1992, I was called to the phone during a meeting in New Brunswick, to be told that my ninety-five-year-old father had died. I arrived at my parents' apartment just as the police was carrying out the body, and as my niece, Michelle, while perching on a footstool in front of the living room window was talking to their lawyer. My brother was in Taiwan. Soon, Sonya arrived—more alive than I had ever seen her. Upon my brother's return, he told us that tears had come to his eyes when he got the news. But then he had thought of "what father would have done," and therefore had attended to the business at hand while waiting for his flight to Newark. Now, he and Sonya made decisions about funeral arrangements, and asked Robert, the son from her first marriage, to take me along to the Riverside Funeral Parlor. In view of the fact that my father, years before, had said that he never would accept him, that blood was thicker than water, I was surprised. Still, in the car, I was tongue-tied as Robert, for the first time ever, asked me about his parents' secret. (They still had not told him that my brother had adopted him at the age of five.)

Because no one, except for the rabbi who barely knew my father, spoke at the funeral service, I felt compelled to give an impromptu eulogy for the father of my childhood. In the limousine to the cemetery I shared with my mother and brother, I started to mourn my father and among other things, reminisced aloud about how happy I had been after he had sent me my first bouquet of roses, in Brussels.

"He never told me about that," stated my mother. My brother did not utter a word. When two days later the family got together for the Thanksgiving ritual, it went off in near-silence. That Saturday afternoon, while William was home with the flu, I met my mother at the Éclair. She was agitated, which under the circumstances seemed almost appropriate, and, among her routine questions about the children, asked whether or not I had received a copy of the will. Since I had not, she dropped the subject.

It arrived that Monday. Its first paragraph stated that anyone who contested what followed would be totally disinherited. Except for a token sum, I was left out. The paragraph about the debt to me was missing. The business and all of its assets were to go to my brother. The considerable personal fortune was to be used to pay the estate taxes on the business. I collapsed. What had I done to have my father betray me? Had this will been doctored? Had his love turned into hate? Or had he simply believed that the business would stand as a memorial to him by its continuation—like Henry Ford's motor company, or J.P. Morgan's bank? True, I had metamorphosed into an intellectual, but was that treason? And if so, why did my family lie to me all these years, since this will was dated June 6, 1984? What ensued was even more painful. For, when I called my brother, asking to meet with him, we made a date—which he soon cancelled, saying that we had to get together in the presence of our lawyers. Since I didn't have one, he told me to hire one. He screamed at William, and refused to speak to Allen. And he dispatched my mother to his posh Florida residence to "protect" her from me. William consoled me, and insisted that I would be fine despite this betrayal. I was unable to properly eat for a week, had trouble getting out of bed, or even thinking about my work. Why had my mother conspired against me, and so frequently told me that I was my father's favorite child? Did I respond so strongly because the pipedream of a loving family that had sustained me during my flight from the Nazis had been rent asunder?

During the following week I drove Doris Lessing to give a talk at Rutgers. I still was too discombobulated to contain myself, and, against my better judgment, by the time we were out of the Lincoln Tunnel, found myself babbling of my sorrow and my predicament. She was shocked. Up to that point, she had been William's friend and I had been very much in awe of her. I had admired her stories, her talent, her frankness, and her dynamic presence. I no longer can recall exactly what she said, only that she was angry for me, full of sympathy, and spelled out the various options I had to act.

Ultimately, I hired an attorney from a white shoe firm, who charged $535 per hour. After two meetings with John's lawyer and some phone calls I owed him over $16,000. So, I decided to settle, partly because I knew that my brother who relishes fights soon would bankrupt me, partly because he had my mother in his power. I was afraid, although it was not clear to me why. A few weeks after my mother returned from Florida, I went to see her. When she asked me to look for an insurance policy in her strongbox, I came across a codicil to my father's will that had not been submitted. But I did not have the presence of mind or the guts to remove it. A week later I tried to do so at my lawyer's advice. But it already was "in the office safe."

From then on, my mother, who lived to the age of 101 years, every so often would question why I had turned away from her, and why I did not want to be in touch with John. When I tried to tell her, saying that all she would have had to do was to inform me of what was going on, she reiterated that she hadn't wanted to cause fights. At that point, she would become agitated, turn on me in a rage, and soon be totally out of control. It was such outbursts that I had feared as a child, and that then had turned me into a spectator not only of her but also of myself.

After a while I no longer tried to explain. Might my father have been on to something when he said that she was "crazy?" My parents had been at one in blaming my paternal grandmother, and the "green eyes" I had inherited from her, for all that had gone wrong in their marriage—and with me. Why did I refuse to recognize, as my brother did, that my highly intelligent father had gotten senile?

When many years earlier, my therapist had said that not I, but my father, was the problem in my family, and that they all needed me as a scapegoat, I had withdrawn. In my mind, I had excused my father, thinking that it was all right for him to live by his own father's beliefs—which were those of the nineteenth century. Even when rereading Thomas Mann's *Buddenbrooks*, I did not yet realize that my family had transported the same values—diligence, duty, tradition, profit and lack of extravagance—to America, and that these had, in fact, been the road to financial success.

My father began to convey some of his family tales only when he was in his eighties. Such stories could have been told, also, by Hanno Buddenbrook of Lübeck, had he not died at the age of seventeen. For instance, that Uncle Sammy's daughter, Trude, found out only after having married a handsome stranger—who said that he didn't trust banks and therefore carried his fortune in his valise—that his valise contained old newspapers instead of cash; that her brother Fritz's womanizing had ruined him. Or was it his university studies? That my grandfather's perseverance had turned him into Austria's largest marble entrepreneur. And, most of all, that my father, himself, had given up on a career in journalism in order to rescue the family enterprise after World War I—which I, a female, in a flawed way, had achieved.

*   *   *

Already before my father's death, William on and off had suggested that "we might as well get married." I felt comfortable with our loose arrangement. After Edna's death, in 1985, he had come "uptown" every afternoon and "gone home" every morning, after I had left for the university.

"It would be so easy for you to move in with me, it's a sunny and roomy space," he kept saying. That was true. But I didn't like the idea of living in what had been Edna's home. I also preferred living across the street from Lincoln Center.

"I don't believe in downward mobility," I cracked, "the services in my building are better, we have a swimming pool, and there wouldn't be enough space for my books and other stuff down there." While I was stalling, William began to get used to my part of town. Lo and behold, after we answered an advertisement for a two-bedroom dwelling in my building, and were told that its owners needed immediate cash, he broke down. We found a buyer for his apartment and, financially, made a more or less even swap. Together, we moved four flights down from my place, which became the New York office of *Partisan Review*—thereby accommodating both of our libraries, as well as occasional visitors. As before, we spent the end of the week in Boston.

But I still was hesitant about legalizing our setup. I was afraid to rock the boat, recalling how much more difficult the relationship with Norman had become after the marriage ceremony. Our lives were extraordinarily meshed. I could not imagine ever leaving William, even when he was in one of his negative moods, or got grumpy. I did not squarely face the fact that he was getting weaker, which I might have recognized had I not diagnosed most of his complaints as manifestations of his not minimal hypochondriasis, which he too joked about. Whenever he made fun of his foibles, spoke of our large age difference or of his imminent death, he seemed to invoke it—as if that might keep it at arms length. But he feared that if he were to get seriously disabled, I might not stick with him. (As if that were possible for a Viennese girl into whom loyalty and duty had been drummed since birth.) By 1995, we had been together for about twenty-two years. Professionally I was known as Edith Kurzweil. I finally felt happy to be standing on my own feet, and did not want to be known as anybody's wife, not even William's. And might I not cut a ridiculous figure at a wedding ceremony, and in an announcement in the *New York Times*?

Allen overcame my ambivalence by arranging the formal procedure, on St. Patrick's Day, at the Town Hall in Storrs, Connecticut—where he then was living. He even found a rabbi to officiate in his living room. His wife, Françoise, seemed in a huff while running in and out "to look in on the baby." We had forgotten to bring wedding bands. Did we not want to think of ourselves as conventional? (Only my first wedding had been by the book, eternalized by a slim, engraved band that I wore next to my perfect, relatively large blue-white diamond. For my second one, Robert had designed a wide golden "rigatto" ring with a platinum rim at Buccelatti's. Norman's sculptured fantasy circle consisted of a beautiful design, whose holes might have stood for that marriage itself, and which he presented to me a few months after the theologian, Lew Mudge, had married us in his kitchen.) On the morning that William spotted Cartier's advertisement of slim rings with a few widely-spaced diamonds, rubies, or sapphires, he said, "You're not really married without my ring on your finger. Since I'm sure my legs will rebel when entering a fancy store, please go there and pick out two of these rings, and wear them together, so you'll feel doubly tied and won't necessarily appear to be married."

I still wear them on the third finger of my left hand.

23

After the Millennium

We listened to the prophecies preceding the millennium. Words, words, words... Was it possible that men from Mars were going to land in our midst? That only those with access to an updated Noah's arc would be saved come midnight of December 31? Was God to punish us all for our excesses—in ways only the media's talking heads had advance knowledge? The French designer, Paco Rabane even envisaged huge planets that would come crashing to earth, and destroy all kinds of life, turning our world into ashes. Since that did not happen, many of his countrymen were celebrating their survival with a glass of wine, "*le pot des survivants*," on January 1, 2000. On that day, our media went all out to announce, among other nonsense, that: "billions rejoice as era begins with few glitches," that "the human spirit [is] at a threshold," that we are "embarking on a new era, where the possibility of progress is almost endless," and that "the ecumenium gears up, led by Pope John Paul II."

"What nonsense," said William in his most deprecatory tone, "but think of the consequences when so many people take it seriously," I pondered.

For some time, William no longer had gone out after dark. I tended to get fidgety when having to spend night after night at home, not only because William was less and less able to stay awake, but because I had to prove to myself that life with artificial heart valves was "normal." So, I occasionally had dinner or went to the opera with friends. Also, William no longer was able to tolerate people not close to his own wavelength. I occasionally vetted some I knew he would be able to enjoy—rather than dismiss. Among them were the Romanian writer Norman Manea, whose intelligence and low-key erudition William came to appreciate. And the painter Jules Olitski—an early friend he had lost touch with. Whenever Jules and William got onto questions of art and literature they carefully listened to one another, but when it came to their ailments, they sparkled.

William was at his best with the Podhoretzes, not only when arguing that Norman was rewriting intellectual history—mostly about the early connections between *Partisan Review and Commentary*, but about current politics. By then, their old friendship dominated. William, for instance, reminded Norman that during someone's overly long memorial service he had asked him what he was going to say about him.

"I'll stand up and say: 'he was a good man, and sit down,'" William recalled. They had a sort of father-son relation, although at times the roles were reversed, since Norman by now had friends in high-ranking political circles, such as Henry Kissinger and George Schultz, and billionaires who celebrated him. He had made the connections he had written about in *Making It*—that William then had dubbed "his gold." Norman also kept suggesting persons who might support *Partisan Review*. (Only now am I fully cognizant that in our polarized political culture few wealthy individuals are willing to underwrite an intellectual publication that doesn't clearly support their own convictions.) Recently, Tama Starr, whom I had brought to our Advisory Board, reminded me that up until his death William had preserved his sense of irony, and even a certain flirtatiousness, although he could get quite grouchy when he was in physical discomfort, or when annoyed at advice by persons who "didn't know what they were talking about."

During nearly ten years, we felt hemmed in by William's attendants who, like occupying forces, had taken over our living room. Before the laid-back Jamaican Dorothy retired, at least the weekends had been without much stress. An old-timer, she was critical of the hot-and-cold running welfare-to-workfare helpers the agency foisted on us on weekdays. Among those who remained more than a month was the restless Lucy who kept rubbing imaginary spots off the furniture or off William; the hyperactive Russian, Natasha, who went to meet her limousine driver whenever he phoned to say that he was in the area (she dropped him whenever she divined that he was not about to leave his [obese] wife); the nattily dressed Shawna, who asserted her independence by taking her time to respond to William's calls for help. The Polish Tania, stole money: after William kept saying that cash was missing from his "secret drawer," I put $200 into it before going to the dining room. When we returned, only $40 was left. I was afraid of confronting a woman twice my size. But after much back and forth, and my proposal to let the police settle the issue, she packed her things, but not without denying her guilt. For two years, we put up with Stacey, an Eastern European woman who pushed every bit of dirt under the living room couch, where she sat, akimbo, for hours on end. I overlooked her attempts to set us against each other, and her bad moods, because she was adept at getting William in and out of chairs. (In July 1999, I did value her presence after my major heart surgery—aneurism and replacement of two valves.) William sent her to the drugstore or the supermarket when he wanted privacy. Of course, I also put up with these women because I did understand that not having a room of their own was as difficult as the troubles they brought with them from their countries and pasts, and that William sometimes did try their patience.

As time went on, William's anticommunism seemed more pronounced, if only because he was frustrated that updated communist slogans were resonating on the news, and that he was no longer able to get into the fray. Also, he was too alert not to regret—sometimes at great length— that we no longer would be able to walk together on the Champs Élysées and the via Condotti, or even to stroll in Central Park. So, he complained.

Before leaving for my New Year's Eve party on December 31, 1999, I lingered at William's bedside. As had become his habit, he was half-re-clining on his hospital bed in his over-heated room, next to a night table that overflowed with pill bottles, Maalox, and other stomach-soothing medications, a glass of water, the remote control for television, magnify-ing glasses, and piles of newspapers and magazines on top of his electric blanket. I again reassured him that I would be home before 1:00 A.M., and would take no chances on public transportation. When I returned, he was asleep. I turned off his light, which indicated to him that I was back.

On the morning of the new millennium I told William about the conver-sations of the night before, which had been chock-full of psychoanalysis and of psychologically driven explanations of political life—to which I had tried, not very successfully—to add a broader dimension. Inevitably, William sputtered about the subversion of true liberalism, but until then had assumed that psychoanalysts would know better, and have more open minds, "like the émigré analysts I used to know—Ernst Kris, Yella and Henry Lowenfeld, Lawrence Kubie, Phyllis Greenacre, and so on."

While sitting at William's bedside, I denied to myself that his strength was ebbing, that his cough was getting more pronounced, and that his legs were getting weaker. Still, he did not totally give in to self-pity, although every time he had yet another ailment, an ingrown toenail, a bump, a muscle spasm, or more indigestion than usual, he took his temperature and wanted me to reassure him, and prove positively, that he did not have cancer. As a rule, he would follow up with a doctor's appointment.

*   *   *

Whenever I arrived home, upon opening the entrance door, William would call out impatiently to have me join him at once. And when I entered his room, his face lit up, he motioned me to his bedside to give me a bear hug, and asked what had taken me so long. Now, I had to sit down and tell him "everything" I had done and thought of during my absence. In detail. Not only about happenings at the magazine, but at the university, on my drive home, with the children and colleagues. His tongue-in-cheek and cynical comments helped dispel my annoyances, and I counted on his approval for having received a good manuscript, having arranged a meeting, or bought a piece of clothing.

William's eyesight was fading. In order to keep up with, and to figure out, where the world was heading, and what kind of literature was being produced, he needed readers. I could manage to get through an editorial, a short notice, or an obituary, but my voice did not carry well enough for his diminished hearing. Among his readers, he truly appreciated Linda Healey, Chris Hurt, Jacob Weisberg, and Fran Kiernan. They responded to his attentive listening, and to his pungent and challenging comments and questions, not because they necessarily agreed with him, but because he set them to think. Unlike William, who had propagated modernism, and its dedication to clear, truthful writing, and to a new kind of psychological sensibility, his younger readers already had grown up with this ethos and were enticed to go beyond it. The tradition of the new was in, with its emphasis only on the new. William did not reject all of it, even though he kept decrying the loss of standards, the adulation of novel devices of form and style, and especially of literary theories that seemed to appeal only because they offered a language for the cognoscenti. He always sputtered when hearing French post-modern rhetoric with its nearly incomprehensible jargon. On the other side of the spectrum, he kept being annoyed at the increasingly low level of television, whose so-called talking heads grated on his nerves, even when they did not "butcher" the English language. He could not help but remark on every one of their grammatical errors, and there were many. And yet, sitting practically on top of his television set provided him with a great deal of—unappreciated —stimulation.

While I was organizing a conference on "Autobiography, Biography & Memoir," William suggested possible participants, and was adamant that I keep out "nudniks." It was a successful event, even though Stanley Crouch arrived late; and Hilton Kramer walked out when Edward Rothstein avoided the showdown about The *New York Times* he had looked forward to. We printed the entire proceedings, and received excellent reviews in the press. Only later, a friend informed me that an ambitious German journalist had used the occasion to pan both me and the magazine, and to use her review to personally impress upon John Silber, Boston University's president, that she would be a better editor than I. Now, I became fearful for our financial safety. William tried to calm me, mostly by repeating that I should stop worrying:

"I'm just staying alive to keep the sharks away from you." Occasionally, he would call them "the wolves." And he would try to console me by elaborating: "They've been trying to wrest the magazine away from us all along, beginning in the early 1940s with Dwight (Macdonald) and Harold (Rosenberg). Just concentrate on putting out good issues."

William was aware of my Achilles' heel, of my propensity to overly trust whoever was nice to me, or maybe to assume that by treating people decently, they would return the favor. Ever so often, I invited a few of these sharks so that William would not feel totally cut off from his peers. As in politics and in literature, he was prescient, and smelled their hidden agendas, and their envy, although even he did not predict the nefarious manipulations some of them already were engaged in. Or that they would see to it that that conference would turn into my Last Hurrah.

*   *   *

William continued to welcome intellectual stimulation, but increasingly found even the best of company exhausting. He preferred stretching out on his bed, on top of his lumpy electric blanket during the day, underneath it at night—wearing a heavy cashmere sweater, and with his electric heater at the ready. That did not allow for much diversion. On September 11, 2001, after breakfast, while I still was in the kitchen and he already sat in front of his TV set, he yelled for me, panic-stricken. It was 8:45 A.M.

"Look," he said in a trembling voice, while grabbing for my hand, "this can't be real," as we watched the explosion of a plane hitting the north tower of the World Trade Center. Like everyone else, we could not take in this ghastly event. William trembled as tears were running down his cheeks, while saying: "What has the world come to?" We held on to one another while wondering how human beings could lend themselves to so horrendous a deed. We stayed glued to the spot—as we saw bodies toppling from that tower, and watched the rest of the drama of that by now unforgettable day unfold.

Partisan Review was about to go to press, and we could not publish it without a comment on this catastrophe. The following was my first (printed) reaction:

> Not only New York and Washington, where suicide bombers crashed into the World Trade Center and the Pentagon, but all of the Western world has been in shock. One man whose windows used to look out on the World Trade Center said, "I've seen all these horror movies, but today's was real." To others, like myself, who lived through some of the real horrors of World War II, the United States was perceived as a safe haven. On December 7, 1941, President Roosevelt addressed the nation to announce that Japan had destroyed over half of our fleet at Pearl Harbor; and that we were determined to fight. He spoke more elegantly than President Bush did on September 11, 2001, but they both sent the same forceful message.
>
> Once again, the United States is not truly prepared to fight its enemies, but is resolved to root them out. Once again, we are divided around domestic priorities and must fight enemies both outside and within our borders. Isolation of ethnic and racial communities no longer is an option: we saw on our television screens that diversity has become the reality and that, racial theories notwithstanding, the workers at the World Trade Center stood together and ran away together.
>
> But our country will never be the same. Since the collapse of the Soviet Union and with it the mythology of a sublime socialist future, we, as the only superpower, have been blamed for all the evils and miseries that exist in the world. We have attempted to right many wrongs, but at times have overreached our capacities and at other times might have acted sooner, or differently.
>
> We have tried to attain our ends while holding on to our liberal values. However, to defend ourselves against terrorist warfare, we will have to strengthen the CIA, the FBI, the police and other security forces rather than continue to weaken them. How to do so without allowing them to go overboard is a big question. We will have to decide at what point the rights of the individual must be subordinated to the public good, to the "rights" of the country. When do we go after the Osama bin Ladens and potential terrorists inside and outside the United States in order to prevent future disasters? And how do we conduct fair trials without being so overly "fair" as to encourage, or condone, more such activities? All of the above dilemmas are part of the Western values we take for granted. Thus we often forget that human life is not as sacred everywhere as it is in our civilization. In societies where children are taught that suicide bombers will end up in a glorious heaven, and where people can dance in the street and celebrate the killing of others, our values are worthless." [41]

*   *   *

We all are only too clued into the changes wrought by September 11. William and I were particularly shocked at celebrities, such as the right wing Reverend Jerry Falwell, who mindlessly blamed these attacks on the decline of Americans' morals, and by Susan Sontag, who put the responsibility on "American imperialism"—which, of course, is the standard line of the far left.

"Susan ought to know better before shooting her mouth off," William fumed. She did retract part of her foolish statement, and we once more "forgave" her.

Still, even while the towers continued to burn, daily life had to go on. Vivien and Jolyon, her Englishman, were planning to get married in Paris, on October 8. A friend and senator, Claude Estier, had set up the wedding celebration at the French senate. How could I miss it? Of course, I wondered about the safety of flying. William was frightened out of his wits, marveling at my determination to attend—which he attributed to my experiences with the Nazis. Annie Cohen-Solal's sister conducted the civil ceremony in the municipal palace on the Place de Panthéon. That evening, after passing through the tight security cordon surrounding the senate, Napoleon's portrait, among others, watched over us. We feasted, danced, and listened to amusing speeches about the newlyweds—in French and English—while looking out onto the Luxembourg gardens.

Just before then, my 101-year-old mother yet again had been hospitalized for cardiac arrest. This time, my brother, with whom I almost never had talked since my father's death, called to say that the doctors wanted to remove her life support, and that I should make the decision. I wanted her to go on living. In fact after I got through to her that her beloved granddaughter, Vivien, was about to be married, she broke out in a broad smile. The doctors agreed to keep her on life-support until my return from Paris. Nevertheless, they sent her home before I got back. She was nearly lucid, and seemed to have waited until after Vivien's wedding to peacefully die in her own bed.

The graveside service opened old wounds, as a few of my brother's employees, and some of Sonya's family surrounded the open grave. My brother had whispered to me that Sonya had not gone to Michelle's burial place since her death five years before. Soon, she sobbed, and my brother also broke down, as everyone recalled the then thirty-five-year-old tennis champion who had succumbed to bone cancer. Under the circumstances, it was easier to say good-bye to my mother; and to forgive my brother's betrayal. We accepted the invitation to his home.

When sorting out my mother's belongings, I recalled how after we were reunited in New York she had shopped for cheap cuts of meat and other groceries and taken care of the household after a full day in a factory, and had studied English—if only to keep up with her husband and children. Her vocabulary notebook included complex words I never had heard her use. In the same carton, she had saved two books from the course on baby care she had attended before my birth. In one of these, she had registered my daily weight, my height and my first words. Suddenly, her early love for me surged up, as I recalled how she spontaneously had

hugged and kissed me, and had helped me sew my dolls' clothing during my many illnesses. Tears flooded my eyes, and I felt remorseful for
having wounded her. I again sympathized with her, remembering how
she used to helplessly stand at the window of the corner room while my
father drove down the Wiednerhauptstrasse—to meet another woman. I
had realized that she was unhappy, while hugging her around the waist.
Sometimes, she would embrace me, other times she would push me away.
She was so desperately hanging on to her marriage. Now, I first caught on
to how she must have felt when I became the more or less independent
woman she would have wanted to be.

Altogether, September 11, 2001 had traumatized me as had my
mother's death five weeks later. Why had I not been able to hold
on to her love after my brother was born? Could I possibly have
done so? What if I had succeeded in convincing her to occasionally
oppose her husband when she was so furious at him? Or had taken
the chance of directly confronting him about his infidelities? My
answers to these futile questions have kept changing. Yes, Viennese
culture did not allow a woman of her standing to leave her husband.
But after her arrival in New York, it would have been possible. Then,
however, she considered herself lucky that he had stuck with her—his
wife—and had not immigrated with the petite Claire to Australia
in 1938. Did she insist that I had always been his favorite child because she thought I had grown into his "intellectual" equal? By the
time she was in her eighties, she told me that she had known of his
affair with her fellow swimmer, Idi, and why she suspected Hedi
Wertheimer as well. I never said to her that I remembered coming
upon him having sex with Emma, my beloved nanny—while she
was giving birth to my brother, in 1927. Or with her friend, Annie,
when I was about nine.

Now, my head was swirling, while, once again, I had to sign papers
accepting my brother's treachery—which since my father's death I had
tried to relegate to my unconscious. More pleasant scenes and incidents
of my childhood came to the fore: I saw my mother bend over me and
take my temperature during my illnesses; *kvell* over my good report
cards; and defend me against anti-Semitic classmates. Why had I not told
her of my love for her, or been more understanding? Might she then not
have pushed me away, as she so often had done? Yes, she not only was
typical of Viennese women of her generation, but given her beauty was
a bit more so than most. What an unenviable existence for a woman so
envied by her friends.

*   *   *

While reflecting and observing the consequences of September 11 in my immediate surroundings, I noted that former Europeans like myself, and war veterans, were less shell-shocked than Americans who never had experienced danger. Especially the young ones.

"The French know better how to protect themselves," I reported to William after returning from Paris. At Charles de Gaulle Airport, we not only had had to open every one of our suitcases and pass through metal detectors, but, one by one, had to traverse a cavernous hall guarded by three heavily armed soldiers. Before boarding, we had to undergo yet more searches. By contrast, the security guards at John F. Kennedy were limiting themselves to pat-downs. I wished, and still do, that we will get to the point of truly protecting our citizens the way the French learned to do, after terrorists were bombing their subways in the early 1980s, and before then, during the Algerian crisis, when police in armored cars were swarming about everywhere until the insurgents gave up. William and I agreed that for us, a touch of national self-interest mixed into our self-serving skills and entrepreneurial know-how might go a long way.

Soon, it seemed to me that most people came to terms with the shock of September 11 by absorbing it into their ordinary lives. For instance, as a panelist at a psychotherapists' gathering that was to help practitioners in downtown New York deal with their patients' trauma, I was given little opportunity to speak: one by one, nearly all members of the audience got up to recount how they had responded to their patients. Clearly, these well-meaning people not only were upset, but intent on showing off their analytic skills, their humanitarian instincts and their liberal politics. Of course, it is easier to judge what we cannot control than to expose ourselves personally. How ridiculous, I thought, that we stress civil rights, anti-profiling and equality, by having guards open the pocketbook of every old lady who has a ticket to the Metropolitan Opera; and by stopping as many blond drivers as minorities and Muslims who use the New Jersey Turnpike. And why can't we elect politicians who put national safety and common sense above their immediate careers?

*   *   *

The previous October I had decided to retire from teaching, in part because I was annoyed at the hurdles the newly appointed Adelphi administration was putting in my path. But I also had too much work at the magazine—work that I now identified with as much as William had done all his life. To celebrate his ninety-fourth birthday, I gave him a surprise party. It was a festive occasion, with speeches, balloons, and a birthday cake, so that even William—however grudgingly— enjoyed it from his wheelchair. The dedicated drawing Jules Olitski made for the event, and which I hung in the living room, remains a daily reminder of that celebration.

Like most of my generation who had read *Anna Karenina*, *War and Peace*, and *The Brothers Karamazov*, and who had identified with Larissa in Pasternak's *Doctor Zhivago*, I wanted to see that sprawling country. When Jolyon, my son-in-law, who had professional connections at MGIMO, Moscow's prestigious university, suggested that I join him and Vivien, we made plans. Even William, who usually did not want me to leave his side, almost urged me to go, partly because we would be given the red carpet treatment that assured our safety, and partly because he wanted to be there, if only vicariously. Lo and behold, when the rector received my visa application, and found out that I was editing *Partisan Review*, he excitedly called Jolyon to make sure that, in addition to his own and Vivien's seminars, I would address the faculty. "No sweat," I said to myself, expecting to tell them about the magazine's history, and about the roots of its anti-Stalinism.

At the airport, we were met by a van with a driver, and a charming twenty-six-year-old guide. She spoke perfect English without ever having left Moscow. From her we learned that MGIMO had been created in 1944, a year before the end of World War II, as Russia's elite foreign policy institution. I became a bit apprehensive. My blood pressure mounted some more, when, just before our lavish lunch we were escorted through the university's museum: its director proudly pointed to the multitude of Soviet medals, decorations, badges, and other paraphernalia, and to the full-dress uniforms Stalin had worn at Yalta, Potsdam, and so on. I truly panicked. Even more so upon entering the formal seminar room, where about twenty corpulent, mostly dour looking, professors sat around a long table, each of them in front of an individual microphone and name plate; students occupied chairs behind them. Two video cameras began to roll and follow me to the opposite end of the room, where the rector, Ivan Tyulin, introduced me in superlative terms. I began to talk about the lack of contact between Russian and American intellectuals in the 1930s; of the American Communist Party's penchant for "socialist realism" that did not coincide with "the best in new writing, and in literary and political criticism." As I went on to outline the editors' disagreements about whether or not to enter World War II, one of my listeners interrupted, saying: "Some of us were reading your magazine over the years. It wasn't easy to get your hands on a copy of *Partisan Review*, not for political reasons, but because it was in circulation only in special departments in our library. (Translate: KBG and Kremlin honchos alone had access.) So, we don't want to hear about the past, we want to know about your current positions."

What could I tell them, I wondered. I knew they had to have been in the nomenklatura and most likely the KGB to be professors at MGIMO; I had no clue to their current beliefs and orientations; or to their internal hierarchy. Professor Shestopal, who had taken over as moderator, explained that nearly all those around our table had belonged to "the 1968 generation" and had read *Partisan Review*—which "was popular and had provided them with topics to discuss." (From what perspective, I speculated.) At the time, he continued, they all had been enthusiastically watching foreign countries, but at present were less optimistic, given the problems posed by terrorism, nationalism, education, and globalization.

"How are you dealing with all these troubles," he demanded, and then started to call on one after another of the professors. He introduced each of them by citing their specialties and achievements. Most had prepared provocative statements —a few of them almost offensive. Nearly all of them spoke excellent English. They jumped from topic to topic, such as tradition and innovation, utopia and religion, generational changes and multiculturalism, education and the role of elites in democracies, the impact of economic and cultural differences, problems of gender and victim mentality. I had to quickly switch gears. Since the moderator saw to it that all my interlocutors would have their turn, I didn't have time to elaborate on any topic. That probably was my luck. I mostly was stumped by their frequent and trenchant questions about religion. These did not focus on Judaism or Islam, but on Russian Orthodoxy and Catholicism—not exactly my specialties. One man said that Marxism had been a religion he never had believed in, and that he would prefer a return to tradition. At that point a number of my interlocutors switched into a heated free-for-all, in Russian. I felt frustrated but somehow managed to keep calm by providing sincere answers, and not simply defending American education or culture. But I was unable to penetrate many of their obfuscations. Soon, I no longer tried. And over vodka we turned into friends.

During the next few days we explored Moscow, and were driven to the newly restored and heavily gilded Trinity Monastery of St. Sergius. The poverty of the people we passed on that barren landscape was appalling: in my mind I can still see the woman in layers of old clothes and wooden shoes, carrying two small grocery bags—between villages that were too far away to see; and the beggars outside the monastery. The contrast between them and the public at the Bolshoi Theater—where we were treated to a most perfect performance of Boris Godunov—was phenomenal. As was that between the academics at MGIMO and the devout Russians—male and female—who kneeled and prayed outside as well as inside every church.

Unexpectedly, our trip coincided with the historical summit between Presidents Bush and Putin. Heavy security had kept us from getting into the Kremlin, and in St. Petersburg delayed our entrance to the famed Hermitage. But it was worth waiting to behold its renowned treasures. A nuclear scientist, who needed to augment his government salary by picking up fares in his private car, drove us to the Mariinsky theatre. Vivien had succeeded in getting tickets to the (adult-oriented) performance of *The Nutcracker*— together with both presidents, their wives, and their top advisors. From our orchestra seats, we alternately looked at the faultless dancers, and turned around to see the world's leaders in the royal box—while Gergiev brilliantly conducted the familiar music.

24

Wellfleet Summers and Their Ending

Ever since the late 1960s, the children and I had been spending part of August at the colony of Wellfleet. After I bought my house, in 1980, we went up from July to Labor Day. The house, located near the center of town, dates from the nineteenth century, although the year of construction has been disputed: it is admired for its mansard roof, its large lawn, and its imposing fir trees. Before moving in the plumbing system had to be replaced, the kitchen moved, and the living room connected to the kitchen. But despite unexpected expenses and delays, we soon basked in the breeze on the old-fashioned porch on steamy summer days. William would cover himself from head to toe and armed with a scythe, would go after weeds. It was he who found the tree surgeon, the gardener, the house painter, the handyman, and the woman to cut the lawn; and he mourned for every tree sapling that needed to be removed.

Within a few years, William insisted that we hire an *au pair* girl to help out. Tina, was an elfin and highly inquisitive Russian sophomore from Wellesley College. When during our meals she didn't query me on psychoanalytic lore, she told us about her American classmates who tried to convince her that Russia was paradise on earth. And she managed already before the Iron Curtain came down to bring her childhood sweetheart and his entire family to the United States.. (They have come to visit us nearly every year—in 2005 with their three children and her mother—bubbling over about their successes as computer programmers. Only in America, I kept reminding myself.)

The Chinese professor of English who had spent two semesters at Harvard's Bunting Center, took her place the following summer. She kept flaunting the women's liberation slogans she had picked up. William listened patiently and occasionally rolled his eyes. But on the day he asked her whether she would teach that newly found wisdom upon her return to Southern China, she responded indignantly: "Do you think

I'm crazy? Do you think I want to get myself into trouble?" She was a wizard at slicing and cubing fruits and vegetables. We ate well that summer. For a number of years, Phil O'Brian, an Irish schoolteacher from Castelleara in Ireland, whose cooking was mediocre but who was sassy, good company, and enjoyed reading to William took that job. When her schedule no longer accorded with ours, and William's legs were giving out, we brought along whoever was with us in New York.

Until sometime in the 1980s, William and I swam in Long Pond, and often ended up sitting on Noam Chomsky's beach, arguing about American and Israeli politics. William tried to "understand" Noam's anti-Israel stance. He also questioned Robert J. Lifton's growing anti-Americanism, which was highlighted by the Hiroshima marches he organized every August 6. After overhearing Noam's and Bob's heated argument on whether the death camps had been located in Poland alone or also in the West, I too tuned out. We broke relations after Bob attempted to "convert" William to support yet another anti-American peace rally, and "reinforced" his position by inviting the activist, Seymour Melman. After Seymour kept preaching and wagging his finger in William's face, William lost his cool. Matching Seymour's aggressive tone, he interrupted, saying: "Who do you think you are, my teacher?"

So we became more or less *persona non grata* to the Lifton's circle—to William's relief. Now we met only with persons we could talk to freely. Basically, we questioned the new orthodoxies. Those who read William's "Comments" in the magazine did realize that his views sprang from root analyses and from moral certainties. By then, however, many of our peers prided themselves on not reading anything that might shake their convictions. Like Senator Henry (Scoop) Jackson, we believed that America needed a strong defense to deter military violence. However, we also thought that the United States needed a better safety net for its poorest citizens, even though we occasionally were critical of one or another program. (I had come across more viable solutions in Europe.) William insisted on what he called sane thinking—even when this militated against old friendships. In 1985, he explained his position somewhat forcefully:

> The sin of moving to the right is, of course, an invention of the left, and often has nothing to do with the classic meaning of either right or left.... It is true that in the last few years our political emphases have shifted, but that is because the political situation has changed. In the last decade the ideology of pacifism and neutralism has reached staggering proportions, in a way somewhat reminiscent of the thirties when fellow travelers and liberals were taken in by pro-Soviet propaganda and the media and the universities were literally swamped with illusion and lies about the promise of communism. There is however a difference today: few illusions remain about the nature of the Soviet Union. [42]

William's irrepressibly sharp tongue could make enemies. When, for instance, at a Wellfleet party packed with people, a light suddenly came on in that darkening room, he said more loudly than he realized: "It's not enough to have to listen to these nudniks, now you have to see them as well."

And when at one of our dinner parties, he joked about a woman we all knew, Rose Coser announced that "the days of denigrating women are over, and you no longer are allowed to joke about them."

William burst out: "Are we allowed to joke about men?"

"Yes," said Rose. "After all, they are the dominators."

Actually, their differences went back to 1977, when Rose had refused to pare down a book review, and William had not asked her to write for us after that. Now, however, Rose had become one of the leading feminist sociologists, and also was working for the coming victory of socialism. William regretted its failure, arguing that it was a doomed ideal. Lew Coser, while flipping his right arm dismissively, declared that he always had been a socialist, so he might as well stick to it. From then on Rose and William stayed away from one another, and intimate dinners and easy banter were of the past.

Soon thereafter, the friendship with Harry Levin, the first Jewish professor of English to be tenured at Harvard, ended similarly. William had criticized a communist sympathizer, whom Harry felt honor-bound to defend, saying: "William, you see a communist or fellow traveler under every bed and under every table." After a moment of dead silence, Diana Trilling pronounced, "When William has seen them, it was because they were there."

She went on to imply that Harry might well be one of them. Elyena, Harry's wife and a Russian by birth, tended to agree with us, but in loyalty to her husband kept quiet. I too stayed mum, while wondering when this polarization might end and regretted the loss of yet another summer friend. We made up for it by inviting more houseguests. Among the latter were Karola Brede's family and Mechthild Zeul and José Antonio Gimbernat from Frankfurt, Claude Estier and Vicki Man from Paris, and sociologists and writers who were passing through. Rachel Rosenblum and Danny Dayan who, too, arrived from Paris, still fondly recall William's patience and encouragement of their son, Immanuel, whom he taught how to swim. According to Danny, "William was soft and kind, and patient, underneath his gruff exterior. At first I had been upset when he expected me to prove myself to him. But then, I came to appreciate him more and more."

*   *   *

Until her death, in October 1996, we saw Diana Trilling on at least one or two evenings a week. She was her customary imperious self, and did not allow her emphysema or her near-blindness to mar her style. Indefatigable as ever, she was writing her memoir,[43] and would often "fact-check" with William about the early days of *Partisan Review*. Thereby, Diana and William also relived disagreements they had had during the days they both had been on the board of the American Committee for Cultural Freedom, which Diana had chaired. So far as I could make out, she had pushed her anti-Communism to the exclusion of other political questions, while William, though equally anti-Stalinist, had defended a more liberal perspective. By now, they had distanced themselves from these "predispositions," wondering, for instance, about the pro-Soviet stance of someone on that board who, as it later turned out had been a member of the CIA, and the inflexibility of another. I heard more about positions taken by Arnold Beichman, Sol Stein, and James T. Farrell than I needed to know, and about the circumstances of that Committee's dissolution in 1963. (Because the magazine's lawyer, William Fitelson, had neglected to file the necessary forms to extend *Partisan Review*'s tax-exempt status, the magazine had come under the umbrella of the American Committee.) At that time, I had not yet read Mary McCarthy's "The Oasis,"[44] that cast Philip Rahv, as the "malicious leader." Now, Diana and William speculated not only about how well Mary had disguised them all, but about Edmund Wilson's influence on Mary after she had left Rahv to marry him. Under the circumstances, I could not help but ingest some of the quarrels that had energized the old *Partisan Review* gang.

My curiosity was sparked. I began to immerse myself in books on Whittaker Chambers, the Rosenberg case, the Hiss trial, and the Columbia uprisings of 1968. Diana's soft side emerged more readily when we were alone, while shopping for clothes and running errands in Orleans. She was most appreciative of me when I offered her chocolates.

Diana knew that she had cancer in August 1996, and said that she might live another six weeks or six years, but was determined not to spend whatever time she had left by focusing on her impending death. Alas, we never saw her again, and her absence left a large void. By that time, William too no longer went swimming, and after Rose Coser (unexpectedly) had died during that month, I continued to swim in her pond, and to recall the olden days by gossiping with Lew and his new consort, Leona Robbins. Most of my many psychoanalyst friends no longer were around either, so that, altogether, our Wellfleet circle was gone. But I still met Jocelyn Baltzell, Aileen Ward, Marietta Hermanson, and a few other women friends for an occasional lunch. By 2003, Lew and Jocelyn too had passed away.

*   *   *

In 2002, Stacey came with us from New York. William was extremely weak, and rarely left his bed. His chest was congested. By August, Stacey threatened to leave every other day, and finally told me that she "didn't want to be there when Mr. Phillips died." I angrily kept that possibility off my radar screen. But I was increasingly worried whenever he succumbed to yet another racking coughing spell. Since he never had had much patience for small talk by "*nudniks*," I was not too alarmed that he rarely was willing to see anyone who stopped by. I was aware that he had lost much flesh. But even then, he retained his classical features with their underlying softness—although his Adam's apple now appeared larger. Indeed, he often resisted shaving; talking quickly tired him, and he kept saying how lucky he was to have found me, or speculated on what might have happened to him if I had not made it to America. He rarely jested. His customary pallor became more accentuated. Increasingly, his words were interrupted with expressions of pain, while grabbing for a pill and a glass of water, or expectorating.

Towards the end of summer, we decided to return to New York, even though our doctor still was away. I had managed to convince Thomas Nash—Eric Nash's son, who now was a prominent internist at New York Hospital—to see him. Our driver raced against the clock. After a thorough examination, Thomas had William hospitalized. As soon as he was settled in intensive care, he relaxed and said he felt better. (He always was calm when under the close care of physicians.) My anxiety was mounting. It reached its high point when I entered our empty apartment without him. Yet, I did still not expect him to die.

During the following two weeks William was hooked up to what seemed dozens of machines. He slept. Whenever he woke up and saw me, his eyes lit up, and, often with great difficulty, would reach for me, motion to have me come closer, and even with the respirator over his mouth, underneath a mask that cut into the bridge of his nose, try to tell me that he was happy to have me there. My anxiety knew no bounds: William's hands and feet were grotesquely swollen; at some moments his breathing was impaired; at others he tried to grab the mask off his face but was impeded by the tubes. Nurses came around to give him injections. Doctors, residents and interns held conferences, discussing possible interventions to improve his breathing. Midge Decter and Norman Podhoretz came to see him. When they said that they looked forward to another dinner with us, I believed that that meant he would get better. Once, six or seven doctors, including Henry Erle and the pulmonologist, were standing around his bed, debating the pros and cons of performing an operation to facilitate his breathing. William said no. He kept sweeping his arms back and forth, horizontally, again and again, motioning that he no longer wanted to suffer; that even if it meant that his life would end by removing his feeding tube he would not mind. What had happened to my William, to the man who had stated at the end of his memoir that he wanted to be there, "if by some miracle of human persistence, the world should become a nicer place to live in—how awful not to know about it."

During the next few days, William was calm: the sedation did its job. I was exhausted, but kept sitting next to his bed, often in near-stupor, and could not imagine life without him. When around 11:00 A.M., on September 12, he was agitated after arousing himself from his slumber he searched for my hand and motioned me to come closer. He wanted to tell me something but was unable to talk. I formulated all sorts of questions, fudging the crucial one. He kept shaking his head from side to side, indicating ever more strongly that this was not what it was all about. Finally, I got it right, when I said, "I suppose you may want to know what I will do if you should die, which you won't for a long time, but just in case you do." He nodded approvingly and tried to smile.

"I think that at that time I will arrange a small graveside burial just for the family, and later on have a huge memorial service for all of our writers and friends." He nodded and nodded, strengthened his hold on my hand, and with much energy brought it close to his mask trying to kiss it, and with even more difficulty took my left hand in his right one, for what I did not realize was his last good-bye.

That afternoon, Henry Erle had summoned me to his office, not to examine me as I had suspected, but to prepare me for William's imminent death. When I got back to the hospital, William was asleep. He did not wake up again and I was called at 12:15 A.M., on Friday September 13, to come in and identify William's body.

*　*　*

William's last words continued to echo in my ears, and I still see his emaciated body and tortured face in some of my dreams. Everything felt unreal, as I began to wonder over and over again what I could have done, and at what moment, to prolong his life. I made frantic phone calls. I did not sleep. My son-in-law, Jolyon, who happened to be in town, went with me to Campbell's Funeral Parlor. I was aghast at the tall and fawning pin-striped salesman who led us into a room with caskets ranging from $199,000 to $149,000. After Jolyon, in his most haughty British accent asked for something "a bit more reasonable," we were guided into the adjoining chamber, where the lowest priced item cost $99,000 and so on down, until we reached the last room, with "the least expensive coffins." Feeling cheap and unfair to William, I settled on "the most reasonable polished wooden casket" rather than on one of the "shabby plastic" ones. Now, Jolyon took over, signing for such items as the preparation of remains, their transfer, room services, supervision, liveries, flowers, limousines, inscription, and so on. Were William to know the cost of this interment, I was sure he would turn over in the grave he was soon to inhabit. For me, he was still alive.

Early that morning, when an upbeat reporter called from the *New York Times*, I got buoyed up and answered his questions at length, hoping for a huge eulogy. The third time he was on the phone, I said that I would tell him something I probably ought to keep to myself—about an evening in Wellfleet, when Diana Trilling had walked into our house while saying:

"William, I have an outrageous secret I shouldn't tell you, and unless you also have one for me, I won't let you have it."

"Well, what is it," William demanded a bit impatiently.

"Can you imagine, I was called by the *New York Times* to advise them on what to put into your obituary. I'm ashamed, because I shouldn't have talked to that reporter, but I did."

"Diana," he responded, "I shouldn't tell you my secret either, but that man got in touch with me as well, about *your* obituary, and I too answered his questions."

"Do you remember when that was," asked the voice at the other end of the line. I was not certain but thought it might have been sometime in 1994 or 1995.

"You have helped me enormously, I am sure to find that material in our archives," this reporter said before hanging up. On that Saturday morning, William's obituary, signed by Joseph Berger, covered almost an entire page. The phone kept ringing: friends, editors and reporters from far and wide wanted to hear about William's last hours. Midge Decter called, asking whether I would allow her, Norman and Neil (Kozodoy) to come to "say good-bye to William." Of course, I said yes. Daniel and Joanna Rose, my three children and a young rabbi from Temple Emanuel came as well. Just before then, Vivien had accompanied me "to identify the body." William looked unwrinkled and serene, in the navy suit and white shirt he had worn as infrequently as he could get away with, and better shaven than he had been in a long time. They had rouged his cheeks and had stuffed his chin and upper lip. We were horrified and quickly left. On that balmy Sunday, William was laid to rest in my plot in Westchester Hills Cemetery—two graves away from Robert. When will I be buried between them?

Now, my children returned to their homes in Boston and Providence. It took me weeks (or months?) before I could open the door to our apartment without expecting William to call out to me, or to start informing him of something that had happened, and that he would have found interesting or amusing. Like other new widows, I was in a daze, although I managed to concentrate on putting together the upcoming issue of the magazine. By then, I had asked Irving Louis Horowitz of Transaction Publishers to reprint his 1983 memoir. Since this book needed a new introduction, I—painfully—relived my days with William. Inevitably, literary and political quarrels came to mind, as did the magazine's history before my time, and its writers' cleverness. For instance, when Irving Howe applied to *Partisan Review* William Dean Howell's observation that the problem for a critic is not making enemies but keeping them, I had read it as a put-down. But given its origin, it is two-edged. Actually, Irving, who believed that his publication, *Dissent*, would help bring about social-ism, continued to publish his literary criticism in *Partisan Review*. He disagreed with William about the future of our world, but we remained personal friends over many a dinner.

While resuscitating William's spirit, I planned the "huge memorial ser-vice" I had promised him. I aimed for his ninety-fifth birthday, November 14, and eventually reserved the auditorium of the Ethical Culture Society for November 12. I asked Joanna Rose to act as master of Ceremonies, which she did to perfection. We ended up with ten speakers, fewer than I considered, and more than Joanna thought I ought to have.

A number of friends, most insistently Jeffrey Herf and Susan Sontag, were upset because they assumed that their special relation to William entitled them to talk. Ultimately, I asked those he had seen after he was housebound or who had been in contact—Saul Bellow, Steven Marcus, Morris Dickstein, John Silber, Cynthia Ozick, Norman Podhoretz, Roger Straus, Jr., Joanna Rose, Rosanna Warren, and Allen Kurzweil. (Alas, Saul already was too weak to make it.) I was too upset to want to hold forth. And I did not believe like Thomas Mann's Hans Castorp, that funerals have something edifying to them, or that they were uplifting.[45] On the contrary. It was the memorial I had promised William, as well as an event I had organized, like a conference, and that had to go off *perfectly*.

25

The Death of *Partisan Review*

We were at Boston University for over twenty-seven years, and its president, John Silber had always treated us with respect. He had favored me with a broad although sometimes rather pinched smile whenever our paths crossed. After I invited him to give a eulogy for William, he went back and forth accepting and rejecting, and finally found the time to speak. That led me to assume that *Partisan Review*'s future was assured. I planned another conference, and worked on the forthcoming issue—a "Tribute to William Phillips." Since Joanna Rose had always expected to resign as chairman of our Advisory Board after William was gone, I had asked Nina Joukowsky Köprülü to take over. I looked forward to a few more years of editing and in the process to groom a potential "young editor." That people kept asking me what was going to happen to the magazine did not make me suspect that they might know something that was being kept from me. I had no qualms telling them all that Boston University now owned P.R., Inc, and that I was William's literary executor.

So when keeping my 4:30 P.M. appointment with John Silber on March 5, 2003, I launched into informing him of my plans. But after five minutes or so, and while grinning from ear to ear, he vigorously swung his (only) arm from right to left and back again, saying, "No, no, we are shutting you down."

Stunned and shocked, I became defensive. Unreflectively, I burst out with the first things that came into my head. He ignored my pleas for writers whose pieces I had accepted, and my wish to close down later, and with dignity. He also did not mention, as everyone had learned from the press, that the university was in financial trouble. He shilly-shallied only about what would happen to the magazine—was it to immediately pass on to another editor, would it be ended at once, or be resuscitated at a later date? To justify his decision, he said that he had asked a number of magazine editors about *Partisan Review*'s standing and repute, and had been informed that it was no longer viable, that others were doing what I was doing, and were doing it better. And he began to read passages from letters he had solicited from editors of the (conservative) *New Criterion*, the (literary) *Hudson Review*, the (leftist) *Dissent*, and the (academic and issue-oriented) *Daedalus*. What could I say? That none of them had my access to the European continent? That our reputation was larger, and international? Or that he ought to read for himself? His trump card was the (unsolicited) letter by Morris Dickstein, pleading that the magazine be kept alive, but with a new editorial board. (Morris had been friendly and solicitous when we had met at my home a few days before. He had not even told me that he had written an unflattering obituary about William in the Times Literary Supplement.) What a finagling and self-serving shit, I said to myself, while freezing inside. Now, Silber got up, saying that he had no time to lose, that his driver already was waiting downstairs to take him to his 5:00 P.M. appointment, and that for contractual reasons I had to terminate my two assistants, Brenda and James, that day. While triumphantly throwing on his coat and rushing to the elevator, I trailed along, trying to have him change his mind. How stupid of me, I realized, while ambling back to our office. And how will I break the news to Brenda and James? That was easy enough: as soon as I opened our office door and Brenda saw my face she asked what was wrong.

How would I continue on, I wondered, now that I no longer could connect to William through the magazine? Who was going to build on, or destroy, its legacy? And what might it be turned into, and by whom? More immediately, I had to decide whether or not to use my (non-refundable) ticket to Italy two weeks hence. I decided to go, but not before writing a letter to subscribers that would be enclosed in the upcoming issue.

Even that backfired. While I was staying with my British-Hungarian friends in Piazzano (Lucca), James unthinkingly spilled the beans by telling a writer that we were going out of business. That man rushed to inform the *Chronicle of Higher Education*. So during my host's Seder services, I was called by the *New York Times*, the *Washington Post*, the *Guardian*, and by reporters for innumerable other newspapers. Because the only phone on that property was in the dining room, my responses had to be brief—yet another handicap. Allegedly, John Silber let it be known that it was I who had decided to stop publication of *Partisan Review*.

In the end, friends and readers found out what had happened, to judge from the hundreds of communications I received. They bemoaned the loss of America's "best intellectual publication," or "the only one that was unpredictable, and did not follow a political line." Many wanted me to restart. The letter from Cynthia Ozick, written, on April 19, 2003, to the New York Times, put it best:

To the Editor:

As long ago as 1935, Edmund Wilson contended that magazines "pass through regular life-cycles. . . .; they have a youth, a maturity, and an old age." In maturity, he wrote, there develops "a force of inertia against which the youngest and freshest editor is as powerless as the oldest and stalest." And then comes death.

This is pretty much the way the closing of *Partisan Review* has been represented: as the natural decline of a periodical Morris Dickstein bluntly calls "obsolete" ["Farewell, Old Partisans of Past Crusades," Arts and Ideas, April 19], and whose disappearance he deems "inevitable"["Journal's Closing Spells the End of an Era," news article, April 17]. Yet this time the diagnosis may have been falsified—a kind of doctors' plot. *Partisan Review* didn't expire of itself; it was executed by fiat. Boston University, which since the demise of William Phillips, Partisan's founder and editor, owns the journal outright, held the power of life and death in its hands—more explicitly, in Chancellor John Silber's hands. Asserting a questionable verdict of "unanimous opinion," Dr. Silber chose termination, and in doing so mistakenly located the magazine's raison d'être not in the literary and cultural arena in which it has chiefly distinguished itself, but solely in its earlier political response to Stalinism and the Cold War.

It has been noted that *Partisan*'s variegated intellectual themes have been taken over by other, later-born, periodicals, and *Partisan* is accorded high praise for these influences and inspirations even as it is dismissed as irrelevant in itself. But those whose seemingly celebratory elegies blinker the distinction between normal mortality and applied asphyxiation might well ask themselves this question: how is American culture better served by our having one less magazine dedicated to the cultivation of intelligent discourse? A look at the current—and final—issue should supply the answer.

Very truly yours,

Cynthia Ozick

Within six months both William and *Partisan Review* had died. My phone still kept ringing: writers came up with schemes to restart; they cursed John Silber and offered help and sympathy. But only William and I had lived with the practical consequences of going against the grain. And with the work it takes to put out a literary magazine without strong, guaranteed financial backing. I was exhausted. As we had feared, the center did not hold in our social and political mayhem, where a grab bag of cultural values is available at larger and larger discounts. After he was bedridden, and I told him of my "conquests," William used to tease me, saying that I was out to change our culture on a one-on-one basis. But I was (and am) as convinced as he used to be, that we need a forum where intellectuals can have serious disagreements, and where preconceived notions and opinions may be challenged openly and honestly. And where literary values dominate.

Almost as soon as I had come to terms about *Partisan Review*'s demise I received a letter from John Silber offering me a year's salary for a "release." Lloyd Frank, a friend who checked into that matter for me, *pro bono*, advised that under the circumstances I too had to be released from whatever demands Boston University might want to make on me. After much back and forth, Richard Grimm, one of our Advisory Board members, accompanied me for a meeting with Silber—to his annoyance. Richard assured him that he was with me as a friend and board member rather than in his capacity as a lawyer. We signed off. Only about two years later, as I visited our archives for the first time—when we had needed anything, Howard Gottlieb, the director of the archives at the Mugar Library, had it copied and sent to us—did I realize that B.U. probably wanted this release because they were holding those of William's personal papers, along with the magazine's, that had been shipped by Rutgers after the lawsuit was settled. I had assumed—erroneously—that William had taken care of that matter years before.

Now that I no longer was either teaching or editing, I wondered where, and with whom, I might sharpen my wits. How, to paraphrase William, would I "use my mind, in order not to use it up?" Occasionally I was too depressed to know whether or not I still had any mind at all. I did not know for sure exactly which of my "friends" had betrayed me, although a few subsequently, and inadvertently, gave themselves away. I busied myself with everyday trivia—renting the *Partisan Review* apartment, deciding what books or knickknacks to keep or get rid of—while waiting to again engage my brain. Gradually and hesitantly, I started to work on portions of this memoir, on a few commissioned essays, and on the publication of the English version of my grandmother's "Letters from Vienna." In 2005, I set up an endowed lectureship at The New School in William's name.

*   *   *

In 2003, a call out of the blue by Bruce Cole, the head of the National Endowment for Humanities, helped snap me out of my inertia. He informed me that I had been chosen as a recipient of the National Medal for the Humanities and would have to come to the White House on November 14; that there would be a reception the night before, a brunch with the First Lady following the ceremony, and that I could bring one escort and four guests.

A handsome Marine read the citation:

The President of the United States of America
awards this National Humanities Medal
to
EDITH KURZWEIL for her scholarly achievement and for her stewardship
of a peerless journal of ideas. With her late husband, she was gatekeeper
at an intellectual crossroads for the century's greatest thinkers. The pages
of *Partisan Review* will remain a testament to the unshackled mind."

While my family looked on, the president hung the medal around my
neck. I looked at the other nine medalists from Joan Cooney to Midge
Decter, from Joseph Epstein to Elizabeth Fox-Genovese, from Frank
Snowden to Jean Fritz, and from Hal Holbrook and Robert Ballard to
John Updike, and noted that except for me they all had been born in
this country, while I barely had managed to make it to our shores. As
memories of Hitler's march into Vienna, of my escape and my botched
teens flitted through my head, I marveled at my good fortune. I had
made it to America, and into America. But I never had even dreamt that
I might set foot in the country's inner sanctum, the Oval Office. And on
William's birthday! Suddenly, I was unable to contain myself. I turned
to the president and said, somewhat haltingly:

"Mr. President, I never believed that I could be here." Startled, he
looked me in the eyes, and shot back:

"Neither did I."

Up to that point, silence had reigned. Now, everyone in the room
erupted into laughter. My habit of breaking up solemnity by bursting
out with whatever comes to mind had turned this formal occasion into
an intimate one for the entire group. To me, it restored my sense of self,
and my customary optimism—at least temporarily.

*   *   *

Before my invitation to the White House, I had spoken of my past
as disjointed segments, as my five or six distinct lives—fewer than a
cat's, but more than most people tend to lead. Gradually I came to note
the connecting threads, which, as everybody knows, reach back to early
childhood. When analyzing my family's dynamics, I realized how that
long-ago history might have shaped my personality, and my particular
way of facing both triumphs and adversities. Friends have pointed to my
perseverance or strength—which my family termed stubbornness. My
never-ending curiosity drew me to books and fed my imagination, which
inadvertently helped shut out unpleasant realities I didn't want to see. I
will never know whether I would have been as nosy, or would have hid-

den behind doors to find out what was going on, if my parents had been less secretive. Nor whether my ambition to accomplish what I set out to do, and to do so in a hurry, ought to be attributed to my running from the Nazis, or to my genes: both my mother and her mother were nearly as attuned to what we now call multi-tasking as I have been.

Was my childish wish to "know everything," at the root of my later inquisitiveness—be it about Italian society, French intellectuals, psycho-analysis, women's psyches, the Holocaust, literature, university politics, and so much more? Is that why I seesaw between expressing quick opinions and avoiding fights?

After *Partisan Review* was abolished and before I was awarded my medal, people kept asking "how do you feel," in a tone that expected me to say "awful." Since then they are more likely to tell me "you look wonderful." When I was young and really looked good, my father found fault with my appearance, so that I would not fall for boys who flattered me. At present, I accept looking my age rather than get a facelift. I have adopted my husband, Robert's resolve to make the most of every day, as well as William's habit of cutting to the core of whatever puzzles me. And when I push myself into too many directions, I eventually ask myself in Italian: "qui te lo fa fare?" (who makes you do it?).

Given our current political and cultural spheres, the gap between academic writing and journalism, the ascendance of the Internet and blogging, the mostly unacknowledged fusion of serious research and flip opinions; and the priority of the bottom line, that is, of profit, no longer sustain a publication like *Partisan Review*. Yes, as William feared, the sharks got me. But then, we have come to live in a society where sharks tend to thrive. Many among them are worshipped and put on pedestals—not just in the magazine and publishing worlds, but in business, sports, law, the media, the universities and in every other realm. My optimistic self predicts that the boundless advantage these bounders enjoy due to political connections, greed and opportunism, that is, to the victory over honesty by scheming and legal loopholes, eventually will catch up with them. But my pessimistic self wonders whether my father's dictum that money trumps all other values might not win out. This paradox of open-mindedness, of course, is the burden of intellectuals.

So, like the three-year-old Ditta, I still am impatient with repetitious and boring routines, and still assume that all aspects of life are worthy of note. My only lasting regret is not having had the guts to defy my father when offered the scholarship to Radcliffe. For, whenever friends tell me of their college reunions, I have to say that I took college courses, but have no college ties. The closest I come to is my Ph.D. from The New School. I no longer am angry at my brother, because I finally have concluded that my life has been so much fuller than his, that foregoing the softer life I might have had by banking on hard marble has opened up my own large and fascinating world. I occasionally give talks, accept writing assignments, and serve on a few advisory boards. I still sleep little and try to keep up with some of my diversified past—its people and their politics, rereading Thomas Mann and Marcel Proust, Franz Kafka and Elias Canetti, Charles Dickens and Anthony Trollope. And I try keeping up with neurobiologists' findings that connect to psychoanalysis, and with my nephew's, Ray Kurzweil's, *Singularity*.[46] Thereby, old age, although slowing me down, seems not to turn out as sadly as I was led to believe. I also wonder what that ever- expanding scientific knowledge might provide for (and take away from) my grandson's, Max's, generation.

   Old habits die hard, but even more so when one expects to hang on to them. To have escaped from the Nazis and from a controlling father, having moved from a disastrous marriage into a glamorous one, having survived that husband's death and gotten into a serious profession, and into intellectual life and another gratifying marriage—while also bringing up three good children—are in themselves triumphs to look back on with satisfaction.

Notes

1. Betty Friedan, 1983, *The Feminine Mystique*, Twentieth Anniversary Edition. New York: Laurel.
2. Bernt Engelmann, 1986. *In Hitler's Germany: Daily Life in the Third Reich.* New York: Pantheon.
3. M. Loring, 1996. *Flucht aus Frankreich 1940. Die Vertreibung deutscher Sozialdemokraten aus dem Exil.* Fischer Taschenbuch Verlag. pp. 118-119.
4. During the summer of 1942, it was estimated that 700,000 Polish Jews had been annihilated by the Nazis, but the extent of the catastrophe was unknown. When that November it came out that two million Jews had been massacred, the New York Times published a seven and one-half inch report on page 10 (Wyman and Medoff, *A Rage Against Death*, New York: The New Press, 2002, p. 29).
5. Edith Kurzweil, *Briefe aus Wien. Jüdisches Leben vor der Deportation.* Vienna: Turia + Kant, 1999, and *Nazi Laws and Jewish Lives: .Letters from Vienna*, New Brunswick, NJ: Transaction Publishers, 2005.
6. Silvie Murray mentions women's actions for more affordable housing; against landlords who arbitrarily increase rental costs; and zeros in on suburban radicals. But she demonstrates that most of the activists—including Betty Friedan—had been engaged in leftist causes before settling in Flushing, Parkway Village, or other parts of Northeastern Queens.
7. C. Wright Mills, 1951. *White Collar: The American Middle Classes.* New York: Oxford University Press.
8. David Reisman with Nathan Glazer and Reuel Denney, 1950. *The Lonely Crowd: A Study in Changing American Character,* New Haven, CT: Yale University Press.
9. Friedan, Betty, 1983. *The Feminine Mystique.*
10. Silvie Murray, 2003. *The Progressive Housewife. Community Activism in Suburban Queens, 1945-1965.* University of Pennsylvania Press. She analyzes Queens housewives' involvement in political issues; and she provides statistics of voting records, the shifts from traditionally Republican districts to Democratic ones, all of these based on the changing demographics due to the enormous influx of housing and the disappearance of farms and previously fallow areas. Still, political actions, for the most part, revolved around local issues, that is, they addressed inhabitants' immediate interests.
11. William H. Whyte, 1956. *The Organization Man.* New York: Simon and Schuster.
12. Luigi Barzini, 1964. *The Italians. A Full-Length Portrait Featuring their Manners and Morals.* New York: Macmillan.
13. Edith Kurzweil, 1983. *Italian Entrepreneurs: Rearguard of Progress,* New York: Praeger.
14. Nathan S, Hale, 1971. *Freud and the Americans.* New York: Oxford University Press.

15. Soon after the *Anschluss*, the psychoanalyst Lawrence Kubie was informed in Washington, that for a family of four, the guarantor had to show at least $5,000 in liquid assets.
16. Edith Kurzweil, 1973. "Encounter Groups: First Facts." *Partisan Review*, vol. XL, no.3, pp. 512-517.
17. Edith Kurzweil, 1980. *The Age of Structuralism. Lévi-Strauss to Foucault.* New York: Columbia University Press.
18. Edith Kurzweil. 1983. *Italian Entrepreneurs.*
19. William Phillips, 1983. *A Partisan View: Five Decades in the Politics of Literature.* New York: Stein and Day.
20. Kurzweil. *The Age of Structuralism.*
21. Edith Kurzweil and William Phillips, eds., *Partisan Review.* 1992, no. 2, and Our Country, Our Culture. The Politics of Political Correctness. 1994. *Partisan Review* Press.
22. Mary McCarthy, *The Oasis*, 1949. Authors Guild Backinprint.com, p. 13
23. *New York Times,* "New Spy Plan Said to Involve Satellite System," Dec. 12, 2004, pp. 1, 44.
24. Edith Kurzweil, 1989. *The Freudians: A Comparative Perspective.* New Haven, CT: Yale University Press.
25. Edith Kurzweil, 1995. *Freudians and Feminists.* Boulder, CO: Westview Press.
26. Henri Lefebvre, 1959. *La somme et le reste.* Paris: La Nef.
27. T. S. Eliot, 1971. *The Waste Land. A Facsimile and Transcript of the Original Drafts Including the Annotations of Ezra Pound.* Edited and with an Introduction by Valerie Eliot. New York. Harcourt Brace Jovanovich, Inc., p. 111.
28. Susan Sontag, "The Pornographic Imagination, *Partisan Review,* no. 2, 1967, pp. 181-212. (Rahv wrote a nasty letter to William for "Susan's erroneous ideas," and attacked him mercilessly for printing it.)
29. Stephen Donadio, "Columbia Seven Interviews," *Partisan Review,* no. 3, 1968, pp. 354-392.
30. Peter Brooks, "Panthers at Yale," *Partisan Review*, no. 3, 1970, pp. 420-439.
31. Ibid., p.425.
32. William Phillips, 1970. "The Weathervane and the Pendulum," *Partisan Review*, no. 3, pp. 418-419.
33. William Phillips, 1982, "Mind Sets," *Partisan Review* no. 4, pp. 487-493.
34. Morris Dickstein, Peter Brooks, Leon Wieseltier, William Phillips, Edith Kurzweil, Dennis Wrong, Steven Marcus, "Intellectuals and Politics," *Partisan Review*, no. 4, 1983, pp. 590–617.
35. Edith Kurzweil, 1996. *A Partisan Century: Political Writings from Partisan Review.* New York. Columbia University Press.
36. Its introduction was published in *Partisan Review*, no. 5, 1951, p. 540-556.
37. *Partisan Review*, 1964, no. 4, p. 515-530.
38. Its edited version was published in *Partisan Review*, no. 4, 1992, pp. 525-651.
39. Edith Kurzweil, 1995. *Freudians and Feminists.*
40. At that congress, William had protested the German Nobel Prize winner's Günter Grass's nasty attack on Bellow's praise of American democracy. On August 14, 2006, *the New York Times* reported that in his upcoming memoir, *Peeling Onions*, Grass, who for sixty years set himself up as a moral authority, confessed that he had been a member of the Nazi's Waffen SS.
41. Edith Kurzweil, "Comment," *Partisan Review*, 2001, no. 4, p. 518.
42. William Phillips, "Stalinism of the Right," Partisan Review, 1985, no. 3, p. 167.

43.   Diana Trilling, 1993. *The Beginning of the Journey*, New York: Harcourt, Brace, Jovanovich.
44.   Mary McCarthy, "The Oasis," issue no. 110, Horizon, vol. 19, February 1949.
45.   Thomas Mann, 1969. *The Magic Mountain*, New York: Vintage, pp. 109-110.
46.   Ray Kurzweil, 2005. *The Singularity Is Near: When Humans Transcend Biology*. New York: Penguin Group.